D0059958

Praise for

IN A FRENCH KITCHEN

"This is the best trip to France you'll ever have—walking through Louviers with Susan Loomis as your appreciative, ever-hungry guide. You'll stop in kitchen after kitchen to meet her friends and taste their glorious home cooking, you'll get a supermarket tour with special attention to the candy aisle, and you'll find out why she's still dazzled by the French art of using up leftovers and why you'll never see her in public sopping up sauce with a piece of bread. And when it's over, you'll head home with a string bag full of Susan's incomparable recipes."

—Laura Shapiro, author of *Something from the Oven*

"With practical tips, delicious recipes, and real stories from real people, *In a French Kitchen* is a wonderful guide for producing honest, simple, and chic meals, *à la française*. Susan Herrmann Loomis has revolutionized the way I cook for my family!"

—Ann Mah, author of *Mastering the Art of French Eating*

"There is wisdom in this book, expressed in stories and anecdotes; in advice, opinions, recipes, and shopping lists; and most of all in Susan Loomis's warmly engaging yet always sternly authoritative writing. *In a French Kitchen* is a crash course in cooking and living well."

—Luke Barr, author of *Provence, 1970*

"A warm invitation to the French table. . . . A tempting and helpful guide to delectable food."

—*Kirkus Reviews*

SUSAN HERRMANN LOOMIS

IN A FRENCH KITCHEN

TALES AND TRADITIONS OF EVERYDAY HOME COOKING IN FRANCE

GOTHAM
BOOKS

GOTHAM BOOKS

An imprint of Penguin Random House LLC
375 Hudson Street
New York, New York 10014

LIBRARY OF CONGRESS CATALOGING-IN-PUBLICATION DATA
Loomis, Susan Herrmann, author.
In a French kitchen : tales and traditions of everyday home cooking in France / Susan Herrmann Loomis.
p.   cm.
Includes index.
ISBN 978-1-592-40886-3
1. Cooking, French.   2. Food habits—France.   I. Title.
TX719.L663 2015
641.5944—dc23
2014035856

Printed in the United States of America
1   3   5   7   9   10   8   6   4   2

Set in Granjon and Harriet Text • Designed by Sabrina Bowers

*This book is dedicated to
my darling sister-in-law, Gayle.*

La bonne cuisine est la base du véritable bonheur.
(Good food is the foundation of genuine happiness.)
—**AUGUSTE ESCOFFIER**

Preparing and serving a meal is a sacred experience, a virtuous
circle begun by the guest who sits at the table.
—**SOPHIE'S UNCLE, PÈRE JEAN-MARIE**

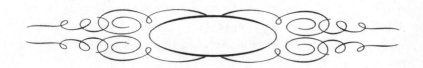

Contents

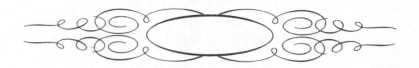

Acknowledgments

A BOOK IS WRITTEN WITH THE HELP OF SO MANY DIF-
ferent people, moments, tastes, aromas, melodies. When I say thanks,
the list is long, the moments glorious.

People: First and foremost, thank you to my children, the
guardians of youth and enthusiasm. Fiona, your endless generosity,
appreciation, appetite, and good humor are such balm and joy.

Joe, your bright presence and crackling phone calls asking, among
other things, "How's the book going, Mom?" are more of the same.

For constancy and inspiration, I thank the friends who sur-
round me in Louviers and Paris. To my sisterhood—Lena, Edith,
Elo, Astrid, Nadine, Betty (your tolerance is unparalleled), Danie
(you are a national treasure), Deborah, Bernadette, Thérèze, Fati-
ma, Patricia, Marie-Lawrence, and Marie-Agnès. A note here about
Sophie: She is my imaginary French cooking friend, a composite of

several people who contribute much to my cooking knowledge and lore on a daily basis, a rich source of inspiration. To my brotherhood, I thank Bernard, Christian, David, Stanley, Louis.

Thank you to Marie, Dominique, Virginie, Emilie, Maude, Leila, Marie-Eve, and Nadège, for all of your insights into daily home cooking—I am so grateful for your help.

I wouldn't be the cook I am without my friend and favorite market gardener, Baptiste Bourdon, who sings his way through each Saturday market in Louviers, enticing his customers with sweet words and gorgeous vegetables. Thanks also go to my neighbor, butcher Stéphane Coutard; my flour-dusted friend, baker Fréderic Bénard; my smart and funny fishmonger, Bruno Richhomme; the best *foie gras* producer in Normandy, Loic Métrot; permanent joker and fine mushroom grower Luciano Martin.

To Hervé Lestage, my dear friend and wine guru—thank you for your poetic, knowledgeable, and generous approach. You enrich my life and appreciation of wine beyond measure.

Thank you, Elisabeth Hyde, for all of the time you gave, for your patience, your deeply hilarious humor, and your fine eye as you read the manuscript.

Thank you, Laura Shapiro, for taking a look at both proposal and manuscript at very crucial moments.

The recipes were first tested in my kitchen, then carefully tested (and often re-tested) in the US kitchens of my wonderful assistant Kelly Lytle, Ellen Cole, and Cathy Arkle. An extra-special thank-you to Kim Wiley, too, for your detailed eye and spatula, and your fine palate. You are such a great team!

Thank-you to all of you who participate in my cooking classes in Louviers and in Paris. Each of you brings such fun, inspiration, and richness of spirit into my kitchen.

For keeping the pieces (of house and home) from flying apart, thank you to Christophe and Nadine.

For melodies: Valerie June at the beginning, Chris Botti in the middle, Paul Simon at the end.

Thank you to Jane Dystel, *l'agent literaire formidable*; Rachel Stout, *assistant hors paire*. A huge thank-you to Charlie Conrad for your support, enthusiasm, and passion, *un editor sans pareil*. Thank you, too, to all the team at Gotham for such a wrinkle-free, humor-tinged experience, including Sabrina Bowers, designer; Andrea Santoro, production editor; and Casey Maloney, publicist.

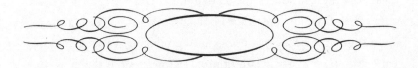

Introduction

THIS BOOK, *IN A FRENCH KITCHEN*, IS INTENDED TO ANSWER the question I hear more often than any other: "How does the French cook do it?" Translated, this means "How does the French cook put a multicourse meal on the table at least once every day, and usually more often than that, and still manage to look great, act normal, and do everything else that needs to be done, from working to raising kids, to taking care of the dog?"

I've asked it myself throughout the years as I'm invited here and there, drop in occasionally unannounced around mealtime, and always sit down to a well-planned, lovely meal that has a beginning, a middle, an end, and the wines to go with it. It is presented without apparent effort, enjoyed with stimulating conversation and appreciation late into the night (or at lunchtime), and repeated every single day on one level or another.

To get the answer, I talked with French cooks, and as you read these pages, you'll meet them—friends, colleagues, acquaintances— each of whom produces meals daily and with style. They don't think they are doing anything special, but they are. They take care choosing ingredients, planning and producing variety, making time and insisting their families make time to sit at the table and enjoy meals. And somehow—and this is simply a statement of fact—they manage to look put together at each moment of the process.

Many French cooks shared their methods and secrets, their recipes and stories; revealed the contents of their refrigerators, freezers, cupboards; divulged their shopping habits; told me their traditions; talked about their families and their origins. I added some of my own, and the results are presented here.

In *In a French Kitchen*, you will be immediately enfolded in warmth and good smells, which will make you hungry and eager to get in front of the stove. There is much here to help you along, from tips to recipes. So, I raise my glass, look you right in the eye as I say, "*Santé!*"—to your health—and urge you along. Cooking like the French, in a French kitchen, is the shortest route to happiness, warmth, pleasure, and delicious times!

CHAPTER 1

Loving Food

THE FRENCH LOVE FOOD.

I know, that's like saying "The sky is blue." But the French love of food isn't just carnal. The French love of food is primordial. They love food the way we love our Grand Canyon, our freedom, and our waves of grain—primitively, instinctively, fundamentally. Their love for food is overwhelmingly universal—it permeates the air, the life, the lifestyle, and the habits of all in this country.

This love of food resonated from the day I set foot in France and smelled butter in the air. It was a chilly day in March, and I had just arrived on an early flight. Nothing was open in Paris that morning, and I walked to stay warm, inhaling that buttery smell that would balloon into intensity each time I passed a boulangerie. When one finally opened its doors, I stepped inside and bought my first French croissant. It shattered all over me when I bit into it, and I've never been the same since.

This buttery, shattery moment led me to a French life. There was, of course, a lot more involved. But that croissant was like a perfect first kiss at the start of a lifelong romance.

Since then, I've discovered just how much the French love food, which has allowed me to openly love it, too. I always loved it, which made me something of an *extra-terrestre* when I was in college and after. Then, friends and colleagues greeted my love of cooking with skepticism and friendly derision, as if to say, "Who on earth would want to spend time cooking?" The minute I came to France I was surrounded by like minds, and my somewhat suppressed passion came fully out of the closet.

Fast-forward to a life in France raising children, writing books, teaching cooking classes, settling myself into a culture where food is the linchpin, the gathering point, the warmth in a cold world of politics, social upheaval, complex religious persuasions, and everything else that composes our contemporary French world. Here, I'm surrounded by people who love food.

Take Edith, my friend and cohort in many an exploit for thirty years. She is the antithesis of the stay-at-home mom, though that's what she's been for nearly thirty years. The thing is, she coddles no one, believes that a harsh life is better than a soft one, wears Birkenstock sandals every day of the year regardless of the temperature, and is always dressed in items of designer clothing that she assembles with the flair of a diva. As for her four kids, they were born, they were fed, they were schooled, and now they're out of the house, all of them strong individuals with passions of their own.

What did Edith do with her time? She painted, landscapes and portraits that enchant everyone who sees them. She has many other passions—remodeling, sewing, hunting down bargains on eBay. One of her most notable passions is her love of eating. I've never encountered anyone who approaches meals with so much gusto. When she sits down in front of something she loves, you'd better be sure to serve yourself quickly because otherwise she is likely to eat it all, with big, appreciative mouthfuls, down to the last crumb.

I see a lot of Edith. For one thing, I often swim in the pool she and her husband, Bernard, thoughtfully put in their backyard. If she isn't making lunch when I arrive, she's about to sit and eat it, and it's always a hot meal. Lately it's been boiled potatoes with mustardy vinaigrette and smoked herring (it's herring season). But it might as easily be thick, herb-rich potage, or pasta with lots of garlic and a shower of Comté, or a mass of vegetables that she pulled from her garden and braised with bay leaf and thyme.

Edith wouldn't dream of eating something she considered less than scrumptious, which for her is heavily weighted to vegetables, garlic, and olive oil. Her refrigerator is mostly empty, but half their property is given over to a vegetable garden where her neighbor, Mr. Harel, has tended the same few crops for at least fifteen years. There are leeks and carrots, lettuces and potatoes, onions, green beans, and a big row of red currants. It never varies (which would drive me crazy because I like variety, but which suits Edith just fine). As long as she has these fresh staples, her life—and her diet—are complete.

What I find fascinating about Edith, aside from her colorful nature, is the time she spends cooking. She has absolutely no passion for it, yet her intense passion for eating drives her into the kitchen twice a day.

She's efficient there like she's efficient everywhere. Nothing she cooks takes long—leeks are washed and cut in seconds, then set to braise in olive oil and garlic; potatoes are put on to boil; cheese comes out of the fridge. Edith loves good bread and while she might not take time to go to the market for vegetables, she'll drive miles for a great loaf. She loves dessert and whips up a chestnut and honey cake in five minutes, or a thick chocolate sauce, which she'll pour over homemade ice cream, or a fruit tart made from the figs off her prolific tree.

Her meals are all impromptu and very simple, whether she's cooking for herself at noon on any old day or has ten people coming for dinner. For a dinner party, she'll just multiply that warm potato and herring salad, preceding it with nothing more than some delicious cured sausage, fresh walnuts (from her tree), and perhaps a chickpea or avocado purée; she might decide to splurge and grill perfect little lamb chops, which she'll cook in the fireplace; these she'll serve with buttery tender green beans or sautéed leeks. If she doesn't want to eat meat she won't serve it and will, instead, offer an extra-ample cheese selection and call it good. Her meals are direct and no frills, like her. And because she's an artist, while guests might be surprised, they allow her this peccadillo.

Most of Edith's dishes are based on memories from her austere grandmother Juliette's farm, where she spent many a summer and school holiday. I swear, there isn't a flavor or food memory she's forgotten. If she's making braised endive, she'll tell the story of how her grandmother forced her, at age twelve, to sit in front of a plate of braised endive every meal for three days until she ate it. (This is a true story. Then, she hated endive; now, miraculously, she loves it.) When she bites into a butter cookie, it reminds her of those the housekeeper made with fresh top cream when she was a girl; when she makes chocolate sauce with water, it's because her aunt at the farm did it that way.

Edith wasn't surrounded by a lot of warmth and affection when she was growing up, so food became the vehicle for emotion. She is much like her grandmother, somewhat austere to those who don't know her. Yet eat at her table and you'll feel as though you're wrapped in a down comforter. Food, for her, is memory and warmth all wrapped up together.

The other day I went to buy candles at my friend Fabienne's boutique, Art, Flo, Deco. Fabienne is my age, thin as a rail, and while she loves to eat, she openly complains about having to cook. "Ah, *non*, Susan, I really don't like to cook," she'll say, with a rueful smile. "But I don't want to eat just anything."

Fabienne loves good tastes, and was waxing poetic about the baguette she had just bought at Aux Délices de Louviers, a bakery down the street from her shop. "It's parfait," she said. "Crisp, soft, and it smells like wheat." Though Fabienne lives mostly alone, she cooks every single day.

Her favorite dishes to make? Sausages with lentils in the winter, a big composed salad with an egg or ham or tuna in the summer. "I love to make osso buco too," she said.

Fabienne grew up around experts in the kitchen. "I come from a family of cooks and bakers," she said. "I should like to cook, but every time I have guests for dinner I feel like I'm taking an exam, so I keep things very simple." But still, she makes osso buco and lentils with sausages. These aren't exactly the equivalent of macaroni and cheese or peanut butter and jelly—they're real dishes that require real time in the kitchen.

Appreciating good, tasty food the way Fabienne does means she just gets down to it, once or twice a day. She knows how because she's French and it's part of her DNA, and because she grew up around cooks who showed her how to choose ingredients and gave her some tricks and hints.

She gives me tips about where to find great ingredients. Her latest was about chicken. "I lean out my window to order mine from Janine," she said, referring to the farm woman who sells produce and chickens under Fabienne's window during the Saturday morning market. "You need to try them, Susan, they're the best at the market." She also directed me to her favorite apple producer, and told me to stay away from the vendor in front of her boutique, because he's "*malhonnête*," dishonest. "He sold me soft clementines," she said.

Mr. Bunel, a rosy-cheeked, bustling man who stops by once a year to service my fire extinguisher, always walks in my front door mid-sentence, as if I see him everyday. The subject of his patter is always food. "My wife and I, we're going to buy a steam oven," he said as he tampered with the extinguisher. "It's expensive, and don't get me wrong, we're not rich, but we love to eat, and besides, we owe ourselves a little gift." I simply nodded, then he disappeared to his truck with the extinguisher to do something that costs 90 euro—I don't know what it is, and I assume it's necessary, yet I never quite trust him because he's a slick salesman who rarely leaves space for a question.

On his return he chatted about the latest dish he's cooked as he wrote up the annual bill. This year it was *blanquette de porc au Sancerre*, sautéed pork deglazed with Sancerre and braised with herbs and small vegetables. It sounded delicious. I realized after he was gone that I'd said three words, listened to his monologue, paid him his money, and forgotten to get a recipe. I'm sure his number is on the receipt so I can call and get it.

Nathalie Souchet is our family doctor. She grew up on a farm in Brittany and has that sweet, open attitude of the Bretonne, which includes a taste for hard work, family values, loyalty, dancing all night, and love of everything that's edible. She likes Louviers, but doesn't feel at home here. She can't—Brittany is a warm world apart. All her childhood friends are there, the air is pure, and there are regular *Fest-Noz*, which are peculiarly Breton fêtes with lots of Celtic music, crêpes, and gorgeous pork sausages. No other French region, except perhaps the Pays Basque, has such ripe and colorful character.

She and her husband, Arnaud—Breton also—make regular trips to see Nathalie's mother, who still lives on the family farm. I always ask what her mother cooked. Each time Nathalie describes the meals, like a peppery pork and cabbage stew or a potato gratin with bacon, her eyes get shiny with nostalgia.

When I visit Nathalie at her office, she treats my case seriously but can't wait to talk about food. The last time I went, she led me through *hachis Parmentier*, a classic family dish that has saved many a harried cook. Named for Antoine-Augustin Parmentier, who introduced potatoes to France in the 1700s, *hachis Parmentier* is a haven for leftovers. Nathalie begins hers with a pot-au-feu.

This begs the question, for me, of how she has time to make a pot-au-feu. It's not that pot-au-feu takes all that long to make, but it's an involved recipe that requires a multitude of ingredients. And Nathalie has three boys under the age of ten, she and her husband work more than full time, and she regularly has evening meetings.

But then I remember she's French, and she has The Secret. Part of hers is a shopping-and-cooking husband. I bump into Arnaud at the market on Saturday morning, their youngest—Leopold—in tow, with a rolling basket overflowing with produce. Nathalie can't go because she's busy treating patients.

Another part is organization. Most weeks, Nathalie makes pot-au-feu for Sunday supper. She puts the leftovers away until Wednesday, which is her day off so she can shepherd her children to their activities. Then, she has time to cook, and she pulls out the leftovers to make *ha-chis Parmentier*. At that point, it's a quick affair—she boils potatoes and mashes them. How is it she has potatoes? Her mother grows them, so Nathalie returns from Brittany with huge sacks full. While the potatoes are cooking, she shreds the meat from the pot-au-feu and chops any leftover vegetables. The mashed potatoes go atop the meat and vegetables; she sprinkles all with Gruyère, and pops it in the oven.

Friday nights are always egg nights. Then Arnaud is the cook, and for the family he makes either a huge omelet, which is served with salad, or a stack of crêpes that will be filled with ham and cheese, or a quiche. This is fun food, and it signals the end of a long week. Saturday is another treat day, as Arnaud makes a market lunch that might include *nems*—spring rolls from the Vietnamese food stand—baked fresh cod, oysters with a spicy sauce. Yes, the boys eat it all, along with lots of bread and cheese.

Yet another part is growing up with a mother who had every-thing on hand, so that Nathalie also knows what to have in her re-frigerator and pantry. She is very organized about shopping, a big part of The Secret. Arnaud takes care of it at the Saturday mar-ket (part of her organization), supplemented by Nathalie's quick stop at the Wednesday market. They always have fresh farm milk, a variety of cheeses, *mâche* and other lettuces, carrots, cabbage, radishes . . . whatever the season dictates, and all from the best growers at the market. Then, they've got their Breton potatoes, and leeks and apples from the farm, too, so they're set.

And finally, there's the one last thing involved in Nathalie's Secret. It is something she shares with every French cook—a healthy appetite and the nostalgia that brings tears to her eyes when she talks about her childhood. She wants to offer something similar to her sons. Food is one way to do it.

Finally, in my selection of French people I know, love, and present here, there is Betty. She's my scion of manners and proper French etiquette, even though she is a quarter English. The product of a comfortable and refined childhood in Paris, she entertains often and with flair. Even the simplest meal at her home includes linens on the table, a proper aperitif hour, a fire in the fireplace in winter, an ice bucket to keep the summer rosé chilled.

Once at table, she likes to serve fish terrine with mayonnaise or a soup decorated with cream. The main course might be *blanquette de veau* or a *couronne de poisson*, a sort of creamy fish concoction. Her food is simple and delicious, and everything is always prepared and ready so that when guests are present, so is Betty. "Our family was *proûte*, slang for almost excessively formal," Betty said. "I learned how to be that way too, though I'm a little more relaxed than they were."

At Betty's table, nothing is left to chance, everything is perfectly ordered, the family silver is always used. I asked her once how she manages to be so perfect. "I took cooking classes in high school," she said. "I still make a lot of the things I learned there." Aha. I hadn't known that French *lycéennes* in the sixties and seventies had the option of learning to cook. The equivalent of our home ec classes was learning how to make dishes like fish terrine and beurre blanc. As for where she gets her style? "My mother," she said. "She was the epitome of elegance."

So you can see that my world, and many of my conversations,

revolve around food simply because I live in a nation that loves it. Edith, Nathalie, Arnaud, Fabienne, Mr. Bunel, Betty, and others you will meet encapsulate the French way with food. They're busy people with careers and houses and children and a million other activities. Yet they devote time and energy to putting good food on the table.

I've watched these people cook. There is a sense of economy and organization about it that never ceases to amaze. None of them have any equipment to speak of. All of them are simple cooks, and they turn out scrumptious food.

Whether or not they like to cook doesn't really enter into it. Food and eating are simply priorities, equal to if not more important in status than work, exercise, entertainment. And it's not just any food that they make a priority—it has to be really good food.

The French ease with cooking, the fact that it seems to be no big deal, has to do with being prepared. They have fresh ingredients on hand. And they have the instinct—garnered from growing up in families that cooked and ate—to know what to do with those ingredients.

It also has to do with actually being hungry. The French truly do not eat between meals. Everyone knows that when you're hungry in the way these people are, thinking about and planning meals is a delightful occupation. And when you're hungry, you're in just that bit of a hurry that makes you cook with concentration and efficiency, anticipating sitting down to something delectable.

There is something else. French people take care of themselves. Eating something delicious isn't enough; to a hungry person, a Snickers bar is delicious. No, the French don't want to just inhale something to assuage the hunger. They want to carve out time to sit—preferably with family and/or friends—and eat something tantalizing, sip wine, start at the beginning and end with dessert. Each moment at the table for my French friends is an opportunity to experience and share pleasure. Each bite is also a call to arms for them, a flavor- and texture-packed reminder of where they come from.

One can get into trouble with such generalities, but I've lived in France a long time, and it is rare to come across someone who doesn't love to eat.

Like my friends and acquaintances here, the French love to eat, so they make time to cook. But cooking isn't necessarily the part that gives them joy. Cooking with quality ingredients, using simple techniques and organization, is simply the straightest path to a delicious, warming moment at the table.

WHY IS THE FRENCH MEAL SO PLEASANT?

There is no tension at the French table; meals are relaxed, open-ended, delicious. This is, I believe, because there is a *cadre*, or framework, to the meal, which means each person has a clearly defined role. The cook is relaxed because she knows right where she is in the organization of the meal. The diners are relaxed because they don't have to do anything but put their feet under the table. Everyone is happy because the meal is so good. Diners preen just a bit because they are being catered to; the cook preens because she is being celebrated along with her food. This frees up everyone to discuss real things like politics and taxes, vacation plans, and the latest good book.

BRAISED ASPARAGUS WITH HERBS
{ ASPERGES BRAISÉES AUX AROMATES }

This recipe offers a whole new spring temptation! If you can find white asparagus, use it; otherwise, use thick green asparagus stalks. For Americans who like their asparagus crisp, this French method of cooking yields meltingly tender—but not mushy—asparagus that gives the fullness of its delicate flavor. If you are using white asparagus, peel off the outer skin, beginning with the leaves just under the tip, where grit may be hiding. Hold each stalk up to the light so you can be sure you've removed all of the tough skin. You may need to peel each stalk twice to be sure. Then, trim off the end of the stem.

> 1 pound (500g) white or green asparagus, trimmed (and peeled, if using white asparagus)
>
> 1 tablespoon (30ml) extra-virgin olive oil
>
> Coarse sea salt and freshly ground black pepper
>
> 1 fresh bay leaf (from the *Laurus nobilis*) or dried imported bay leaf
>
> 4 sprigs fresh tarragon
>
> Chive blossoms or herb sprigs, for garnish (optional)

1. Sort the asparagus by thickness.
2. Place the oil and ¼ cup (60ml) water in a large, heavy-bottomed skillet over medium-high heat and add the thickest asparagus pieces. (If all of your asparagus are the same size, add them all to the pan at the same time.) Turn the asparagus so it is coated with the oil and water mixture, season generously with salt and pepper, and lay the bay leaf and tarragon sprigs atop the asparagus. When the water and oil come to a boil, reduce the heat to medium-low, cover, and cook the asparagus until it begins to to turn tender, about 5 minutes. Add the thinner asparagus stalks and tips, toss and stir gently so they are coated with the water and oil, then continue to cook, stirring and shifting the asparagus in the pan so it cooks evenly, until all of the asparagus is nearly tender, an additional 4 to 5 minutes.
3. Uncover the pan and cook, shaking the pan and stirring, until any liquid in the pan evaporates and the asparagus becomes golden.

4. Remove the asparagus from the heat, remove and discard the herbs, transfer to a serving dish, and garnish with the chive blossoms (if using). Serve immediately.

SERVES 4 TO 6

SEASONAL VEGETABLE SOUP
{ POTAGE }

This soup sustains the entire French population for at least six months of the year. Served either as a one-dish supper (with salad and cheese and, of course, dessert!) or as a first course, it changes every time a French cook makes it, depending on which vegetables are in season. The typical garnish is crème fraîche, stirred into the hot soup right before serving, or a drizzle of extra-virgin olive oil.

Here, try a light red, such as a Beaujolais, or a white with some body, like a Gaillac.

> 1 large bunch Swiss chard with ribs (1 pound; 500g), rinsed, ends trimmed, coarsely chopped
>
> 2 large carrots, cut into rounds
>
> 2 large leeks, rinsed well and cut into thin rounds
>
> 1 medium (3 ounces; 90g) starchy potato, peeled and quartered
>
> 2 Jerusalem artichokes (or sunchokes), peeled and cut into chunks
>
> 2 cloves garlic, green germ removed
>
> 10 whole black peppercorns (preferably in a tea ball so you can extract them easily)
>
> 2 fresh bay leaves (from the *Laurus nobilis*) or dried imported bay leaves
>
> 20 sprigs fresh thyme, tied with kitchen twine
>
> 1 teaspoon coarse sea salt
>
> ¼ cup (60ml) crème fraîche or non-ultra-pasteurized heavy cream, for garnish (optional)
>
> 2 tablespoons (30ml) extra-virgin olive oil, for garnish (optional)

1. Place all the ingredients in a large pot and add enough cold water to cover by 1 inch (about 6 cups; 1.5L). Cover and bring to a boil over

medium-high heat. Reduce the heat to medium and cook gently and slowly until the vegetables are completely tender, 25 to 30 minutes. Check them occasionally to be sure they are covered with liquid, adding more water if necessary.

2. When the vegetables are cooked through, remove the peppercorns, bay leaves, and thyme. Purée the soup directly in the pot using an immersion blender, if you've got one. If the soup is very thick, add a bit of water to it. Stir in the cream (if using) and adjust the seasoning. Divide among six warmed soup bowls. If using olive oil as a garnish, drizzle some over each portion right before serving.

SERVES 6

WHY DOES THE FRENCH COOK ALWAYS LOOK SO GOOD?

Sophie is my favorite example. She gets home from a long day at the office, drops off her briefcase, goes into the kitchen. In an hour, dinner is almost ready; she has the appetizers on the table and her husband, Jean, has poured the wine. She's still wearing heels, her hair looks great, and before she takes a sip she puts on lipstick. It's simply a habit with Sophie, and most of the women I know. They don't dither about their looks, their clothes, their shoes. Wherever they're going in the morning, they just show up looking great and stay that way all day. For the record, the men I know are the same. Like the women, they don't get home and change into sweats; they just keep their nice clothing on and wear it until they finish their day. In fact, I'm not sure sweats really exist in France (they do; they're available at Decathlon, the huge sports store chain, but they have a specific role—they're worn when one is *sporting*, doing sports).

THE GREEN GERM OF GARLIC

Garlic is considered "fresh" for two to three months after harvest, which, in the northern hemisphere, is generally in the month of July. After those couple of months, the garlic clove—which is the seed of the garlic plant—gets the urge to grow, and the tender, immature germ inside it begins to flesh out and turn green and slightly tough. This is the green germ that needs to be removed from the clove before cooking. It won't harm you, but its texture might harm whatever dish you're using it in.

HUNGER BEATER
{ MATAFAN }

The name means, literally, "hunger beater," and this dish is just that! Originally from the Savoie, it was served to field hands in the afternoon, to keep them going until late in the evening. Some say it originally included apples and was seasoned with sugar and cinnamon. Others insist it had a hint of walnut oil in it, along with onion tops. I like this version, which I got from my friend Fabienne's mother, who used to make it for her family. It's a great midweek supper, served with bacon and chives as it is here, or with apples and walnut oil. I love to serve a fruity Bergerac with this dish.

While matafan *was traditionally fried, this one is browned and baked, leaving time to prepare the rest of the meal. While baking strays from tradition, it results in a lovely light and savory bread/cake that is perfect with a green salad.*

4 ounces (120g) lightly smoked bacon, cut into large dice

1⅓ cups (200g) all-purpose flour

3 large eggs

2 cups (500ml) milk

Pinch of fine sea salt

1 small bunch fresh chives, or 4 scallions, green parts only, minced

3 tablespoons (45g) unsalted butter

2 ounces (60g) Gruyère, grated

1. Preheat the oven to 425°F (220°C).
2. Place the bacon in a small, heavy skillet over medium heat and cook, stirring often, until it is golden at the edges. Remove from the heat.
3. Place the flour in a large bowl and make a well in the center. Break the eggs into the well, then add 1 cup (250ml) of the milk and a large pinch of salt. Whisk together the eggs and the milk, then gradually whisk in the flour until all is blended. Slowly whisk in the remaining 1 cup (250ml) milk. The batter should be quite liquid and make a thick ribbon when you lift out the whisk.
4. Stir the chives into the batter.
5. Melt the butter in a large, heavy-bottomed skillet. When the butter is hot and foaming, pour the batter into the pan and pull back on the edges of the batter just to make sure all of the batter is in the butter, and none is sticking to the bottom or sides of the pan. Cook until the batter is golden on the bottom, tipping the pan gently back and forth, for about 4 minutes (lift the edge of the *matafan* to see if it is browning). Sprinkle the bacon over the batter, then bake until the *matafan* is puffed and golden, 15 to 20 minutes. Remove from the oven and sprinkle evenly with the cheese. Serve immediately.

SERVES 4 TO 6 AS A MAIN COURSE

POT-AU-FEU
{ BEEF AND VEGETABLE STEW }

This recipe is a combination of one given to me by Nathalie Souchet, a friend who grew up in Brittany and loves to cook, and one from my neighbor, who is the best butcher in town. Nathalie gets beef from her uncle. I get mine from my neighbor, along with his thoughts on how I should cook it. I combined these recipes here for one reason—Nathalie uses a pressure cooker to make her pot-au-feu, because she has no time for long, slow cooking. But before the butcher would let me walk out the door with his carefully tied pot roast and oxtail, he looked me in the eye and said, "Three hours cooking." There is no way I would have crossed him. This dish calls for a red with personality, but not overly strong, such as a Languedoc from Domaine du Poujol.

NOTE: *You will cook the beef with half the amount of vegetables, discard them, and add the remaining vegetables for the final part of cooking the beef.*

2½ pounds (1.5kg) boned beef shank

2 pounds (1kg) oxtail or beef short ribs

2 fresh bay leaves (from the *Laurus nobilis*) or dried imported bay leaves

24 sprigs fresh flat-leaf parsley

6 sprigs fresh thyme

1 leek leaf

4 medium carrots, trimmed and cut into rounds

4 leeks, rinsed well, white and green parts separated and cut into 4-inch lengths

2 large onions, cut into eighths

6 cloves garlic, green germ removed

10 whole black peppercorns (preferably in a tea ball so you can extract them easily)

Coarse sea salt

6 medium potatoes, preferably Yukon Gold, peeled and cut crosswise into thirds

GARNISHES AND CONDIMENTS:

Coarse sea salt

Mustard

Horseradish

Cornichons

Flat-leaf parsley

1. Place the meat in a 20-quart (20L) heavy stockpot and add water to cover by 2 inches (5cm). Bring to a boil over medium-high heat and cook for 5 minutes.

2. While the meat is cooking, make a bouquet garni by wrapping the bay leaves, parsley, and thyme in the leek leaf and securing the bundle with kitchen twine.

3. Remove the meat, discard the water, and return the meat to the pan with the bouquet garni, half of one of the carrots, the green parts of the leeks, 1 onion, 2 cloves garlic, 10 peppercorns, and 1 tablespoon salt. Add water to cover by 2 inches (5cm) and bring to a boil over medium-high heat. Reduce the heat so the water is simmering and cook, partially covered, until the meat is tender, about 2½ hours. Check from time to time and turn the meat; the meat should remain submerged in the liquid, so add water, if necessary.

4. Remove the vegetables from the pot and discard. Add the remaining carrots, leeks, remaining garlic cloves, and onion and cook for 30 minutes, then add the potatoes and cook until the vegetables and meat are very tender, 30 minutes more.

5. To serve, remove and discard the bouquet garni. Transfer the meat and vegetables to a shallow platter and keep warm. Taste the broth and adjust the seasoning. Ladle the broth into four to six soup bowls and serve.

6. When everyone has finished the broth, cut the meat into serving-size pieces, either chunks or slices. Arrange the vegetables around the meat, and garnish with a parsley stem or two. Serve immediately, accompanied by coarse sea salt, mustard, horseradish, and cornichons.

SERVES 4 TO 6

WATERCRESS PESTO
{ PESTO DE CRESSON }

This recipe was offered by a watercress producer at the Louviers market, with the suggestion that it be served with raw oysters. I use it for much more than that! I love to dip vegetables into it, use it on pizza right out of the oven, as a sauce for a tartine, on a steak straight from the grill, or even on a cheese sandwich. It will keep just a couple of days in the refrigerator. A sparkling Crémant de Bourgogne is great with this.

You can make this in the food processor, though the rough texture when all is minced by hand makes it livelier and more tasty.

4 cups (about 3½ ounces; 105g) watercress leaves (from about ½ bunch)

½ cup fresh flat-leaf parsley leaves

2 shallots, minced

Zest of 1 lemon, preferably organic

1 clove garlic, green germ removed, coarsely chopped

1 tablespoon balsamic vinegar

3 tablespoons extra-virgin olive oil

Fine sea salt and freshly ground black pepper

1. Mince together the watercress, parsley, shallots, lemon zest, and garlic. Place in a bowl and immediately stir in the vinegar, then the oil. Season with salt and pepper. Cover and let sit for at least 30 minutes before serving.

MAKES ABOUT ¾ CUP (180ML)

GOÛTER AND HEALTHY EATING

Everyone knows the French don't eat between meals. But they do snack. In fact, the snack is institutionalized under the name *goûter*. This is the name for the famous "fourth meal" in the French gastronomic repertoire. Though intended to keep school-children from fainting before dinner, plenty of adults indulge in it as well, mostly moms, I believe, who can't resist their own temptations! I usually snack with my kids; Edith, my French sister, snacks with or without her kids. A neighbor with five children filches a bite or two when her brood sits down to their after-school *goûter*. And should there be an adult in my home at *goûter* time (between four thirty and five P.M.) they always— and I mean *always*—have at least a taste.

I learned, early on in my French career, to serve really great *goûters*. Edith was one example; my time on farms provided another. When I saw that a *goûter* could be fresh strawberries mashed into fresh baguette and sprinkled with sugar, and realized how luscious this was, I followed suit. Fresh apple compote with plenty of vanilla is another favorite (see page 288). Edith makes a chocolate cake or her chestnut cake for *goûter*; I sometimes make yogurt cake, almond cookies, or brownies (*brooneys* in French). If I'm in a rush, I resort to fresh baguette with semi-sweet chocolate tucked into it, or a perfect piece of cheese. Whatever I offer, I think about fun, memories, and health, in that order.

My ideas about health have changed radically during my French lifetime. I entered France a vegetarian, non-white-sugar eater. My early nutritional informants were Adele Davis and Dick Gregory. My habits were formed, but after living in France I was slowly but surely won over by the flavor and pleasure brigade known as the French cook. What might have left me feeling guilty and made me fat in America, somehow left me feeling great and has kept me lean in France. I'm not sure of the whys, really, though I suspect it all has to do with all the things we've heard so much about. When food tastes incredible, you eat less because you're satisfied faster. When you have four meals a day, you eat less. When you don't eat between meals (because you're satisfied), you eat less. When you have to move to do everything, the food you do eat is used to good purpose.

Another thing about the *goûter* is that it is eaten sitting down. I have a friend François Olivier, a cheese *affineur* or "ager" who thinks that cheese is the ideal *goûter* and talks about eating this way. "If ever my grandfather caught me eating while standing, he would look at me and say, 'You wouldn't fill the gas tank of your car while the motor is running, would you? Sit down and take the time to eat.'" This is excellent wisdom.

Children learn, as soon as they can eat, that food is to be eaten within a *cadre*, or framework. That framework is being seated, and taking time. The time taken may be just fifteen minutes, but it is time wholly given over to eating. Everyone is better off for it.

CHAPTER 2

It All Begins with Mamie

"THE DISCOVERY OF A NEW DISH DOES MORE FOR HUMAN happiness than the discovery of a new star." Or so said Jean Anthelme Brillat-Savarin (1755–1826), lawyer and gourmand. While I cannot speak for humanity, I can for myself, and I agree. And when I discover a new dish, I do my best to find out where the inspiration came from.

More times than I can count, the answer is Mamie, or Grandma.

I've heard this from the mouths of starred and un-starred chefs, great home cooks, moderately great home cooks, irrespective of gender. The French are slavish in their devotion to Mamie and the way she did things in—and out—of the kitchen.

Mamie is the heart of the French family. She's the one to transmit tradition, feed the family, cluck over the children who run outside and get dirty. Unlike the image of an American grandmother, though, Mamie is not there to spoil. She's there to do what she has to do; her grandchildren are along for the ride. Mamie is picking and trimming beans? The grandchildren are, too. Mamie is making an apple tart? The kids are, too, down to peeling, chopping, rolling out pastry.

Mamie isn't planning special activities for her grandchildren, nor do meals vary to include tiny taste buds. That she produces flavor-packed dishes, which stay in the memories of her progeny for generations, is just part of her role.

Because I'd heard so much about Mamie, I expected to meet many Mamies in my peregrinations throughout France, in and out of farms, restaurants, and home kitchens. I've met some, but not as many as I might have expected. This is a hazard of aging, I realize. But it also, I think, has something to do with myth. Not that Mamie is a myth. She was and is real. But while Mamie sightings may have been few to many a small French child, the phrase *"Mamie a fait comme ça"*—Mamie did it this way—is oft repeated.

Mamie falls into a category of what you cannot see. Of course she exists or existed. And she cooked, gardened, and knew herbal remedies galore, all of which she transmitted. But you won't often find her sautéing potatoes in goose fat or whipping egg whites for a floating island, because she has more than likely passed away, sometimes a very long time ago. Her spirit, and her gifts, however, remain. So sometimes, when someone says that Mamie taught them all they know in the kitchen, they are speaking of the spirit of Mamie.

And what is the spirit of Mamie? It's all the things that make the French cook so good at what she (or he) does. It's attuned to the seasons, to the region, to the traditional. It's organized and efficient. It's intent on putting a good, solid meal on the table including salad, cheese, dessert. It's unsentimental, yet filled with caring that is evident in the taste of the dishes she made and passed down.

Philippe is a gourmand—and the most talented florist in Rouen—who barely knew his mamie, yet cooks with her spirit. She was a shadowy figure as he was growing up, cooking away while his parents worked in the family florist shop around the clock. Mamie cooked hearty, traditional Norman dishes loaded with cream, butter, and beautiful golden eggs for Philippe and his eight brothers and sisters. Like all mamies, she had to follow the seasons, so Philippe's family ate sea scallops with cream in the winter, mussels in cream with tomato salad in the summer, and leek soup (with cream) in the fall. Roast turkey with chestnuts was always on the menu for Christmas, roast lamb for Easter, and a salad was served at the end of every meal. The family ate enough Camembert to keep the Norman cheese industry alive. When Philippe cooks, he instinctively does what Mamie did. "Basically, I use a lot of cream," he said with a wink. "It makes everything better!"

Philippe learned what might be called an old-fashioned style of cooking from his mamie, because it is rich and amply generous. His meals are ordered with multiple courses like hers, but he is more precise and formal, with fine china and silverware set at each place by twos. His style is enhanced by the frame of his sixteenth-century manor house, which he shares with his partner, Alain, a former lawyer turned goat cheese maker. But the spirit of Mamie is his guide.

My friend Eloise is a single mom with twin daughters and a son all under the age of ten. She loves to cook and somehow fits in making fun and tasty meals for herself, her kids, her friends. Eloise is organized to within an inch of her life, putting her menus on a spreadsheet for the upcoming three months. "I have to, I run like an idiot and this way I'm organized," she said slightly breathlessly. "I can't help it. It's just who I am."

Sample menus from Eloise include honeyed raw beet salad with sausages and *frites*, three-cheese tart with green salad, broccoli gratin with fried eggs. Every menu is based on the season. "The kids help me decide the menus," she says. "I make it a project for them."

Who taught her the most about organization, and who gave her a love for cooking and food? She'll refer to the mamie she never knew, but whom her father talked about all the time. "Mamie was a plain and simple cook, and she was always cooking for a big group," Eloise said. "I don't really remember her, but Papa and Tante Jacqueline cook the way she did."

Eloise's father, André-Louis, is a determined gentleman who spent his career making paper and his leisure time planning vacations that included fishing and hunting with his son. They would bring back their catch to cook for the family. André-Louis is retired now. He keeps chickens, has a huge garden, and still hunts and fishes. He visits Eloise often, always arriving on her doorstep with food in the form of fresh garden produce, a pâté he's just made, a chicken he finished roasting as he walked out his door. His food is often complex, always delicious, and while he instinctively refers to his mother's cooking, he spends time on the Internet searching out new ways to prepare things. His sister and Eloise's aunt, Jacqueline, is the keeper of the traditional family recipe flame. She loves to bake, and her cakes are like a treatise on simple, old-fashioned cooking for a big family. Eloise is a marvelous combination of the two.

Eloise spent a lot of time at her aunt's home, and from those visits she gleaned dessert recipes like *gâteau cocotte*, a simple cake studded with apples or pears that is baked in a covered stew pot. "*Gâteau cocotte* is revered in our family," she said. "I make it all the time." While her children are doing their homework at the table near the window in her contemporary kitchen, Eloise mixes up the batter, adds an apple or two that she's diced, puts the mixture in a heavy *cocotte*, or casserole, and slides it in the oven. She looks over the kids' homework, then prepares a simple dinner like *rougail* or roast guinea hen or chicken and by the time they've finished eating, the cake is ready to sample. "We eat the leftovers for breakfast," she says.

Eloise also makes *gâteau semoule*, a caramel-flavored pudding from her mamie that she first tasted at Tante Jacqueline's. As for food memories from her dad, all she can do is laugh. "I love his food and sometimes it was a normal dish like boeuf bourguignon that he learned from Mamie. But lots of times it was weird," she said. "One of his real specialties and our favorites was *nems*, Vietnamese spring rolls. I know, what French dad ever makes those? But he had a friend in college who was Vietnamese and she taught him how." Another dish that Eloise remembers fondly is squid in tomato sauce. "Yep, he made it all the time. We were the only kids I knew who ate squid for supper." They also enjoyed their dad's braised wild boar, his homemade pâtés and rillettes, and the foie gras he made—and still makes—each year for Christmas. "Those dishes he learned from his mother. My dad is a great cook," Eloise said. "I think he taught me all I know, and he learned all he knows from his mom—and his Vietnamese college friend!"

My friend Sophie is *cadre*, an executive at an importing firm near me. She's French, yet because she works internationally and conducts much of her work in English, she's developed a quick wit and a relaxed Anglo-Saxon attitude that many French don't have.

For instance, she never minds if her kids get their clothes dirty when they play, unlike so many French moms who send their kids outside with the admonishment to return perfectly composed.

Sophie is in her mid-forties, has two teenage children, wears high heels with jeans, has shoulder-length hair that is just the right color of blond, and wears sunglasses most of the time. When she isn't at home, she's negotiating contracts for her company with presidents of countries; when she is home, often as not she has an apron around her waist and she's making dinner.

She isn't in the kitchen because she has to be—she's there because she loves it. Despite consorting with international deal makers in her job, she lives simply, in an old house not far from my town. Her sparely furnished home includes her grandmother's furniture and crystal glasses and her favorite recipes—all for homey, comforting dishes that have nothing to do with the elegant restaurant fare she is accustomed to for her job—begin with "Mamie told me if you do this . . ." To say that Sophie is attached to her French roots, which began in the Drôme, near Provence, where her parents still have the home that belonged to Sophie's mamie, is an understatement.

In Sophie's case, Mamie was around long enough to teach her granddaughter a hoard of wonderful cooking tips and leave her with rich food memories. Sophie, like Eloise, is organized to a T. She thinks ahead, and is never without certain things that she can use to create a simple, delicious meal based on the way her grandmother cooked. While her grandmother made tapenade, Sophie buys hers and always has some on hand, made with either black or green olives. She loves spicy food and has harissa, a north African pepper paste, to spice up things. Her grandmother had lemon trees, and Sophie always has lemons; she planted herbs outside her back door so fresh bay leaf, thyme, rosemary, and sage are steps away. Sophie's mamie kept chickens and always had a basket of their eggs on the kitchen counter, and so does Sophie. It wouldn't occur to her to refrigerate them. "I grew up eating eggs twice a day," Sophie said, laughing. "They don't last long enough in my house to be refrigerated."

Sophie's mamie grew up on a farm, but she wound up living with Sophie's grandfather in a small town. She had space for her chickens and some rabbits, was known for her legendary omelets, her rabbit stew with fresh tomatoes in the summer and apples in the fall and winter, and a special walnut cake that she served with strawberries in the spring.

Sophie makes these dishes to similar acclaim. She barely whisks the eggs for an omelet, just like her mamie did, and fills it with a drizzle of cream and minced chives. She serves this for lunch or dinner, with a green salad. As for the rabbit dishes, Sophie loves to make them, usually on a weekend when she has a bit more time. She cuts the rabbit into serving-size pieces and browns them in peanut oil, then adds onions that she's cut into chunks with a tiny paring knife. When these are almost tender, she pours white wine in the pan, scrapes the bottom to lift up the browned juices, then adds herbs, salt, and pepper. She makes sure the wine is simmering, covers the pan, and gets along to the salad or dessert.

She loves to make her grandmother's version of *raclette* by boiling potatoes then smothering them in melted cheese and serving them with cornichons, pickled onions, and air-cured ham on the side. The walnut cake? "I use a mixer; Mamie didn't because she didn't have one," Sophie said, almost guiltily. "If I didn't have a mixer I'd make it once a year. But I make it once a month—everyone loves it."

Sophie branches out in her cooking, incorporating ingredients her grandmother might only have dreamed of. Take broccoli. It's a relatively recent introduction to the French vegetable repertoire. Sophie braises it with garlic and herbs, or cooks it to death, then turns it into a beautiful puree. Sophie uses avocados a lot, mixing them with cilantro and a touch of harissa. While her grandmother grew endives under the table in the kitchen and Sophie loves them in a salad with blue cheese and walnuts, she'll often substitute freshly picked iceberg lettuce that she gets from the market. "Iceberg's got that great, juicy crunch like endives," she said. "My grandmother would have loved it; I know she'd serve it the way I do."

Plenty of French cooks did know their real-life mamies. Danie Dubois, a small, attractive, generator of a woman now in her late sixties, is one of the finest cooks I've ever met. She created one of the Dordogne's highest-quality foie gras productions on her farm in the Dordogne, and after cooking constantly for friends, family, and guests at her bed-and-breakfast there, she finally opened up a farm restaurant. People flock there to taste her garlicky *pommes sarladaises*, potatoes cooked in goose fat with abundant garlic and parsley, her foie gras, her confit. It's the stuff of dreams, and she produces it with one hand while directing her business with the other.

"My mamie and my *maman*, they taught me how," says Danie.

Danie's mamie was real and present, because on French farms in the 1960s, families all lived and worked together. By the time Danie could stand on her own, she was helping her mamie and mother in the simple farmhouse kitchen that looked out over the farmyard, where chickens pecked and cages held rabbits. Danie's incredibly delicious, classically regional cuisine—prepared in a thoroughly modern farm kitchen that overlooks a walnut grove and a flower-filled front garden—is testament to this.

Danie naturally does things every year that she watched her

grandmother do. I remember one spring she handed me a nicked-up old knife and a bowl and told me we were going to harvest dandelions. We traipsed through the woods to the neighbor's pasture and there we dug them up, small little balls of dandelions that were just getting ready to bud. As we crouched over the field, Danie recounted how when she was small she'd do this with her grandmother and sometimes a stray lamb would come and investigate what they were up to. "The farmer never minded that we were here," Danie said. "As long as we didn't scare away his sheep."

When we got home we dumped our substantial harvest in a big sink of cold water and they balled up even further. We trimmed and cut them in half, and they wound up on the dinner table later, dressed with walnut oil, vinegar, and garlic, one of the finest salads I'd ever tasted.

Danie makes pastry that she rolls out paper-thin, spreads with prune purée, and drizzles with cream the way her mamie did; she takes the huge, red-orange squash her husband, Guy, cultivates and cooks them in water for soup. If she has a spare goose carcass, she'll throw it in the pot the way her mamie showed her.

Baptiste, a market gardener who grew up near his grandparents' farm in a tall stone-and-timber house in the Norman countryside, has vivid, real-life memories of his mamie, too.

"Her food was indescribable, and I can't replicate it no matter how hard I try," he said. He specifically remembers her pork chops. "I will never forget them. She fried them in butter and they tasted sublime. I can't do that even if I try because she raised her pork and it was butchered just two days before she cooked it." He remembers making his first crêpes with her, and how she made sure there were no lumps in the batter. She boiled potatoes before peeling, then doused them in cream before serving. Baptiste does the same.

MAMIE'S RULES FOR LIFE

- Make dessert first.
- Peel your vegetables into a bucket and not on the counter.
- Eat peaches in summer and apples in winter.
- Add a carrot or an apple to your soup for sweetness.
- Keep potatoes in the dark.
- Serve salmon with sorrel. It melts the bones and cuts the fat.
- Eat garlic. It's good for everything.
- Add butter to vegetables right before you serve them; then you can really taste it.
- Add some oil to your butter when you cook things; it keeps them from burning.
- It's winter? Eat Belgian endive and lots of leeks; they'll keep you healthy.
- Add chocolate to your red wine sauce to make it smooth and deep in flavor.
- Use apple cider for roasting a chicken (or doing anything else, for that matter).
- Have stale bread? Make *pain perdu*, French toast, or creamy onion soup.
- Tired? Eat lots of garlic and drink fresh lemon juice with water every morning.
- Down? Eat green vegetables.
- Getting a cold? Use thyme in everything.
- Add a bay leaf to the water when you boil potatoes— they'll taste better.
- Be sure meat and poultry are at room temperature before cooking.
- Pour vinegar on the roasting chicken fifteen minutes before you take it from the oven and it will have crisp skin.

- Save chicken, rabbit, and guinea hen carcasses and freeze them. When you have several, make stock with the mix.
- Use sea salt. It's evaporated sea water and it's full of minerals.
- Use fleur de sel to season dishes right before you serve them, and put it on the table.
- Don't worry about crying when you cut onions; it's good for the eyes.
- Feel a sore throat coming on? Eat honey.
- Got the sore throat? Cook sliced onions in sugar and drink the juice.
- Have a fever? Drink thyme tisane and go to bed.
- Have a wart? Soak organic orange peel in vinegar for twenty-four hours, then put the white side of the peel on the wart every day until the wart is gone.
- Have a crick in your neck? Spread *argile*, wet green clay, on your neck, wrap it in a scarf, and wait until the crick goes away (it works).
- Heat olive oil just until it's hot and pour it over lemon zest. In three days, you'll have lemon oil.
- Plant seeds in the garden with the waning moon.
- Cut your hair then, too.
- Make a nice Sunday lunch and invite your mamie.
- If something isn't working, call the *rebouteux*.

A Few Tabletop Tips from Mamie

- Never seat thirteen at a table. It's very bad luck.
- No water glasses on the table, because the French don't serve water with meals—just a glass for red and a glass for white.
- Glasses go above the table setting in the center, not to the right.
- Feed the children first if you're having guests.

- Don't have music playing during a meal. It's distracting.
- Set the silverware 1 inch (2.5cm) from the edge of the table, and each piece of silverware should be 1 inch (2.5cm) apart.
- Always put plates on the table (also 1 inch [2.5cm] from the edge of the table), even if you're just going to whisk them away. A table without plates looks undressed.
- Avoid serving the same ingredient twice in a meal.
- Avoid serving the same textures and colors in the same meal (unless you are preparing a "theme" meal, such as one that is all white).
- If setting a plate down in front of a guest, set it down from the right.
- If serving a guest from a platter, serve from the left.
- Use edible flowers in the centerpiece.

"I watched and absorbed what she did, though it was all very simple," he said. "She probably gave me my love for food. But one of my favorite things to make now is a poached egg that I set on top of salad, and she would never have made that. It's way too fussy."

Edith knew her mamie, and Betty knew hers. "My grandmother always lived with us," Betty said. "She was an elegant, rather snobby Englishwoman who married my French grandfather. She loved making desserts and taught me how."

Betty's grandmother's desserts were mostly English—trifle, roly-poly pudding, bread and butter pudding, mince pies.

"She made French cakes and tarts, too, and she also made Yorkshire pudding to go with roast beef," Betty said. "We were a very proper French family, and our meals were very traditional." Betty's favorite French dessert, the one she makes most often, is crème caramel.

Louis, Betty's husband, is that rarity—a Frenchman who loves to cook. He was raised in Algeria (then part of France) by his grandmother, whose parents immigrated to Morocco from Spain. "I spent my first five years in the kitchen with my grandmother," Louis said. "She didn't 'teach' me to cook, but I watched her and learned."

When Louis cooks, he's right back there in that kitchen with his grandmother. As he browns chicken and sausages for paella, he remembers the kitchen in Morocco. "Certain things are my 'madeleine de Proust,'" he says. "The crackling sound of meat frying, the aroma of paella rice, the way she cooked semolina with chorizo—it all takes me back to those happiest of moments."

Even professional chefs rely on Mamie for their inspiration. They may spend their time today dipping olive oil crackers in gold leaf, foaming sauces, and flavoring air, but yesterday they were standing at the kitchen door watching Mamie work her culinary magic.

Mamie transmitted more than her culinary secrets, though. Because she cooked with what she had or could easily get, her ingredients were the freshest. Seafood came right off the boat; meat and poultry were from the farmyard; vegetables and fruit were from the garden or the orchard. Mamie didn't have to think about variety, nor did she worry about the seasons—they simply dictated what she cooked and what her family ate, so her charges grew up knowing what was seasonal and how to find the best ingredients.

When I see someone like Sophie, who has traveled the world and can buy anything she wants, be happy with the five or six vegetables in her garden that she eats day after day, I see her mamie. "Everything fresh is so good," she said. "My grandmother was a woman of principle—she never bought any vegetables or fruit, but always ate from her garden. If that was good enough for her, it's good enough for me."

Edith is now a mamie herself (albeit a young one who bicycles and swims daily, wears flamboyant head scarves and sandals, is always ready for a *ballon de rouge*, glass of red wine, in the afternoon, or a *bière blanche*, white beer, with lemon in the early evening). Her two teenage granddaughters, Eve and Ambre, and her baby grandson, Abel, are learning so many secrets, hints, and tips, culinary and otherwise, from her. They'll repeat what they've learned, with nostalgia.

Real or myth, Mamie looms large in the French culinary and cultural landscape. Along with her savory food, she demonstrated strict *règles de vie*, rules for life. These included herbal and culinary cures, kitchen tips and tricks, universal flavor combinations that are the warp and weft of every French cook's life.

SUNDAY LUNCH

We roll through the tall, wrought-iron gates, past the pond where geese are floating until they spy the car and start flapping their wings, at twelve thirty, right on time. A clutch of dogs runs to greet the car as our hosts, Alain Madonna and Philippe Sanjean, emerge from their sixteenth-century manor house, clapping their hands to rein in the herd. It's Sunday, and we'd been invited to lunch.

Sunday lunch in France is a ritual that defies time. Formal, it is a meal designed to occupy the entire afternoon into early evening. When invited to Sunday lunch in France, one must have nothing else on the agenda, except for a large appetite. Sunday lunch is not for the faint of heart.

Our hosts are friends we see, on average, once a month. I did the unthinkable many years ago and gave them our furry, energetic dog, which they'd been pining over for all the years we'd had her. She is a mutt with lots of hunting dog in her, and my tiny, urban garden was no match for her instincts. Nonetheless, I admit that my act was unthinkable in the eyes of everyone I know—most important, my daughter. She may never forgive me, even though the paragraph explaining my reasons, which I've included in my last will and testament, is convincing.

It's an ideal arrangement for me, because I no longer worry about the dog running out in front of a car and killing an entire family. It's perfect for Alain and Philippe because they have five dogs already, and now, with ours as number six, the whole tribe has fun on the couple's ten-acre property as they hunt rabbits, sniff after fieldmice, and generally keep the place in order.

The other thing I love about it are the gastronomic benefits. As part of our deal, I asked for and received visitation rights(!), and each time we visit we're treated to a gorgeous meal. I protest, because I am in their debt already, but Alain and Philippe don't listen. They make our visit the occasion for a big Sunday lunch, and that is that. And Alain and Philippe do Sunday lunch like no one else. All the stops are pulled, all the silver put on the table, all the crystal set to the left of the knives. Bottles of wine are on the side table; whiskey is in the decanter; fires are lit; peanuts, olives, and chips are at the ready.

We spend an hour over the aperitif with the peanuts, olives, and chips; then Alain, a retired goat cheese producer, ushers us next door into the dining room. A fire burns in this room, too, its flames reflecting in a large carving knife, the handle of which is a goat hoof, set on the table.

We begin our meal with quickly sautéed coquilles St Jacques, fresh sea scallops from the English Channel, on a tangy salad of mâche that Philippe, a florist, has prepared in the time it took us to walk from one room to the next. We linger, sipping a beautiful Quincy that Philippe has chosen specifically for the dish. Everyone begins to relax in the warmth, including the dog, whose shiny black nose sniffs along the edge of the table.

Some time later, Alain rises to put the finishing touches on the main course, which he brings in moments later—a dish mounded with crisply fried potatoes and green beans, accompanied by a rosemary-redolent leg of lamb. Sometime later, we are served cheese, from a laden tray that includes Camembert and Neufchâtel, Ossau Iraty, a sheep's-milk cheese from the Pays Basque, a Brie that threatens to run right off the plate, and my favorite Roquefort from Carles. There is no goat cheese, and I suspect there never will be. Fifteen years of making—and eating—the region's best has left Alain jaded. Either his, he says, or no one's!

Along with the cheese is a choice of fresh, crusty breads, one dotted with walnuts, another with figs, another with rye flour and hazelnuts.

After cheese, we decide to walk the property before it gets dark. Trailing dogs, my daughter and the *copine*, girlfriend, she brought with her, gamboling about around us, we walk under apple trees, visit the *pigeonnier*, pigeon house, circle the goose pond, and finally return back to the house at dusk. It's time for dessert, a fluffy confection called *gâteau Russe*, which is a multi-layered cake filled with hazelnuts and cream.

By the time we say our good-byes, sated with petit fours and coffee, I note we've spent six hours at Sunday lunch. Even the dogs are tired. Dusty, our little darling, who hurled herself at us on arrival, doesn't lift an eyebrow as Fiona fondly tells her good-bye. Off we drive, satisfied, warm, and happy, into the night of a Sunday lunch.

JACQUELINE'S APPLE CAKE
{ GÂTEAU COCOTTE DE JACQUELINE }

This cake is legendary in the Peissel family, in which my friend Eloise grew up. Her father's grandmother made it, and when she was gone, her daughter—Eloise's Tante Jacqueline—continued to make it whenever Eloise came to visit. "This is the 'big cake' of our family," said Eloise. "It is the most memorable one we have, not just because it's the best but because it represents the happiest moments we had with our grandmother and our aunt."

That said, this simple, hearty cake is delicious. It's the kind you make in a flash for dessert, have leftovers for breakfast, and then more for goûter, or snack time. The recipe calls for apples, but do as Eloise does, and use the fruit you have on hand.

Butter and flour, for the baking dish

1¼ cups (200g) all-purpose flour, plus more for the baking dish

1 teaspoon baking powder

1 teaspoon ground cinnamon

Fine sea salt

4 large eggs

1 cup (200g) vanilla sugar

1 teaspoon pure vanilla extract

Zest of 1 orange, preferably organic, minced

8 tablespoons (125g) unsalted butter, melted and cooled

3 large apples or pears (about 1 pound; 450g), peeled, cored, and diced

1. Preheat the oven to 350°F (180°C).
2. Butter and flour an 8-cup (2L) cast-iron pot or baking dish with a cover.
3. Sift together the flour, baking powder, cinnamon, and salt onto a piece of parchment paper.
4. In a large bowl or the bowl of a stand mixer fitted with the paddle attachment, mix together the eggs and vanilla sugar (on high speed if

using a mixer) until they are light and pale yellow. Mix in the vanilla extract and orange zest, then fold in the flour mixture until combined. Fold in the melted butter and, finally, the apples. Pour the batter into the prepared dish, cover, and bake until the cake is springy when you touch it with your finger, about 45 minutes.

5. Remove the cake from the oven, remove the lid, and let the cake cool to room temperature before serving.

SERVES 8 TO 10

SAUSAGES WITH TOMATOES AND GOLDEN RICE
{ ROUGAIL CREOLE }

Eloise makes this often for her three young children, and they love it. Simple and full of flavor, this dish is based on a Creole dish from the Île de la Reunion, a French protectorate. There are as many versions of it as there are cooks, each with its little touch of spice and condiment. If you like a spicy dish, crush the birds'-eye pepper, or add the pepper of your choice to give the dish some heat. This is hearty and spicy, and I love to serve a Corbières from Clos de l'Anhel with this.

FOR THE RICE:

> 1 cup (195g) basmati rice, rinsed
>
> 2 teaspoons ground turmeric, or as desired
>
> ½ teaspoon fine sea salt
>
> 1 fresh bay leaf (from the *Laurus nobilis*) or dried imported bay leaf

FOR THE *ROUGAIL*:

> 1 pound (500g) fresh smoked pork or chicken sausages (preferably not lean), pierced with a skewer in several places
>
> 2 large onions, diced
>
> 2 large cloves garlic, green germ removed
>
> 1 (½-inch; 1.25cm) round fresh ginger, peeled

1 (28-ounce; 840g) can whole tomatoes (I recommend Muir brand)

Zest of 1 lime, minced

10 sprigs fresh thyme

1 fresh bay leaf (from the *Laurel nobilis*) or dried imported bay leaf

1 birds'-eye pepper or other hot pepper (optional)

Fresh herb sprigs, for garnish

1. To make the rice, place the rice grains in a medium saucepan. Add 2 cups (500ml) water, the turmeric, salt, and bay leaf and bring to a boil over medium-high heat. Reduce the heat so the water is boiling gently and cook until there are holes in the top of the rice and the water has evaporated below the surface of the rice. Reduce the heat to low, cover, and cook for 10 minutes. Remove the pan from the heat and do not remove the cover. Let stand until you are ready to serve, at least 10 minutes.

2. To make the *rougail*, while the rice is cooking, brown the sausages on all sides in a large, heavy-bottomed skillet over medium-high heat, about 6 minutes. (If you are using lean sausages, you'll want to brown the sausages in a generous tablespoon of extra-virgin olive oil.) Remove the sausages from the pan and transfer them to a cutting board.

3. Place the onions in the pan and cook, stirring, until they are golden, 6 to 8 minutes. Add the garlic and ginger, stir, then add the tomatoes with their juices and stir, breaking them up into large pieces as you stir. Reduce the heat to medium and add the sausages, lime zest, thyme, bay leaf, and hot pepper to the tomato mixture. Season with salt and pepper, stir, and cook until the mixture is boiling, then reduce the heat to medium. Cover and cook, stirring from time to time, until the sausages are thoroughly cooked through and the sauce has thickened, 25 to 30 minutes.

4. Remove the herbs and the hot pepper from the *rougail*. Adjust the seasoning. To serve, divide the rice among four shallow soup bowls. Season the *rougail* to taste and divide it among the bowls, placing it atop the rice but leaving some rice to show, as it has a lovely color. Garnish with the herbs, and serve immediately.

SERVES 4, GENEROUSLY

MADAME KORN'S QUICK LEMON CAKE

{ GÂTEAU AU CITRON RAPIDE DE MADAME KORN }

This recipe comes from Dominique Léost, a rare Frenchman who cooks daily and loves it.

This simple, delicious cake comes from his childhood. He grew up in Le Havre, in an apartment building that was a melting pot of cultures. "During the 1960s, when Algeria was given back to the Algerians, all the French there had to leave," he said. "Many moved into our apartment building. They had nothing because they'd been given twenty-four hours' notice, but that didn't stop them from being the happiest, warmest people."

Those French, called Pieds Noirs, *were of every culture, and from living on the Mediterranean, their food was rife with color and flavor. This recipe holds happy memories for Dominique, and it comes from their neighbor across the hall Madame Korn who, with her family, eventually emigrated to the United States. "This cake was our favorite," Dominique said.*

I can see why. It's light and satisfying, and tastes like the Mediterranean sun! I like to serve it with sliced strawberries in the spring.

Butter, for the pan
1 cup (150g) all-purpose flour
½ teaspoon fine sea salt
1 teaspoon baking powder
2 large eggs
1¼ cups (250g) vanilla sugar
⅓ cup (75ml) milk
Zest of 1 lemon, preferably organic, minced
4 tablespoons (60g) unsalted butter, melted and cooled
Confectioners' sugar, for garnish

1. Preheat the oven to 400°F (200°C). Butter a 9-inch cake pan, then line it with parchment paper.

2. Sift together the flour, salt, and the baking powder onto a piece of parchment or waxed paper.

3. In a mixer or a large bowl, beat the eggs and vanilla sugar until they are thick and pale yellow. Add the dry ingredients to the eggs and sugar alternately with the milk, beginning and ending with the dry ingredients. Fold in the zest, then fold in the melted butter.

4. Pour the batter into the prepared cake pan, and bake in the center of the oven until the cake is golden and slightly puffed, about 30 minutes. Check it after 25 minutes—if a cake tester stuck in the center of the cake comes out clean, it is baked. Let cool to room temperature on a wire rack. To remove the cake from the pan, run a knife around the edge of the cake, place the wire rack on the pan and flip it. Shake firmly, and the cake will drop from the pan. Remove the parchment paper and let the cake cool, right side up.

5. To serve, transfer the cake to a serving platter, mounded-side up, and dust with confectioners' sugar.

SERVES 6 TO 8

CRISP GREEN SALAD WITH POACHED EGGS

{ SALADE VERTE CROQUANTE AUX OEUFS POCHES }

This makes a delicious lunch or dinner. For dinner, I often serve it with Baptiste's oven-fried new potatoes (page 266). Here, you can vary the lettuces and the herbs, of course, and serve the salad with one egg or two, depending on your eating public!

Generally, wine isn't terrific with a vinaigrette, but if you would like to serve wine with this, I suggest a red Touraine.

10 cups (260g) lettuce leaves (I like a blend of iceberg, Batavia, and curly endive), rinsed, spun dry, and torn into bite-size pieces

1 large shallot, peeled and cut into paper-thin rounds

2 teaspoons white wine vinegar

4 to 8 large eggs

6 ounces (180g) slab bacon, rind removed, cut into 1 by ¼ by ¼-inch (2.5 by .5 by .5cm) pieces

3 tablespoons olive oil (optional)

1 large clove garlic, green germ removed, minced

2 tablespoons red wine vinegar

Fine sea salt and freshly ground black pepper

Chives, for garnish

1. Place the greens and the shallot in a large, heatproof bowl and set aside.

2. Bring a medium pan of water to a boil over medium-high heat. Reduce the heat so the water is boiling merrily, add the white wine vinegar, and break an egg into the bubbles in the water. Spoon the water around the egg as it begins to poach, then let it cook until the white is opaque, 3 to 4 minutes. Using a slotted spoon, carefully transfer the egg to a shallow bowl or plate. Trim off and discard any excess egg white. Repeat with the remaining eggs.

3. Place the bacon in a medium skillet over medium-high heat, and when the bacon begins to sizzle, reduce the heat to medium and cook, stirring frequently, until the bacon turns golden, about 5 minutes. If the bacon doesn't give off a great deal of fat, add the olive oil. If it gives off quite a bit of fat, you won't need the oil. Add the garlic to the pan, stir, and cook for about 30 seconds, then add the red wine vinegar to the pan and stand back as you stir and scrape the pan, because it will give off eye-stinging steam. Pour the bacon and the juices and fat over the lettuce, then toss, toss, toss until the leaves are coated. Season with salt and pepper, then toss again.

4. Divide the salad among four plates. Using a slotted spoon, transfer an egg to each salad, patting it dry before setting it on the lettuce. Garnish each egg with plenty of salt and pepper, and 2 or 3 chives. Serve immediately.

SERVES 4

CHAPTER 3

Order in the Kitchen and a List of Equipment

OUR IDEA OF THE FRENCH KITCHEN INCLUDES COPPER pots hanging over a long farm table, lots of counter space, an expansive stove with brass knobs, a cooking fireplace. There is a nice round table with a crisp tablecloth that gets changed every day, another table off to the side holding a toaster, a bowl full of sugar cubes, a glass with small spoons, and a selection of pretty bowls, all for morning coffee.

Near the stove, there is likely to be a string of garlic hanging somewhere, and there will surely be a basket of shallots and one of onions. Various electrical appliances will be sprinkled about, from a mixer to a juicer to an ice-cream maker. Pretty ironed tea towels hang from the stove, and there's a window topped by a lace valance over the big, stone sink that looks into the courtyard, where a few chickens peck, flowers bloom, herbs thrive.

Off to the side of this dream kitchen and behind a vintage lace curtain is a big, cool, walk-in pantry with a screened window. In there, shelves lined with more vintage lace hold just the basics—a kilo of dried beans, one of rice, one of couscous, perhaps garbanzo beans, surely stone-green lentils. There is a jar of sugar, several bags of flour, a bag or two of salt, and ample coffee.

There are bottles of oil—olive, peanut, rapeseed—and a vinegar barrel, jars of cornichons and mustard. There are many jars of different kinds of honey, an assortment of homemade jams, a jar or two of chestnut puree. Cheeses wrapped in paper are set under a *cloche*, or bell, and dried sausages hang from brass nails. The only cans hold tomatoes, tuna, and sardines (these last are turned regularly so they age well). There are crocks of olives, a few jars of tapenade, some of rillettes.

On the floor sits a big crate of potatoes covered by a heavy towel (so they don't turn green and poisonous), and far from the potatoes, a crate of apples (it is said that apples make potatoes spoil, but this may be folklore).

The refrigerator is small and holds the bare essentials: crème fraîche, unsalted butter, milk, mustard, oranges and lemons, smoked salmon. A narrow shelf near the stove holds jars and pots of herbs and spices.

This is the ideal French kitchen, like Monet's at Giverny in Normandy, where the artist and gourmand did everything right, from the white-and-blue tiles to the mile-long stove to the fireplace. And it's like my kitchen, which I planned for efficiency and warm comfort.

My own kitchen does resemble Monet's, in some fashion. But it wasn't always so. When I bought my house in Normandy, what passed for the kitchen was a dark, triangular room with two big, low windows that looked out on a muddy courtyard. I worked in it that way long enough to realize exactly what I needed to transform it into the warm heart of my home, and an efficient teaching kitchen.

My list was long—a sturdy, beautiful professional stove, a center island, lots of light, expansive counter space, several sinks, cupboards for everything from baking pans to the millions of tiny dishes I use for *mise en place*, organizing recipes. I needed a big refrigerator that I could see into, and a fireplace for grilling; and I wanted my utensils at hand, so I could grab them fast.

I got it all. My six-burner and two-oven stove, hand-built by Cometto, a small company in Burgundy, has gotten hours of use every day over the past twelve years, and it looks brand-new. The island is a two-hundred-year-old butcher block with huge drawers in it. The large, boxy refrigerator, built in the 1920s, once lived on a farm, and what sold me on it was when the farmer opened the door and said, "You can hang half a sheep in here." It's all wood and tile inside and works like a dream. A section of the kitchen is all glass, which pulls in the exterior light. The floor where I work is wood, because wood is easy on the legs, and when you drop something on it, it doesn't break. The rest of the kitchen has a tile floor, which is beautifully esthetic, but, as the French would say, *bienvenu les dégâts*, "welcome the damage," the minute something falls on it.

I hung copper pots above the stove at easy reach, and a few hidden but open shelves that face the stove—under the central island—give me instant access to pots and pans, while all my other equipment and accessories are in roomy drawers. I have a coffee sink, a vegetable washing sink, and a dishwashing sink. Above the coffee sink is my fanciful array of vintage coffee bowls that I buy when I find them at *foires à tout*, town-wide garage sales, frilly tea-cups from my grandmother's collection, and a collection of espresso cups that I've picked up here and there.

I love the space and light in my kitchen; my copper, which I polish after each use (much easier and more efficient than it sounds); my pretty mix of contemporary and antique accessories, which include a wrought-iron candle holder attached to one of the wooden beams near the sink, which sheds a warm glow after I've climbed up on the kitchen counter to light the four candles in it; my multiple sinks and custom-made cupboards. I love the big butcher block, the cracks in which I fill with melted beeswax when they start to open up; I love my trash drawers under each sink.

Efficiency is vital to both my mind and my work, and to that end I have a dishwasher that does a quiet load in seventeen minutes, and my tongs, peelers, mixing blades, and other indispensable miscellany hang on either side of the stove for easy reach. Peppers and braids of garlic hang on hooks looking—and tasting—beautiful, and sometimes they're joined by air-cured sausages, too. My baking sheets have their own tall, narrow drawer; I have a woodstove and a fireplace in the kitchen, each of which serves a specific purpose. The woodstove provides heat and acts as a plate warmer; the fireplace is my barbecue.

It's all so pleasing to my eye, and so efficient and comfortable to work in, and it's been put together with such care, using artifacts and treasures that I've found all around me. Of course it's a French kitchen. But then, I'm American in a French land, so it's really my romantic version of a French kitchen. And since I love to not waste time or movement, it is efficiently designed and very well equipped. My French friends? They just want to get great food on the table.

Thus, Monet's kitchen and mine bear little relation to the real French home kitchen, which all too often seems to have a similar status to the toilet—it is relegated to a small, dark space. The cook has to be efficient or nothing edible would ever emerge from it.

Sophie's kitchen is shoved in a corner of a living/dining room area, separated from the dining table by a tall bar. There is one small window that lets in shadowy light. The countertops are uneven gold-colored tile, there is a small double sink that fills up fast, a rack for drying dishes, a few shelves for spices and herbs. A narrow pantry off the kitchen is Sophie's lifesaver—there sit pots and pans, baking dishes, staples. It's organized, but small and dark.

Sophie has made concessions to modernity in this, her kitchen that was recently remodeled. She put in a wall oven and bought a bread-making machine. She put in open shelving, but to my surprise didn't enlarge the kitchen one centimeter. She may as well live on a boat for the space she has.

Sophie's equipment is basic, her knives aren't very sharp, and she uses cracked pottery bowls to mix things in. But the thing is, she doesn't care, either about the state of her equipment, or about having more space or amenities in the kitchen. She's organized, she knows where everything is, her knives cut, and her bowls hold things. Besides, cooking is a means not an end. She wants to do it, she is happy while she's doing it, but ask her and she'll tell you that what really makes her sing are flavor and company. She loves bringing everything to the table, and sitting down to enjoy it with her family and friends. She's economical and efficient in her small kitchen, which she leaves behind for the fun part of eating. She does things the old-fashioned way, like her mamie taught her.

She does, though, love to try new things. Currently she's caught up in the furor of the *verrine* movement, which has the French home cook putting everything but a roast leg of lamb in an odd-shaped glass, and calling it an amuse-bouche.

The *verrine* is a French obsession. As far as I can tell, it began in Lyon where a young chef, Nicholas Lebec, started serving his homemade pâtés in small jars. Each diner got a jar of pâté and took home whatever was left, jar and all. This led to other things served in glass containers until now, one can hardly sit down at a French table—in a restaurant or a home—and not be served something in a sweet little odd-shaped glass container.

The *verrine* has revolutionized French dining more than just about anything else. It has allowed the home cook to serve like a pro—what's prettier than a puree of parsnip topped by a few rounds of fried carrot, garnished with tonka bean (the aromatic seed of a teak tree) and a sprig of chervil, the whole served in a short glass tower and accompanied by a teeny spoon? Or a puree of avocado topped with a layer of smoked salmon, a lime mousse, a pesto of cilantro. It's fussy but simple, and the effect is dramatic.

Sophie has served me the parsnip and the avocado terrines. She makes a delicate lentil salad topped with minced cucumbers and puts it in a wine glass, and her mashed potato and foie gras *verrine*, which she puts in a martini glass, is beyond belief.

Sophie invested in a food processor and, about a year ago, a KitchenAid mixer (that she bought on eBay—the French cook is a thrifty one). When she comes to my house, she drools over my heatproof spatulas, a relative novelty in France. On the other hand, one look at my copper pots and she starts breaking out in hives. "I would never have those," she said. "They're way too much work."

That's the mamie coming out in her. Why spend (money or time) when you don't have to? "What was good enough for her is good enough for me" is Sophie's operating principle. Thus the slightly battered aluminum pot (Alzheimer's be damned), the heavy old cast-iron crêpe pan, the thin, light, stainless-steel saucepan.

Edith's kitchen is long, narrow, and cramped beyond belief (my opinion), though very lovely and efficient once you're in there. She's done tastefully creative tile work on the walls, and has open shelving, a counter between the kitchen and the dining area so she can slide things from one side to the other, and a four-burner stove with a garage-size oven. That she can barely turn around in her kitchen suits her just fine. "I don't want anyone in there with me," she said. The crowning glory of Edith's kitchen is her double stainless-steel sink, along with the window in front of it that she surrounded with her own bright mosaic and which opens onto her herb garden.

Betty and her husband, Louis, just moved into Betty's mother's home, a rambling old place with an acre of land that is dotted with rose gardens, a tennis court, a chicken coop, and a variety of fruit trees and berry bushes. The first thing they did was remodel the kitchen. Like Sophie, though, they didn't make it bigger, just different. It's a light, tidy, pretty little spot with an induction stove (that Betty dislikes intensely because she says it's either too hot or too cool), a wall oven abutting the door, a tall center island that accommodates stools, and all the dishes that Betty has prepared for supper, ready to serve. To one side of the kitchen is Betty's singular nod to nostalgia, an exquisitely beautiful, antique woodstove that doesn't work but is a perfect prop.

Lena is another cooking friend, whose kitchen has a huge, overstuffed armchair in it so she can sit and read in front of the fire. Lena's kitchen also accommodates an imposing refrigerator, a three-burner stove that doesn't always work very well, and a long table where she and her kids eat all their meals and manage all their homework. The thing is, Lena, like so many French cooks I know, doesn't think about the best piece of equipment or a powerful stove. She just cooks using what she has. Not that she doesn't love her kitchen toys—she just bought a fancy French fry maker that uses just 1 tablespoon of oil to produce crisp *frites*; she has a milk foamer and a Nespresso machine; a fancy ice-cream maker; and a complicated radio that receives stations from all over the world (not quite kitchen equipment, but music is important to every cook!). Still, her basic equipment is humble, which proves that you don't need a battery of fancy equipment to produce great food.

Nadine, one of the best home cooks I know, has a huge kitchen that includes space for a big table, a woodstove that burns daily all winter, and a very small work area built at one end. She has minimal countertop space and a very tiny sink that sits in an island across from the stove. I've never figured out how she is so calm about producing such delicious and imaginative dinners for good-size groups. Because she and Christian travel, her menus reflect their latest trip, like the seared tuna and crisp-cooked vegetables with a sweet soy sauce she made after their recent return from Japan.

Not long ago, I helped her prepare a dinner and was astonished to find that her kitchen works perfectly. That's because she designed it for her style of cooking, which is relatively simple. And, Nadine is very efficient. First, she has shelves above her counter next to the stove where all her equipment sits. She cleans up after every dish, keeping her work area free. And the minute a dish is ready to bake or eat, she whisks it out to the pantry, her "holding area." Her knives are all small and mostly dull, like most French cooks I know, but she doesn't even notice this as she cuts and slices away.

Like any cook anywhere, French cooks I know have their indispensables, each of which is personal and unpredictable. Sophie couldn't live without her bread machine and a wide array of wooden spoons. Edith, the simplest and quickest cook of them all, has an electric grater, a professional ice-cream machine she uses daily, and a silver-handled knife with a blade shaped like a scimitar. It belonged to her grandmother and doubles as vegetable peeler, chicken carving tool, and just about everything else. Eloise uses her KitchenAid mixer many times each week, Betty has a double steamer that is her lifesaver, and Lena wouldn't consider life worth living without her grandmother's old-fashioned mixer. As for Nadine, with one knife and a few battered pans, she can make a meal fit for kings and queens.

Here I've compiled a list of must-haves in the kitchen. I admit that I've added many indispensables of my own to help make your life in the kitchen easier. I cook all day long, and I count as French— I've had French nationality for more than five years. So my list is authentic, and will lead you to cooking *comme les français*!

Attention! You don't have to get all this equipment right now. Accumulate it as you need it—that's the French way!

LIST OF
ESSENTIAL KITCHEN TOOLS

The Truly Very French List

Stainless-steel whisk (Okay, Sophie uses a fork to make her vinaigrette and you can, too. But a whisk is quintessentially French!)

10-inch stainless-steel chef's knife

Paring knife

Vegetable peeler

Melon-ball maker

Cheese grater

Juicer (either electric or hand)

Wooden spatulas

Wooden cutting board

2 colanders

Salad spinner

Series of mixing bowls—at least 4

Oyster knife

KitchenAid or other mixer

Food processor

Milk steamer

Siphon

Glass baking dishes—13 by 9 inches and 18 by 9 inches (32.5 by 22.5cm and 45 by 22.5cm)

10½-inch removable-bottom tart pan

Baking sheets

Jelly roll pan

A selection of *verrines* (odd-shaped glass containers—this will make you very French)

Many tea towels, ironed and carefully folded

My Additions, for Really Easy Cooking

2 additional stainless-steel whisks—1 balloon, for egg whites; 1 small balloon, for general everyday things

2 additional stainless-steel paring knives

3-inch stainless-steel knife

Zester

Heatproof spatulas (lucky you—available everywhere in the United States!)

Plastic scrapers

Metal scraper

Fish spatula

Offset spatulas—1 small and 1 large

Springform mold

SOPHIE'S LENTIL VERRINE
{ LA VERRINE DE LENTILLES DE SOPHIE }

Sophie borrowed this recipe from one of my books, and adapted it to her inimitable verrine *style. She changed the seasoning but stuck with the garnish of cucumber and cornichon granité, which I applaud. This pleases everyone who tastes it. I often serve a Crémant de Bourgogne or a wine from Alsace with this lovely little appetizer.*

NOTE: *Properly cooked lentils are "al dente"—that is, cooked to a tender crispness—rather than soft. The most flavorful lentils are the slate-gray* lentilles de Puy, *from the flinty soil of the Auvergne.*

FOR THE GRANITÉ:

> ½ cup (about 16) cornichons (small French pickles) or baby dill pickles
>
> 1 (1½ by 1½-inch / 4 by 4cm) piece fresh cucumber, seeds removed, diced

FOR THE LENTILS:

> 1 cup (190g) small French lentils (*lentilles de Puy*)
>
> 4 coins fresh ginger (each about the thickness of a dime), unpeeled
>
> 20 sprigs fresh lemon thyme or other thyme
>
> 2 fresh bay leaves (from the *Laurus nobilis*) or dried imported bay leaves
>
> 1 small onion, diced
>
> 2 (2 by ½-inch / 5 by 1.25cm) pieces lime zest

FOR THE SALAD DRESSING:

> ½ cup (5g) flat-leaf parsley leaves, minced
>
> 1 tablespoon freshly squeezed lime juice
>
> 1 teaspoon Dijon-style mustard, preferably Maille brand
>
> Sea salt and freshly ground black pepper
>
> 3 tablespoons hazelnut or walnut oil
>
> 1 tablespoon extra-virgin olive oil
>
> 1 shallot, sliced paper-thin

1. To make the granité, place the cornichons and the cucumber in a food processor and process until the mixture is very fine. It won't be a purée, but will be very finely chopped. Place the mixture into an ice cube tray—it will fill about six spaces—and freeze until solid, which will take several hours.

2. To make the lentils, place all the ingredients for them in a small, heavy saucepan. Add enough water to cover the lentils by about 3 inches (7.5cm), which will be about 3 cups (750ml). Bring to a boil over medium-high heat; reduce the heat so the water is simmering merrily and cook, partially covered, until the lentils are tender but still slightly crisp, about 30 minutes. Drain the lentils, reserving the cooking liquid. Remove and discard the herbs and the lime zest.

3. To make the salad dressing, while the lentils are cooking, in a large bowl, whisk together the parsley, lime juice, mustard, and salt and pepper to taste. Add the oils slowly, whisking continuously, until they have emulsified into the vinegar. Whisk in the shallot.

4. When the lentils are cooked, fold them into the bowl with the dressing until they are completely coated. Divide the lentils among eight to ten martini-style glasses, and let sit (if possible) for up to 2 hours before serving.

5. Just before serving, grate an equal amount of the cornichon granité on a fine-holed grater over the glasses so that it looks like a mound of green-white snow. Serve immediately.

SERVES 8 TO 10

VERRINE OF CUCUMBER PUREE WITH HERBED FRESH CHEESE

{ CERVELLE DE CANUT, CONCOMBRE EN PURÉE EN VERRINE }

This delightful first course wakes up the palate with its herbal freshness. Nothing could be simpler, or more lovely! Here, a rich Sauvignon Blanc from Domaine de Mont d'Hortes is ideal.

2 long European cucumbers, peeled, seeded, and cut into chunks

1¾ cups (435ml) fromage blanc (fresh white cheese—you can use pureed large curd cottage cheese)

1 tablespoon white wine vinegar

Sea salt and freshly ground black pepper

1 bunch fresh chives, minced

1. Puree the cucumbers in a food processor. Transfer the puree to a sieve, and set the sieve over a bowl. Chill for at least 1 hour and up to 3 hours.
2. In a medium bowl, whisk the fresh cheese until it becomes slightly lighter. Whisk in the vinegar and season with salt and pepper.
3. Fold the chives into the fresh cheese. Taste and adjust the seasoning; set aside.
4. To serve, pour off (but reserve—it is delicious to drink!) the juice that has drained from the cucumber purée. Season the cucumber purée lightly with salt, then evenly divide it among eight small glasses. Top with an equal amount of the seasoned cheese, and serve immediately.

SERVES 8

LENTILS WITH SAUSAGES

{ LENTILLES AUX SAUCISSES }

My friend Fabienne makes this dish at the drop of a hat, because it's quick, simple, satisfying, and delicious! Traditional vegetables in a dish like this are carrots, celery, onions, and perhaps fennel, which make it so flavorful. Sometimes it's fun to go a bit wild, though, as Fabienne says. "I use red bell pepper," she said. "It gives the dish exciting color and flavor." Whichever vegetables you use, be sure to dice them so they blend in nicely. This calls for a hearty red, from Cahors.

NOTE: *You need delicious pork for this recipe. I've suggested kielbasa and slab bacon; use pork belly or unsmoked bacon, salt pork that you've boiled in fresh water twice first, or fresh pork sausages.*

---

1 tablespoon duck fat or extra-virgin olive oil

2 medium onions, diced

1 small red bell pepper, seeds and pith removed

Sea salt and freshly ground black pepper

1 large clove garlic, green germ removed, minced

1 cup (250g) green lentils (ideally *lentilles de Puy*), picked over for small stones, rinsed

1 bouquet garni

1 (8-ounce; 250g) Morteau or kielbasa, cut into ½-inch (1.2cm) rounds

2 to 3 fresh sausages (about 8 ounces; 250g total), cut into 2-inch (5cm) pieces

6 ounces (180g) lean slab bacon, cut into 1-inch (2.5cm) chunks

Fresh flat-leaf parsley, for garnish

Grainy mustard, for serving

---

1. Melt the duck fat in a medium, heavy-bottomed saucepan over medium heat. Add the onions and bell pepper and stir. Season with salt and black pepper and cook until the onions are translucent, stirring frequently so they don't stick, about 6 minutes. Add the garlic and stir.

2. Add the lentils, stir, and add water to cover them by 1 inch (2.5cm). Add the bouquet garni, pushing it under the water. Raise the heat to

medium-high and when the water boils, reduce the heat to medium so it is simmering, partially cover, and cook until the lentils begin to soften, about 15 minutes.

3. Add the meats, pushing them into the lentils, and additional water if necessary to make sure that the lentils are moist. Return the liquid to a boil, then reduce the heat to maintain a simmer and cook, partially covered, until the lentils are "al dente" and not too soft, 15 to 20 minutes more.

4. Remove from the heat and ladle into four shallow soup bowls. Garnish with a generous grind of black pepper and a parsley leaf. Serve immediately with the mustard alongside.

SERVES 4

CHAPTER 4

Intimacy Amid the Produce

IN GENERAL, THE FRENCH SHOP DAILY. HISTORICALLY, it has been easy to do this at the proliferation of butcher shops, charcuteries, cheese shops, bakeries, pastry shops, fish shops, poultry shops, fruit and vegetable shops, and markets that dot neighborhoods and town centers. This shopping tradition is alive and well in France, and it is one of the best parts of French life.

When I chose to buy my home in Louviers, a town just more than an hour northwest of Paris, many things went into the decision. Not the least was that to one side of the house was a butcher shop, next to that was an *épicerie fine*, a small grocery with a fine wine and spirits selection, and across the *parvis*, in front of the church, was a fish shop that stayed open and lit—casting a briny glow on the stone courtyard in front of the church—until well after dark. There was a big farmers' market every Saturday morning in the main town square three minutes from my house, and a smaller market on Wednesday mornings, too. That three bakeries were within a five-minute walk helped, as did the café kitty-corner from the front gate.

So despite crumbling walls, no heat, the suggestion of a kitchen, and hostile neighbors who were convinced we were the Antichrist, the house became ours and my life as it should be, in a small French town, *sans voiture*, without a car (because all of my immediate needs were within walking or bicycling distance), began.

Now, I'll admit that Louviers isn't the cultural hub of the universe, though we do have a national theater company, a five-theater cinema, a museum, an aqua center rivaling Disney World, and a former mayor who had delusions of grandeur that resulted in streets lit up like the Champs-Élysées. I'll admit, too, that occasionally when I see the streets rolled up firm at eight P.M., I want to lock my door and run screaming for the next train to Paris (which I do, frequently, though without screaming). Nonetheless, Louviers and its *commerçants*, merchants, and its *marchés*, markets, have sustained my soul.

I do most of my fresh ingredient shopping at the farmers' market on Saturday morning, where I employ a certain strategy that allows me to avoid lines, shop efficiently and well, yet feel as though I've just had a little vacation at a great outdoor fair.

My strategy is well honed. I go early—I'm usually there by eight thirty—so that I can avoid the lines and head toward my favorite *maraîcher*, market gardener, Baptiste. I stop by the egg man first, drop off egg cartons, and order and pay for large, gorgeous, brown eggs because there won't be any left if I don't do it immediately, and they'll get buried and broken besides. I'll pick them up on my way home. If there is no line at Baptiste's, he and I slip away for a coffee where we're often joined by a trio of chefs from local-area restaurants, some of them honored with Michelin stars. The ten minutes we spend over coffee is a chance for all of us to laugh (I hear a lot of raunchy jokes at this regular rendezvous, not all of which are translated for my benefit!), share work notes, gripe if necessary.

Back at Baptiste's I point to what I want, and he weighs it out and puts the produce in my basket. "That will be thirty euros and sixty cents," he'll say. "Just thirty euros for you, my dear." This, and an extra black radish or handful of mâche is his appreciation for my patronage, what the French call *bon poids*, good weight.

The exchange made, I go straight to the mushroom man for my weekly supply of shiitakes and button mushrooms, maybe some *pleurottes*, oyster mushrooms, or chanterelles. I crane my neck to see if there is a line at the cheese truck—if it's long I get other things done until I spy that it's short and then I make my way there to spoil myself, relying on the cheese mongers to choose the very best. My last stop is usually the fish stand where Xavier, the burly fishmonger, always yells, "Heeeey, Suzannnnne!" and tries to get me to buy something outrageously expensive like St. Pierre turbot. I do buy this occasionally, but my regular choices are modest because I am a mackerel, sardine, and cod lover.

I make my way home back through the market where I inevitably pick up a few more items—persimmons if they're fat and ripe, apples if their perfume grabs me, gorgeous Israeli avocados (I know, not local, but a girl's got to live), and finally, those beautiful eggs. At this point, my rolling basket is full, I've got another full basket balanced on top of it, and another hangs from my shoulder. Fortunately, the walk home takes five minutes.

Since my fresh produce comes primarily from the market and

the hands of those who produced it, Chez Clet, the grocery next door, serves as stopgap. And what a stopgap—the fruit and vegetables are gorgeous, temptingly spilling out onto the sidewalk. Inside, there are exotics from the French *Doms-Toms*, their former colonies, like passion fruits, black pineapples, mangos, and mangosteen and every possible variety of rum.

When I go in, there is one major rule to respect, aside from the obligatory *"Bonjour, Messieurs/Mesdames"* that took me years to perfect. That rule? *"Ne touchez pas,"* don't touch. The customer asks, the merchant delivers. It is a more than fair exchange, as accountability reigns supreme. No self-respecting merchant would try to pass off anything but the best, nor charge overly exorbitant prices because customers would complain, and the merchant's reputation would suffer.

In our frantic and frenzied world it's sometimes easy to forget that merchants are at the mercy of their customers. Not in France, at least not in my town. The *épicier* used to try to sell an occasional vegetable that was less than fresh, and he was roundly criticized. Since his son has joined the business, filled with youthful enthusiasm, contemporary marketing ideas, a sense of "kitsch" and nostalgia (he's brought in old-fashioned wooden carts to display fruit, has instituted uniforms for all the vendors, has a shelf of artisanally produced cookies all tied with little ribbons), this practice is gone and the shop's reputation has soared. At Chez Clet, as at our other wonderful *épicerie*, Prim'Eure, a ten-minute walk across town, accountability reigns supreme and you don't touch. Should there be a problem—a moldy clementine, an overly bruised pear—it is exchanged, no questions asked.

There is a charming intimacy about the interactions in these food shops. I never tire of it. For a minute, at least, while you're discussing a cut of meat, a type of cheese, the very best clementine, you are part of the social fabric of the entire country. You are called upon to discuss your taste, the tastes of your family and your guests. You reveal your plans. In exchange you get exactly the right ingredient, usually with a tip or two on how to prepare or use it. You are also likely to walk away with a personal anecdote or a little story that advances your relationship. Little by little, you're allowed to get to know these people who serve you, and they you. While you may never socialize, you are clearly part of the same community.

I notice this particularly at the butcher shop next door. The butcher, Stéphane, and his wife, Christine, work inhumanely long hours, stashing their two children in the house behind the shop. They are professional in their black-and-white-striped coats, attentive to the finest detail of their clients' desire. They've been my neighbors for seven years (they took over from the other couple who had no children and kept even longer hours), and while they know what I put on my table many nights for supper, I know little about them.

I see Madame Coutard walk her children to school twice a day—in the morning and at noon. I run into her often at the bakery, where we end up talking about subjects of universal interest—school, children's activities—with Nadège, the *boulangère*. Yet she has never been in my home, and I've never been in hers. I never see Mr. Coutard outside his shop because I think he lives in his *laboratoire*, kitchen. Yet, there is a familiarity among us that is hard to describe.

Example—not so long ago a close friend asked if I'd make the main course for his wife's sixtieth birthday party. There would be one hundred guests, and it promised to be great fun. I decided on beef cheeks, and went to order them from Mr. Coutard.

At my request, his eyebrows shot up to hairline. "*Oh la la la la,*" he said. "*Impossible. Maintenant il est trop difficile de les obtenir, ça sera impossible,*" he said firmly. "Impossible. It has become way too difficult to find them. It's impossible." I was floored. I was in a meat palace. Every part of every edible beast should be available. I had my heart set on beef cheeks, a piece of meat that turns into the richest, most succulent almost candied confection after being marinated for hours, then cooked for hours more.

I stood in the chilly butcher shop in front of hunk after hunk of gloriously healthy-looking meat, my mind working, my breath short. What would I serve, what would I serve? *Magret*, fattened duck breast? No, everyone serves that for group meals. Lamb shanks? "Eeemposseeble," I imagined. I looked up at the butcher and he was on the phone. When he turned to me he said, "*Ca y est, j'ai trouvés les joux.*" "It's all worked out, I found the cheeks."

My heart skipped a beat, my breathing took on a normal cadence. This was a lesson to me in the Norman—perhaps the French—attitude toward life. Say no first, then say yes. Everyone's happy, the heart beats faster. It's an exhausting way to live, but it's the Norman way.

That "yes" began a rollicking road through relationship building as the number of guests for the party I was "catering" continued to increase. From 100 it went to 125; then 150, then 175. I held tough, running to the butcher each time. He became my partner, getting on the phone and securing me beef cheeks. "Madame, I will trim and wrap them individually," Mr. Coutard said. "They'll take up less room in your freezer."

The first shipment of thirty pounds arrived; I paid for them and put them in the freezer. The second shipment of sixty pounds was on the way. I was getting increasingly nervous, and so was the butcher. He offered to loan me buckets for the marinade, pans for the baking. Pretty soon, he offered me his ovens, and was just about to offer himself as my co-chef when the number of guests shot above two hundred, and I got hives.

It wasn't the number of guests that made me cry uncle and back out. Nor was it the many pounds of beef cheeks in my possession. I'm not a quitter. But a hot dish for two hundred people in a remodeled barn, which I learned late in the game had an oven the size of a small television, was looking like a disaster in the making. I called the friend who'd asked me to do the job; he was behind me 100 percent in my decision to desist from the challenge, confessing that the whole thing was getting beyond even him. (He ended up hiring a professional caterer who made chicken in cream sauce. The only consolation I had was that it was boring and my dish would have been explosive. Oh well.) I then had to go tell the butcher, who had sixty pounds of beef cheeks ready to hand over to me.

I screwed up my courage and, checkbook in hand, went and told him. He looked at me. "Madame," he said. "You have made a courageous decision. Your reputation was *en jeu*, on the line, and you must think of that before loyalty. You had no way of knowing it would be so many people." I asked him for the beef cheeks, and began to fill out a check. When I looked up to ask how much I owed, he had a vacant look in his eyes for a moment, then he snapped back and said, "Madame, I can sell these beef cheeks here. People clamor for them and I hardly ever have them."

I didn't believe him. I thought he was just being kind and I insisted that it was no problem for me (lie).

"Madame, if I cannot sell them then I will tell you," he said. "Let me try."

I cried as I walked out the door. How could I have known that this butcher, who rarely cracks a smile, can be brusque and short, works the livelong day six and a half days a week, never allows himself to overstep the professional boundary between service and client, could have been so GOOD? We may not have a warm and neighborly relationship as my American vision would have it, but when the chips are down, he proved himself stalwart. He sold every last beef cheek.

Meanwhile, I had thirty pounds of trimmed, individually wrapped cheeks in my freezer. To give you an idea of what that represents in quantity, it was about a cubic yard of meat. Because I often host lunches and dinners for groups in my home, I prepared them as the main course for several months until I exhausted every one. Each time, they were a roaring success. For a while I wasn't sure I could look at another beef cheek but, like anything, the pain fades and the pleasure returns. I've got some marinating in red wine downstairs right now!

I wouldn't trade my relationship with these shopkeepers for the world. But whether it is going to the *boucher*, where Mr. Coutard refuses to do anything in advance so each client waits while he painstakingly trims, flames, pats, arranges, ties, or to the *épicier* where he or she hand-picks each apricot, or the *fromagerie*, where the virtues of each cheese are carefully detailed, each transaction takes time, sometimes maddeningly so.

This is where the supermarket comes in. Not often for me, but for the shopper who cares less about intimacy and social fabric and just wants to get the shopping done, it's the answer.

French supermarkets don't leave me unaffected. They are universally vast and unattractive, completely lacking in warmth and personality, resembling Costco without the ceiling height and happy bustle. They act as a town center under one roof. It is common to find knots of people in the aisles discussing affairs of the day, bags or baskets on their arms since the supermarket doesn't give them away anymore, just as they might in the local town square. These groups cause traffic jams, as shoppers wheel around them as best they can, fighting the French grocery cart, which is designed to be perennially out of control unless packed to the gills.

But the French supermarket is fun, because—and I say this after twenty-plus years of life in France—they have all these exotic French products on the shelf. I never quite get over it. And I do depend on the supermarket for a few things. Coffee is number one. I've sampled every possible type in France, I believe, from Hédiard's hand-roasted and gorgeous beans (starting price 18 euros a pound) to Carte Noir, from the supermarket, which goes for about 6 euros a pound. I've settled on Malongo brand (6 euros a pound), a delicious blend of Arabica beans that is part of a *commerces equitable*, fair trade, network, and is associated with the group Max Havelar, which ensures that coffee producers benefit fairly from their work. It's absolutely delicious coffee.

I get a few other things there—yogurt, sometimes milk, always butter for baking, a few dry goods. And while I'm there I love to investigate. The dairy aisle is my favorite—I have never gotten over the array of yogurts and milk-based puddings (Flanby, an industrialized sort of crème caramel that I've never tasted and hope I never have to, became famous when its name was attached to the French president whose character was compared with its texture), fresh cheeses and creams, varieties of milk (organic, buttermilk, a cultured milk from north Africa, farm-fresh milk), and many brands of butter.

I buy chocolate in the candy aisle, which ends up being a spot where I sometimes feel as though I'm taking a class in current

French culture. I'll explain. From my point of view, the French have a huge sweet tooth. They don't just eat gorgeous little cream-filled pastries and tarts, either. They love candy. I'm not a candy eater, but because everyone I know here grew up eating candy, and because I have French-raised children, I know the names of some, but not all, the popular French candies. I am actually fundamentally opposed to candy, but nonetheless a steady flow of Carambars (caramel sticks with jokes and riddles on the inside of the wrapper), Malabar (bubble gum with more jokes and riddles), and Dragibus (like Dots) made its way through my house, often thanks to teachers who reward students with candy. I usually discover just the wrappers, my kids being canny enough to consume what they are given.

The French have great nostalgia for the candy of their childhood. Take this case in point. I was with a group at a lovely restaurant in Rouen called 37. The chef had prepared us a special meal with a surprise dessert, which he served himself. It was three crème brûlées. "They each have a flavor of childhood," he said proudly. "You need to find them." He stood there while we all—Americans down to the last—tasted. I found one, because it was licorice and obvious. The other two? Impossible to even take a guess. Why? Because our flavors of childhood and French flavors of childhood are totally different. All three crème brûlées were flavored after three different candies—*fraises tagada*, *Carambar*, and *réglisse*, or licorice. If we'd been in the United States, I figured the crème brûlées would have been flavored with peanut butter, Oreos, maybe Tootsie Roll. The chef, so proud of his idea, couldn't believe how uncultured we were. And that's one reason I stand in front of the candy aisle sometimes, becoming cultured.

I also like the exotic food section, where the Old El Paso brand reigns supreme, thanks to the French fascination with tacos, and the excellent distribution system of the parent company, General Mills. Depending on the supermarket chain there are more exotics— delicious Patak chutneys, peanut butter, often lemon curd, usually brands of what an Irish friend calls "Builder's Tea," Yorkshire Gold. Just today I bought McVities digestives, Oreos recently broke the culture barrier, and I'm waiting for the day I see graham crackers and organic Cheetos. When those arrive, I'll never have to go back to the United States.

Finally, I love living in a country where speculoos butter and Nutella sit on the shelves as proudly as peanut butter does at home. I rarely buy either, but it's just fun to see them there.

Supermarket employees, on the other hand, rarely know anything about the food they sell, nor do they seem to care. They are, I almost hate to say this, typically French in that their faces are permanently set in neutral-to-dour, and if you ask for help they'll stare at you just long enough to make you uneasy, then they may or may not come forth with an answer. I say this with sincerity, yet very recently I've noticed a change in supermarket employee attitude. Not all the time, and not at all supermarkets, but enough that there may be hope. I wonder if there is some team building going on.

Our supermarkets have recently installed the self-checkout spots, which allow the average shopper to pretend he or she is a cashier. I love them. They take me back to my early childhood, when I dreamed of being a cashier so I could hear the clang of a cash register, handle goods, count out change, tap lots of buttons. Of course, the automatic cashier just has you swipe the bar code, but the sound when you do is so satisfying—just like a cash register. It's not politically correct to use these automatic cashiers, because they have effectively cut the workforce. But they beat standing in line for forty minutes while the always seated human cashier moves as though underwater. If the line is short at the human cashier, of course I wait in it. If it's multi-shopper and over-stacked-shopping-cart deep, I head for the automatic cashier and a chance to relive my youth.

Aside from *supermarchés* and *hypermarchés* (giant *supermarchés*), there is a proliferation of other stores that I call "package stores," with names like Lidl, Dia, Aldi, Leader Price. These are discount (pronounced "deeskoont") stores that act like supermarkets, though they're smaller and tend to offer either generic brands or others one has never heard of. Merchandise sits in cardboard boxes that are stacked on shelves, and everything has a pilfered rather than organized look. Their prices are right if they happen to have something you need. The other day, for instance, I stopped into a Lidl near my home because they usually stock delicious *lebkuchen*, chocolate-dipped spice cookies from Germany (the company is German-owned). There were none, but I found gorgeous *rose de Roskoff*, gourmet onions from Brittany at a plebian price. I snapped up a string of them, delighted, as they're hard to find. Why were they at Lidl? I don't even want to know, in case the answer is that the growers are having trouble getting rid of them, so they've lowered the price to make them attractive to discount grocers like Lidl.

Though there is an increasing number of discount supermarkets, none of them come close to something like Costco except for a chain of huge supermarkets called Métro, which is reserved for professionals. I shop there and often see local chefs, the owner of the *épicerie* next door, and some of my town's café owners. At Métro things are sold by the case, from avocados to lemons, nuts, melons, mushrooms. You can buy huge cans of olives; jugs of premade caramel; big boxes of Haribo candies; bags of chocolate pastilles that are used by bakers (and sometimes by me). I go to buy certain things—large cans of anchovies from Collioure, the very best in the world, I think, which I use up in everything from tapenade to aperitifs; chocolate and cocoa; sea salt, flour, sugar; and my favorite thing, candles. The candles at Métro are French-made, they burn forever, and I use them by the ton. That Métro isn't open to the public doesn't seem to bother anyone. The French simply don't buy in bulk. Because they have the daily shopping gene, they buy smaller quantities and use them up rapidly.

Supermarkets can be efficient. They can also eat up more of your money than you want to spend, something I've learned through experience. I have gone in for a tube of toothpaste, and come out with a set of four wrought-iron garden chairs and a table. Did I need the latter? Maybe, but life was all right without them. So, what the supermarket shopper gives up in favor of efficiency is a balanced budget, further knowledge about ingredients, cooking and household tips, culture, and the illusion that all is available all the time.

None of this matters to the shopper trained by Mamie, because that person makes a beeline for the best wherever he or she goes. And that person generally prefers to frequent the market and the smaller shops, if time permits. It does matter to the general culture of France which is, while frayed, for now still intact. Small shops offering information and quality help it stay strong, and when I see the *épicerie* and *boucherie*, the patisseries and boulangeries near me so crowded there are people on the street waiting to get in, my heart soars. I'm not the only one who wants French culture to thrive. Sixty percent of the French buy their groceries at the farmers' market or at the *épicerie fine*. They all agree with me that intimacy among the produce makes for better meals and, quite simply, a better life.

BRAISED BROCCOLI
{ BROCCOLI BRAISÉ }

Every time I eat broccoli, I think it's my favorite vegetable. Of course, then I eat another vegetable and think the same thing. But there is something deeply satisfying about broccoli, and when it is in season (early spring, how exciting!), I cook it often. Usually, I braise it as here, because it's so flavorful this way, and it's so quick and easy.

Use the stems on the broccoli if they're nice and fresh.

2 bunches broccoli (generous 1 pound / 540g), florets separated into bite-size pieces, stems peeled and cut into ½-inch (1.25cm) chunks

4 small (about 1-ounce / 30g) spring onions, trimmed and quartered

2 cloves garlic, green germ removed, cut in matchsticks

2 tablespoons extra-virgin olive oil

Coarse sea salt (or fine if that is all you have) and freshly ground black pepper

10 fresh thyme sprigs

1 fresh bay leaf (from the *Laurus nobilis*) or dried imported bay leaf

1. Place the broccoli and the onions in a heavy-bottomed skillet. Strew the garlic over all, then add ½ cup (125ml) water and drizzle with the oil. Shake the pan so everything is combined. Season generously with salt and pepper, then lay the herbs on top. Bring the liquid to a boil over medium-high heat, then reduce the heat to medium-low, cover the pan, and simmer just until the broccoli is tender, about 8 minutes, shaking the pan occasionally and checking once to be sure the broccoli isn't sticking to the bottom of the pan.

2. Remove the cover from the pan, raise the heat to medium-high, and dry out the broccoli, shaking the pan so it moves around in it, until it is golden brown, 3 to 4 minutes. Remove from the heat. Remove the herbs and serve immediately.

SERVES 4

SUCCULENT BEEF CHEEKS
{ JOUES DE BOEUF SUCCULENTES }

*I like to serve these succulent beef cheeks atop a puree of either squash,
potatoes, Jerusalem artichokes, or celery root. They're satisfyingly delicious, so easy to prepare, and something you and your guests will remember and dream of eating again. So elegant, so lovely, this dish begs
for a carefully constructed and elegant wine from Clos de l'Anhel, Les
Terrasettes being my first choice.*

> 1 pound (500g) beef cheeks, nerves and fat trimmed
> 4 cups (1L) hearty red wine, such as one from the Languedoc
> 4 fresh bay leaves (from the *Laurus nobilis*) or dried imported bay
>   leaves
> 10 sprigs fresh thyme
> 10 whole black peppercorns
> ¼ orange, preferably organic
> 2 carrots, diced
> 1 tablespoon extra-virgin olive oil
> Sea salt and freshly ground black pepper
> 2 to 4 cups (.5 to 1L) beef stock
> Squash or potato puree, for serving
> Braised carrots, for serving

1. Cut the beef cheeks vertically into three pieces each and put them in a
   nonreactive bowl. Cover with the wine; add 2 of the bay leaves and the
   remaining herbs, the orange, and the carrots. Cover and marinate in
   the refrigerator for 24 hours, or at least overnight, turning the cheeks
   once or twice.
2. Preheat the oven to 270°F (130°C).
3. Remove the beef cheeks from the marinade and pat dry. Strain the
   wine, discarding the solids, and pour it into a saucepan over medium
   heat, and when it is hot, flame it. To do this, simply light a match right
   over the hot-to-simmering wine. The alcohol given up by the wine will
   catch fire, and you'll have a nice blue flame roving over the top of the

wine, until the fire has consumed all the alcohol. When this bit of artistry is finished, remove the pan from the heat.

4. Heat the oil in a skillet over medium-high heat. When it is hot but not smoking, brown the cheeks, seasoning them generously with salt and pepper. Transfer the cheeks to a 6-quart (6L) roasting pan. Pour the wine over the cheeks, add the remaining bay leaves and 2 cups (500ml) of the stock, or as much as you need to cover the cheeks. Cover the pan and cook until the cheeks are tender and melting, at least 4 hours. Check from time to time, turning the cheeks and adding additional stock if necessary to cover the cheeks.

5. Uncover from the pan and let the cheeks cook an additional 1 hour, turning them two or three times.

6. When the cheeks are fully tender, remove them from the pan. Place the cooking liquid over medium-high heat and cook until it has reduced to about 1½ cups. Taste for seasoning.

7. To serve, use two forks to shred the beef cheeks. Add enough reduced cooking liquid to moisten the meat, and serve atop squash or potato puree and braised carrots.

SERVES 4

SPICED CHICKEN WINGS
{ AILES DE POULET AUX ÉPICES }

Inspired by the chicken wings that come my way from the butcher next door, Stéphane Coutard, I put this little recipe together one night when time was short and appetites were big. The French occasionally use spice mixtures like this one, thanks to the French colonial presence in Martinique and Guadeloupe, as well as the Île de la Reunion, where these spices are common. They add a lilt to this simple preparation, giving it a slight exotic aroma. A wine as fun as this dish is called for: I recommend a sprightly white, such as a Sauvignon Blanc and Chardonnay blend from Réthoré Davy in the Loire.

*I like to accompany these chicken wings with a fresh cabbage salad
(page 291).*

NOTE: *The hot pepper is really to your taste—add more if you like spicy
wings.*

1½ cups (225g) all-purpose flour

1 teaspoon ground cinnamon

2 teaspoons powdered ginger

1 teaspoon ground turmeric

½ to 1 teaspoon piment d'Espelette, or pinch of cayenne pepper
(see Note)

1½ teaspoons fine sea salt

Freshly ground black pepper

2½ pounds (1.25kg) chicken wings, wing tips tucked under the
drumstick, at room temperature

2 tablespoons duck fat or extra-virgin olive oil

1. Preheat the oven to 425°F (220°C) and position a rack in the center.
2. Place the flour, cinnamon, ginger, turmeric, piment d'Espelette, salt,
and pepper to taste in a brown paper bag and shake the bag until they
are thoroughly combined. Add the chicken wings by twos and shake
until they are thoroughly dusted with the flour blend. Place the wings
on a wire rack and, if you have time, let them sit for 30 minutes, then
dust them again. If you don't have time for the waiting period and
second dusting, just go ahead and bake them immediately. The second
dusting just makes them a bit more crisp.
3. Place the duck fat in a large, heavy baking pan and place it in the oven
for 5 minutes. Remove it, make sure the fat is spread evenly across the
bottom of the pan, and place the chicken wings in the pan. Bake for 15
minutes. Turn the wings, and bake until they are crisp, golden, and
cooked through, 15 to 20 minutes more. Remove from the oven.

SERVES 4

TRIO OF FISH IN PACKETS
{ TRIO DE POISSON EN PAPILLOTE }

I was served this for dinner at the home of Sandrine and Roch Balouka, teachers both, neither of whom likes to spend a lot of time in the kitchen—their idea of a good meal is a fast and easy one. Yet they enjoy eating and want good, fresh food on the table.

I've adapted their recipe by using radishes instead of cherry tomatoes because they were in season. You do the same—use the vegetables in season, remembering to cut them in thin slices. You can adapt this recipe any way you like it—use oil instead of butter, any herb that you've got in the garden, spices that make you happy.

I like using different colored fish—it adds to the visual interest of the dish. Again, use what is best and most fresh. Serve a Chardonnay with this dish, even if it's a weeknight!

8 ounces (250g) salmon fillet, bones removed

8 ounces (250g) firm white fish fillet, such as lingcod, snapper, tilapia, bones removed

8 ounces (250g) halibut or other delicate white fish, bones removed

¼ cup (about 3g) fresh tarragon leaves, minced

Fine sea salt and freshly ground black pepper

2 shallots, sliced paper-thin

2 medium radishes, cut into paper-thin rounds

1 generous tablespoon unsalted butter, cut in 4 equal pieces

Fleur de sel, for garnish

1. Rinse the fish and cut each piece on the bias into four even pieces so that they are flat rather than chunky. This will allow them to cook more evenly. Refrigerate.

2. Preheat the oven to 450°F (225°C) and position a rack in the center. Cut four pieces of parchment paper that measure about 12 by 6 inches (30.5 by 15.24cm). Cut four pieces of aluminum foil that measure about 18 by 11½ inches (45.7 by 29cm). Place the parchment in the center of the foil.

3. Arrange one piece of each fish in the center of the parchment paper, arranging them so they are touching but not overlapping, in a sort of flower pattern. Season generously with salt and pepper. Top each with equal amounts of shallots and radishes, then sprinkle with tarragon. Season again with salt and pepper, and set a piece of butter on top. Bring the foil and the parchment together above the fish and gently twist so it makes a closed packet. Repeat with the remaining ingredients.

4. Place the packets on a baking sheet, and bake for 15 to 20 minutes, or until the fish is opaque through. (You may need to check by removing one of the packets from the oven and deftly opening it to see if the fish is cooked. If just about, but not quite, cooked, give the aluminum a twist and let the packets sit while you call everyone to the table for dinner. If not cooked at all—doubtful—return to the oven for 3 to 5 minutes.)

5. Remove the packets from the oven, immediately remove them from the baking sheet, and open them. Assemble your plates, giving the fish a few minutes to sit, then carefully remove the fish and vegetables from the packets with a slotted spatula, and place them in the center of a warmed dinner plate. Drizzle with a bit of cooking juices, season with fleur de sel, and serve. Don't serve the packets at the table—it ends up being complicated for the diner, because they have to figure out what to do with a pile of paper and aluminum foil on their plates.

SERVES 4

CHAPTER 5

Always Salad

GREEN SALAD IS FUNDAMENTAL TO THE FRENCH MEAL, so much so that it is often taken for granted, like the fork or the wineglass. Yet it is worthy of a chapter, a mythic poem, an epic tale, for it is a rare work of art, a simple creation and a perfect one.

Tender, crisp, green salad comes after the main course. It is just perfect lettuce dressed with a vinaigrette that is usually spiced with mustard, a sprinkling of chives, shallot. The lettuce is so tender, the vinaigrette the perfect balance of tart, salty, smooth. There is nothing else to confuse the issue—no nuts, no apples, no chunks of potato.

The reasons for serving this treasure after the main course are varied. Some say it's a palate refresher. Others claim that the vinegar helps the transition from salty to sweet; still others insist that the greenery helps digestion. In my experience, the little green salad does a bit of all of those.

I was discussing salad with my friend Betty, who is also my arbiter of taste. "I always serve salad after the main course," she said. "But you know, there is a trend to serve *salade* before the meal. Honestly, this is so silly. We say that the vinaigrette in a salad dulls the taste buds so you cannot serve it before a meal. Who would do this, anyway?"

So far, no one I know.

There is so much that goes into making a French salad special. Most important is the lettuce, called *salade* in French. There is a panoply of tender varieties with names like *rougette, feuille de chêne,* mâche, *laitue, lollo* and *lollo rossa, Batavia,* and then there is iceberg (pronounced "eisebehrg") and *sucrine.* Each holds dressing perfectly, and they're all gorgeous.

Like anything worth enjoying, a perfect green salad takes time to make. The time is lettuce-dependent. Lettuce in France is filled with grit and soil, and if you get yours from the market like I do, chances are that your life will be as well. So, lettuce of any worth needs serious rinsing.

Before I explain how to do this, some advice: Rinse and refrigerate lettuce you get at the market as soon as you get home; that way you are always prepared to make a salad. Use up the more fragile varieties right away—butter, oak leaf, romaine—then move along to those that keep a bit longer. To keep lettuce as fresh as possible, keep it refrigerated in the lettuce spinner, or in a big plastic container or a plastic bag lined with paper towels. Rinsed lettuce will keep about three days.

"Rinsing lettuce is nothing," you say.

Well, I'm so sorry, but you're wrong. Rinsing lettuce is primordial to the quality of the salad you serve, and to your worth as host or hostess. Just think. You take a nice bite of beautiful salad, tempted by its alluring aroma, and "Crack!" Your tooth hits grit, your entire brain feels like someone is piercing it with a needle. No guest, no being, wants such violence done to them.

So, rinsing lettuce is important. To do it properly, you need to look at each leaf. You never know when a stem or a wrinkle might harbor some grit.

Of all the lettuces, mâche is the most difficult to rinse. I have friends who won't buy it because it's so much trouble, but oh! what pleasure it gives! Its small, dark green, spatulate leaves grow from a teeny central stem in a kind of whorl, which is a universe of fleshy, tender, violet-flavored leaves. Nonetheless, I dread the rinsing process, too, which is due, I think, to a mild case of post-traumatic stress syndrome.

Here is the scenario: When I was a cooking apprentice at La Varenne Ecole de Cuisine in Paris, I pretty much stayed out of the way of the head chef, Fernand Chambrette. He scared the living daylights out of me even though I was a good head taller than him. He'd yell—and I mean yell—and scowl, pinch, throw, and grimace his way through the days.

One of the things that made him boil was finding grit in the mâche. "Rinse it seven times," he'd yell, coming up behind whomever was at the sink and breathing down their neck as he watched them. "Seven times, seven times, seven times."

Even now I tremble just a bit when I rinse mâche, though I religiously follow the method I learned from Chef Chambrette (who never, ever turned out to be anything but who he was, yet whom we all adored). This method works for all lettuces.

Fill a sink two-thirds with water. Gently push the mâche into it and swirl to dislodge the grit. Leave it for five minutes, come back, lift out the mâche into a bowl, feel the bottom of the sink to see if there is grit (there will be), and repeat until there is no more grit. As you're rinsing and observing the mâche, you can trim off stems and gently break apart whorls so they are relatively bite size (keeping the leaves intact). Once you are satisfied, gently spin the mâche dry and use it in a salad, or put it in a plastic box or keep it in the salad spinner in the fridge. It will keep longer than most lettuces.

When it comes to leaf lettuce, the process is similar. Take *rougette*, a small, firm, almost chocolaty-colored lettuce that looks like a big rose. It gets soil stuck down near the base of the leaves, so as you tear the leaf gently away from the stem, going right to the clustered heart of miniature leaves, first rinse each leaf there to remove the soil. Put the leaves in water. Swirl, lift out of the water, feel the bottom of the sink. As long as there is grit, continue to repeat the process.

While Chef Chambrette was a stickler for tradition and perfection, when it came to lettuce rinsing, he was just teaching what he'd undoubtedly learned from his mother and grandmother. Every French cook does what he does, without the yelling. Take Edith—she goes out to the huge garden in front of her house, pulls a head of lettuce from the ground, tears off any damaged outer leaves and slices off the root end, so she won't carry half a garden's worth of soil back with her into the kitchen. She fills one of her stainless-steel sinks with water, carefully removes each leaf from the head of lettuce, and begins swirling and rinsing. She does this without thinking. "I can't stand grit in the salad," she says. "If I find some, I won't eat the salad."

Tightly packed lettuces like *sucrine*, which is fleshily juicy and sweet with white to yellow leaves, and its torpedo-shaped cousin, Belgian endive, are simple to rinse because grit can't get into them. A quick trim and rinse, and they're ready to go. So is *scarole*, or escarole, because its leaves are huge and they rinse quickly, though you may need to rub soil off the stems. Curly endive can be challenging because it has so many places for grit to hide, so you have to be more vigorous as you swish it around in the water.

Iceberg seems like a slam-dunk when it comes to rinsing, but what I get at the market is disaster waiting to happen. Despite a firm head that seems as though it might be impervious to grit, it can be chock-full as I discovered recently after I'd rinsed a head only twice.

Pre-rinsed lettuce is available at the supermarket in France. I don't know anyone who buys it, but I understand those who do. I've just described the time-consuming task of rinsing lettuce. The lettuce in a bag is a huge time-saver and it is pretty on the plate. But it will never offer you the flavor of lettuce from the market.

When you make your little green salad, consider mixing lettuce varieties. Try *lollo* or *lollo rosso*, whose slightly firm, frilly leaves have a mild flavor, with *rougette*, which is a bit crisp and quite sweet; you can toss in some *laitue*, which tends toward pistachio green in color, is very tender and has a tannic quality. Or, you might want to do a mix of *feuille de chêne*, which is delicate with just the slightest bitter hint at the end, and *batavia*, which is crisp with a curly edged leaf, is closely related to iceberg, and has a wonderful "green" flavor. If you can find it, use *sucrine*, a small variety of romaine that has an almost buttery texture, and again a slight bitterness. And don't underestimate iceberg (no, I am not joking). If you can get some fresh from the ground, try it. There isn't another lettuce that is so crisp and refreshing, with such a delicate "chlorophyll" flavor.

While green salad made with these varieties of lettuce is always served after a meal in France, there is a whole other category of salads that is uniquely and marvelously delicious. Called *salades composées*, these are generally based on the more gutsy lettuce varieties, loaded with lots of other ingredients, and served as a first or main course.

Among the gutsy lettuces I count Belgian endive, a crisp, ivory white torpedo tipped in either scarlet or yellow; *scarole*, escarole, with its fleshy white to green and often pleasantly bitter leaves; frisée, curly endive, also of the slightly bitter family with a tickly, fringed edge; *roquette*, arugula, a southern lettuce with its spicy smokiness that has made its halting way north; and *romaine*, whose French version is darker of leaf, with an almost perfumey taste.

The *salade composée* is the mainstay of the café and bistro lunch menu. It is a meal on a plate, and a perfect foil for a *ballon de rouge*, a glass of simple red wine, and a basket full of crusty bread.

There are classic *salades composées* and among my favorite is the *salade Landaise*. Its base is frisée. It's dressed with a mustardy vinaigrette that is usually spiked with garlic, and then loaded with many of the things I love best—thin slices of smoked duck breast, sautéed *gésiers*, gizzards, from a force-fed duck, a fat slice or two of foie gras, perhaps even a few slices of air-cured ham. Toast is usually served on the side, and a better winter meal cannot be made.

Other typical composed salads include endive topped with Roquefort and raw walnuts; the famous *frisée aux lardons*, curly endive dressed with vinegar and hot bacon fat, then topped with hot bacon and a poached egg. There is the *salade Niçoise* with green beans and anchovies, *salade Norvegienne* (page 97) with smoked salmon, freshly poached shrimp, potatoes, cucumber, and dill, and a salad of escarole topped with slabs of Cantal, Bleu d'Auvergne, and Laguiole.

Salades composées are often on my menu because they're such a great blend of textures, colors, and flavors. One I made the other night was a blend of iceberg and red oak leaf lettuce that I'd torn into large bite-size pieces and dressed in a lemony vinaigrette that included some walnut oil. I sautéed leftover potatoes that I'd cut into rounds, and some strips of duck breast—the fillet part—that I'd rolled first in piment d'Espelette. I put the salad on plates and when both potatoes and duck were golden, laid them atop the lettuce. I deglazed the pan with a tiny bit of red wine vinegar, and poured a bit over each salad, then seasoned it with pepper and fleur de sel. So delicious, so satisfying.

A *salade composée* is also quick (if the lettuce is already rinsed). I always have eggs and I usually have a pot of *confit* shallots on hand, too. It's so easy to poach an egg, sprinkle it with the shallots, and voilà! A great dinner is made. For something more formal, I'll cook skate wing after dredging it in milk and flour and frying it until it's nice and crisp, then set it on a spicy salad. I get duck sausages at the market, and those are just great after being cut in bite-size pieces and sautéed, on dressed lettuce. The sky is really the limit, with one caveat. Whatever goes on the lettuce has to be blistering hot. The hot ingredients just slightly melt the cool salad, making for great textures.

There is another important thing to remember about *salade à la française*, French salad, whether it is served before a meal as a *salade composée,* or after as a *salade verte.* It is unacceptable to cut lettuce on the plate. It is equivalent to *saucing* your plate with a piece of bread, an indication of poor breeding. If you are served a salad that includes large lettuce leaves (not good), you can fold them with knife and fork into a packet that will fit into your mouth. When you're making salad, be kind to those who will eat at your table, and tear the lettuce leaves into bite-size pieces before dressing and serving.

There is an art to the tearing. First, don't tear any leaf that is small enough to fit into your mouth whole, nor those closest to the "heart," which, for reasons I cannot even try to understand, most people want to discard. They're the best, sweetest, and most tender part of the lettuce. Never discard them—they are the vegetable equivalent of the sinfully exquisite interior of a molten chocolate cake.

Traditionally, you tear off the green part of the leaf and discard the stem. I'm not for this—I like the crunch of the stem. So tearing includes the stem, but it never includes twisting the leaf. When you do that, the leaf is bruised and has lost its delicate quality. To tear

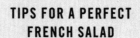

TIPS FOR A PERFECT
FRENCH SALAD

- Buy perfect lettuce (it's okay to buy bagged, pre-rinsed once in a while, if it's organic—remember to rinse it well before you use it).
- Have shallots on hand.
- Have good vinegar and extra-virgin olive oil on hand.
- Carefully rinse the lettuce leaves.
- Use a salad spinner to dry the leaves.
- Tear them gently into bite-size pieces.
- Toss thoroughly, right before serving.

Oils that make great *sauces*:

- Extra-virgin olive oil
- Canola oil
- Peanut oil
- Walnut oil
- Hazelnut oil
- Almond oil

Vinegars and other complements that make great *sauces*:

- Red wine vinegar
- White wine vinegar
- Soy sauce or tamari
- Rice vinegar
- Balsamic vinegar, white or dark
- Freshly squeezed lemon or lime juice

lettuce, you snap off large, bite-size pieces, letting them float down into the bowl. It's easy; it just takes a little time and attention.

Another key to a perfect salad is the *sauce*, or vinaigrette. Most people don't think of vinaigrette as a sauce but it is one of the most important in the French repertoire. It always includes mustard, and shallot, garlic, or chives, either vinegar or lemon juice, and most often peanut oil, though olive and canola oil are rapidly becoming more common. The proportions are 1 tablespoon vinegar, 1 teaspoon mustard, ¼ cup (60ml) oil, a pinch of salt.

There can be more to a vinaigrette. Try adding a bit of soy sauce (1 teaspoon) when you add the vinegar, mix oils or use just a nut oil—hazelnut and walnut are my favorites, but almond and peanut oil are delicious, too. You can add different herbs aside from the traditional chives—try tarragon, mint, thyme, basil, or fennel fronds—a flavored mustard, a mix of ground peppercorns.

One vital tip for making a great salad, whether green, composed, or otherwise, is to thoroughly toss the leaves in the vinaigrette. Some people ask me if they should toss salad with their hands. My resounding response is "Ugh." Apparently someone at some time said the French do this but I've never witnessed this behavior and cannot imagine anything worse. The best utensils for tossing salad are a wooden spoon and fork, though you can use whatever is easiest for you. The point is to *fatiguer la salade*, tire out the lettuce, by lifting it up and out of the bowl, turning it, and letting it fall back into the bowl as many times as it takes for the lettuce leaves to begin to feel heavy. When they do, they're perfectly dressed.

And finally, toss the lettuce right before you plan to serve the salad. You cannot do this in advance. The acid in the vinaigrette begins to "cook" the leaves almost immediately—they'll soon be wilted and soft if they're left to sit.

SPICED TENDERLOIN
OF DUCK SALAD

{ AIGUILLETTE DE CANARD
ÉPICÉ SUR SALADE }

The aiguillette, *or tenderloin, of the duck breast is the strip of tender meat that tucks up under the breast and lines the breastbone. It separates easily from the duck breast and is perfect in this recipe. I call it the tenderloin—it's also called the fillet. Two of these choice pieces make a lovely serving atop this robust salad. Note: There is a tough strip of fibrous tissue that runs down the center of the* aiguillette *and should be cut out. To remove it, slit the* aiguillette *almost in half on either side of the tissue, pull it out, and cut it at the end to remove it.*

This salad is delicious and easy; just make sure the duck is blistering hot when you put it on the lettuce—the contrast of the hot and garlicky and crisp and shallot-rich will win you over! The vinegar may fight with the wine, but it's the "good fight." Try a rich Côtes du Rhône, such as one from Sablé.

FOR THE SALAD:

> 2 tablespoons best-quality red wine vinegar
>
> Pinch of fine sea salt
>
> 1 teaspoon Dijon-style mustard
>
> 2 shallots, sliced paper-thin
>
> ¼ cup (60ml) extra-virgin olive oil
>
> 10 cups (260g) robust lettuce, such as escarole, arugula, curly endive, and romaine, rinsed, spun dry, and torn into large bite-size pieces

FOR THE DUCK:

> 2 tablespoons piment d'Espelette or hot paprika, or to taste
>
> 8 duck or chicken *aiguillettes*
>
> 3 tablespoons extra-virgin olive oil
>
> Fine sea salt
>
> 2 cloves garlic, green germ removed, minced
>
> 2 tablespoons best-quality red wine vinegar

Fresh flat-leaf parsley leaves, chervil, and tarragon, for garnish

Fleur de sel, for garnish

1. To make the salad, place the vinegar in a large bowl and whisk in the salt, mustard, and shallots. Slowly whisk in the oil. Taste for seasoning.
2. Thoroughly toss the lettuce with the vinaigrette, and divide it among four large plates. Reserve.
3. To cook the duck, place the piment d'Espelette on a plate or a sheet of parchment paper and roll the *aiguillettes* in it.
4. Heat the oil in a large, preferably nonstick skillet over medium-high heat. When the oil is hot but not smoking, add the *aiguillettes*, season with salt, and cook, shaking the pan and turning the *aiguillettes*, for 2 minutes. Add the garlic to the pan and continue turning and shaking the pan so the *aiguillettes* and the garlic cook evenly, an additional 2 to 3 minutes. Remove the pan from the heat, and quickly transfer 2 *aiguillettes* to each salad, crossing one over the other. Add the 2 tablespoons vinegar to the skillet, which will still be very hot, and scrape up any caramelized juices from the bottom of the pan. Drizzle the juices over each salad as you scrape out the garlic from the pan.
5. Garnish with the herbs and fleur de sel and serve immediately.

SERVES 4

MELON SALAD WITH SHALLOT VINAIGRETTE

{ SALADE DE MELON À LA VINAIGRETTE AUX ECHALOTES }

I returned from a trip to China with a suitcase filled with Szechuan pepper. It's an ingredient one occasionally finds in a restaurant dish in France, but not a typical home ingredient. I love its floral perfume and the way it numbs the tongue briefly, and it is delicious with melon; if you don't have or cannot find Szechuan pepper, though, any flavorful pepper (Tellicherry black, Voatsiperify, white, green . . .) will do. I like to serve a Sauvignon Blanc from Château Turcaud with this dish.

You can make the melon balls and the sauce a couple of hours ahead, then mix everything right before serving. Be sure to whisk the sauce before using, if you've made it ahead. The melon is served on a bed of grated zucchini—this should be prepared at the last minute.

2 ripe melons, peeled, seeded, and cut into ½-inch (1.25cm) squares or scooped with a melon baller

FOR THE VINAIGRETTE:

2 tablespoons freshly squeezed lemon juice

3 shallots, diced

Fine sea salt

½ teaspoon freshly ground Szechuan pepper or other flavorful pepper

⅓ cup (85ml) plus 2 tablespoons extra-virgin olive oil

¼ cup (3g) fresh mint leaves

FOR THE ZUCCHINI:

1¼ pounds (600g) zucchini, grated on the small holes of a box grater

Zest of 1 lemon, minced

Fleur de sel, for garnish

Fresh mint leaves, for garnish

1. Place the melon balls in a medium-size bowl and refrigerate.
2. To make the vinaigrette, in a small bowl, whisk together the lemon juice, shallots, salt to taste, the pepper, and the oil.
3. Just before serving the salad, cut the mint leaves into very thin strips and whisk them into the vinaigrette. Pour three-quarters of the vinaigrette over the melon balls and toss gently.

4. To make the zucchini, in a large bowl, toss together the grated zucchini and the lemon zest with a fork so it is well mixed. Add the remaining vinaigrette and toss thoroughly.

5. To serve, divide the zucchini among six plates, making a circle of the zucchini in the center of the plate. Evenly divide the melon salad among the plates, placing it in the center of the zucchini circle. Garnish with fleur de sel and mint leaves, and serve.

SERVES 6

MUSHROOM SALAD WITH CAPER VINAIGRETTE

{ SALADE DE CHAMPIGNONS À LA VINAIGRETTE DE CÂPRES }

This is the most refreshing little salad, and I love to make it with the fresh mushrooms I get at the market from Luciano Martin, who grows them in his cool, deep mushroom caves north of Rouen. His are the best mushrooms I've ever eaten, because they're so fresh, so firm, so juicy. Try to buy locally raised mushrooms. Otherwise, any very fresh, very firm mushroom—cremini are excellent if you can find them—is delicious in this salad, which makes a fine first course.

If you can't find capers packed in salt, use those in brine, rinsing and patting them dry first. Try a Bordeaux Blanc here, from Château Panchille.

2 tablespoons capers, preferably packed in salt

1 pound (500g) fresh firm button or cremini mushrooms

1 medium (5 ounces; 150g) red onion, peeled and very thinly sliced

1 tablespoon freshly squeezed lemon juice

1 tablespoon soy sauce or tamari

Pinch of fine sea salt

½ teaspoon sugar

1 teaspoon Dijon-style mustard, preferably Maille brand

Freshly ground black pepper
⅓ cup (85ml) extra-virgin olive oil
1 thick bunch fresh garlic chives or regular chives
Fleur de sel

1. If using capers packed in salt, put them in a small bowl and cover them with warm water. Let sit for 30 minutes, then drain and pat dry. If using capers in vinegar, rinse and pat dry.
2. Trim the ends of the stems from the mushrooms. Wipe or brush the mushrooms clean, then slice them very thin. Place them in a large bowl with the onions. Very carefully mix the mushrooms and onions together, being careful not to break the mushrooms. Your hands are the best tools here.
3. In a small bowl, combine the lemon juice, soy sauce, salt, sugar, mustard, and pepper to taste. Whisk in the oil.
4. Mince the capers and add them to the vinaigrette. Taste for seasoning.
5. Just before serving, separate 4 chives from the bunch and reserve them for garnish. Mince the remaining chives and add them to the vinaigrette.
6. To serve, evenly divide half of the mushrooms and onions among four plates. Spoon half the vinaigrette over the vegetables. Top with the remaining vegetables, and spoon the remaining vinaigrette over it all. Season with fleur de sel and lay a chive over each serving.

SERVES 4

GREEN SALAD WITH CLASSIC VINAIGRETTE
{ SALADE VERTE CLASSIQUE }

This vinaigrette is delicious as-is, though it can serve as a base as well. Add minced shallot or garlic, minced fresh herbs, lemon zest and juice, and/or cracked black pepper. Use this vinaigrette with grated carrots or beets, fresh tomatoes, or any other vegetable mixture.

NOTE: *If you don't use all of the vinaigrette, save the leftover to use as a base for another vinaigrette; use it to drizzle over steamed fish, chicken, or vegetables; or use it as a dip for fresh bread.*

2 teaspoons Dijon-style mustard

4 teaspoons red wine vinegar

Sea salt

3 tablespoons (45 ml) mild oil, such as peanut oil

1 tablespoon extra-virgin olive oil

Freshly ground black pepper

1 small bunch fresh chives, minced

10 cups (260g) mixed salad greens, such as oak leaf, batavia, arugula, and craquerel, torn into bite-size pieces

Fleur de sel

1. Whisk together the mustard, vinegar, and a pinch of sea salt in a small bowl. Slowly whisk in the mild oil until the mixture has emulsified, then whisk in the olive oil. Taste and adjust the seasoning with salt and pepper.
2. Stir the chives into the vinaigrette. Taste and adjust the seasoning.
3. Place the greens in a large bowl, pour over the vinaigrette, and toss, toss, toss. Divide the salad among six small plates, sprinkle with fleur de sel, and serve immediately.

MAKES ENOUGH VINAIGRETTE FOR 6 TO 8 AFTER-DINNER SALADS

NORWEGIAN SALAD
{ SALADE NORVEGIENNE }

One would think every French person had a Norwegian relative, so typical is the salade Norvegienne *on the French table. One finds it in homes and on café and bistro menus, in dozens of different variations. This simple version came to me from Marie-Eve Bourgouin, a schoolteacher and mother of three who loves to cook and eat, but is often short on time.*

This is one of her quickest meals. She can make it right when she comes home, and it will have a chance to sit and mellow until dinnertime. This is a very child-friendly recipe, and yet it pleases adults as well. This salad is full of rich flavors and it goes well with a white Burgundy such as a Mâcon-Prissé from Domaine de la Pierre des Dames.

NOTE: *Cold-smoked salmon is lox style. It's thin and almost creamy, ideal for this salad.*

FOR THE *SAUCE*:

>1 tablespoon white wine vinegar
>
>Generous 1 tablespoon freshly squeezed lemon juice, plus more as needed
>
>½ teaspoon fine sea salt, or as desired
>
>1 tablespoon creamy horseradish
>
>2 tablespoons extra-virgin olive oil
>
>2 tablespoons milk, preferably whole
>
>Freshly ground black pepper

FOR THE SALAD:

>1 pound (500g) new or small waxy potatoes, with skins, washed
>
>1 fresh bay leaf (from the *Laurus nobilis*) or dried imported bay leaf
>
>Coarse sea salt
>
>1 small (8-ounce; 250g) cucumber, peeled and diced
>
>1 small (2-ounce; 60g) red or white onion, diced
>
>4 large slices cold-smoked salmon (about 5 ounces; 150g total), diced
>
>Two 2-ounce (60g) fillets smoked herring (kippers), diced
>
>1 avocado, peeled and diced
>
>⅓ cup (3g) fresh dill fronds, minced
>
>1 grapefruit, for garnish
>
>Fresh dill sprigs, for garnish

1. To make the sauce, place the vinegar, lemon juice, and salt in a bowl and whisk together. Whisk in the horseradish and the oil, then whisk in the milk. Adjust the seasoning with salt and pepper.

2. To make the potatoes, place the potatoes, bay leaf, and about 2 teaspoons salt in a small saucepan, add water to cover, and bring to a boil over medium-high heat. Reduce the heat to medium and cook until the potatoes are just tender throughout, 15 to 20 minutes. Remove from the heat. When you can handle the potatoes, peel them and cut them into ½-inch (1.25cm) rounds, dropping the cut potatoes right into the *sauce*. Fold the potatoes and the sauce together and set aside.

3. Add the cucumber and the onion to the potatoes. Add the salmon and the herring and fold them all together. When the salad has cooled to room temperature, fold in the avocado.

4. Fold the dill fronds into the salad, and adjust the seasoning. Add lemon juice, if necessary.

5. If you have the time, let the salad sit for at least 1 hour before serving, to allow the flavors to marry. Prepare the grapefruit while you wait. Remove the peel using a very sharp, small knife, cutting all the way through the white pith so that none remains on the grapefruit. To remove the sections, cut down between the section and the membrane; then cut up on the other side of the section and "pop" it away from the membrane. Continue doing this, working over a bowl to catch the juice, until all the sections are free from the membrane. (Drink the juice—it's delicious!) Then, divide the salad among four plates. Garnish with the grapefruit sections and dill sprigs.

SERVES 4 AS A MAIN COURSE OR 6 AS A FIRST COURSE

CHAPTER 6

Cheese, Oh Cheese!

I LOVE WATCHING PEOPLE CHOOSE THEIR CHEESES AT the cheese truck in our Saturday morning market, or at the *fromagerie*, cheese store, on our main street. They are so very serious as they consider the offerings, then ask for a cheese for a certain hour, a certain meal, a certain day. As the request comes in, the cheese mongers behind the counter thoughtfully pick up a cheese, and pinch or squeeze it to see if it fits the bill. There is nothing speedy about the process.

Almost every person buying cheese includes a bag of freshly grated cheese in their selection, because grated cheese is the glue holding the French home meal together. It might be French Gruyère or French Emmenthal, which are very different cheeses yet interchangeable in the French mind. Both are made in the Alps in different regions. Both are huge, and both have holes. Their flavors are different, though. Emmenthal is sweeter than Gruyère, which is nuttier. Both melt beautifully, which is why they are interchangeable, and both are used with abandon—sprinkled over a gratin, added to soup, folded into eggs, stirred into béchamel. Ask a French cook what her staples are, and she will always include *rapé*, grated, slang for grated Emmenthal or Gruyère.

Watching people buy cheese in France is to get a glimpse of something intimate, like the kiss of a long-married couple. One might think it had all settled into sleepy familiarity, but no. It's as alive and passionate as ever.

Sophie grew up eating cheese at every meal. "Oh my God, Susan, I love cheese," she said the other day. "I eat it for lunch most days, and I always try to find a new one. And I never share!"

Edith is similar. She gets so excited over cheese that sometimes she'll call to tell me about it. "Susan, I bought a kilo of Comté," she will say. "You have to come try it—it's the best I've ever had." A kilo (two pounds) of Comté is a lot, but it won't last for long because Edith and her family will eat it abundantly, then with the last chunk she will make at least one quiche or omelet.

Eloise is in love with cheese, too, and she is always ready for something new. She shops at the Tuesday-evening market in her tiny village of Puymirol, where the *fromager* obliges. "Let's try that one," she said when I was visiting recently. It was from a local monastery, it had a pocked gray crust, and it was sure to have plenty of flavor. We decided to take just half. The *fromager* cut it and sliced off two shards so we could taste. "Good choice," Eloise said as he wrapped up her half.

What happens with all the cheese the French buy each week? Most of it is eaten after the main course of a meal, either with or just following the salad. Why, you may wonder, would cheese come

A PERFECT CHEESE TRAY—
FIVE DIFFERENT CHEESES

A soft goat cheese

A Camembert-style cheese—Pont l'Évêque, Brie, Livarot

Two hard cheeses—Comté, Cantal, a great cheddar, Beaufort, Ossau Iraty, Abondance

A blue cheese—Roquefort, Bleu d'Auvergne

TASTING ORDER:

Always begin with the mildest cheese and end with blue, or whichever cheese has the most intense flavor.

after the meal in France? I've often wondered this myself. After all, one is nearly sated after the main course, and then arrives the gorgeously tempting cheese platter. As a friend of mine said, "Just when you think you can't eat another bite, along comes the cheese."

The French tradition of serving cheese after the main course goes back a very long way. Some say its roots were with Hippocrates in 5 BC, who had a theory about hot, cold, humid, and dry foods and how they affected the heat properties in the body. From that, eventually, came the idea of cheese being a food that closed the meal, aiding to digest all the "hot" foods that had come before it.

In the Middle Ages, cheese was often served after the fruit, along with dessert. From this practice comes the French expression *entre la poire et le fromage,* between the pear and the cheese. This expression describes a relaxed moment of moratorium, when any subject can be discussed.

I learned a valuable lesson about the usefulness of cheese for digestion in, of all places, Sardinia. There, I was researching sheep's-milk cheese and after a particularly long, hot day of meals, tastings, and sippings, I was under the weather. My host offered me a piece of sheep's-milk cheese so aged it crumbled in my hand. "Eat this," he said. Desperate, I followed his instructions and almost immediately felt better. "It's the enzymes in the cheese," he said. "They help with digestion." This experience set me to thinking about the French and their end-of-meal cheese. What I hadn't understood, I understood.

But still, I was curious about what the French thought about the whys of cheese at the end of the meal. So I started asking around and was met with blank stares, until I asked my friend Betty. She always knows everything. "Well, Susan, cheese is the transition from salty to sweet," she said. "That is what was always said in my family."

Edith had to think about it a moment. "I think it helps digestion," she said. "But honestly, it's just always been that way and I haven't given it much thought. I wouldn't really think about serving cheese at another moment."

As for Sophie, cheese after the meal is like icing on the cake. "The meal has to be great," she said. "And the cheese has to be outstanding, too, because by then we're all relaxed and we want to take our time nibbling on something delicious."

I think there is another, subconscious reason to serve cheese at the end of the meal. It's a nod to moderation. The French adore cheese. If they served it before the meal, when their palates were fresh and they were hungry, they would overdo it. After the main course there is little danger of that. A small piece here, a smaller piece there, and they call it good.

CHEESE CONSUMPTION

More than half of the French population eats cheese daily; only 10 percent think they can survive one week without it. What's more, the average French person eats more than fifty pounds of cheese a year.

Personally, I think this is a conservative estimate. After all, every French meal—or most of them—includes a cheese course, not to mention all the *goûters*, or snacks, and pounds and pounds of it melted over potatoes and bacon, sprinkled atop gratins of every type, added to pizzas, mixed into béchamel, grated into soup. It is an understatement of considerable proportion to say the French love cheese. They revere it.

And finally, here is a fourth reason for eating cheese after the main course: Cheese is the embodiment of luxury and well-being, even to a French person accustomed to its strange beauty, flavor, and texture. Yes, its purpose is to aid digestion, make the transition, contribute to moderation, all of which is a question of enzymes and flavor. But like a wrapped gift under the Christmas tree, cheese is the surprise, served as a final delight to a wonderful moment.

When creating a cheese platter, one must respect the seasons. For instance in spring, don't plan to put a Vacherin Mont d'Or (creamy and pine-scented) on your platter because it's a winter cheese; and at Christmas, don't be disappointed if you cannot find a fresh goat cheese, because many of the goats are pregnant then.

Seasons are a bit less distinct than they once were. I remember when you couldn't get fresh goat cheese in the winter, because all the goats in France were following their natural cycle. Now, most herds are manipulated by being subject to light for varying amounts of time so they fall pregnant in a rotation, making milk available all year. Also, much goat milk is frozen so there is always a supply. Still, pay attention to the seasons when planning.

Beyond that, the idea is to offer variety in taste and texture. A typical cheese platter almost always includes Camembert, which has become the universal symbol of French cheese. This dates to the First and Second World Wars, when soldiers billeted with families in Normandy returned home with the memory of its magic flavor. They looked for it, couldn't find it, and eventually learned how to make it. To this day, the name Camembert isn't protected, so it can be—and is—made all over the globe. A true Camembert made in and around the town of Camembert and honored with an A.O.P., *Appellation d'Origine Protégée*, or pedigree, is called Camembert de Normandie. There is always one on my cheese platter.

There should always be a blue cheese on the platter. I love Roquefort Carles, from a very small production near Roquefort in the Rouerge in southwest France, or Gabriel Coulet, another small production (both softish cheeses made with sheep's milk). Sometimes I include Bleu d'Auvergne, another of my favorite blues, which is made with cow's milk and is smooth, creamy, and elegant.

A mild, fresh cheese is vital, too, and my choice for that category is always a flat, soft round of fresh goat cheese I get at my market, which tastes like a tender, bright cottage cheese and is so pure it can make you weep.

Once these are chosen, it's time to look for a hard cheese. This opens up a lot of possibilities. France has a lot of mountains, where hard cheeses are made and aged. This category is my favorite of all French cheeses, so bear with me while I extol their virtues.

My favorite of the mountain cheeses is Comté, from the Jura, which I love when it's aged at least thirty-six months. Then, the flavor of the summer flowers in the milk it was made with concentrate into a heady, buttery, hazelnut perfume that instantly evokes images of high-mountain pastures. Beaufort, a very tall, round from the Savoie, is sweeter and slightly more floral than Comté, and I always taste a hint of ground walnuts in it. Abondance, from the Haute Savoie, is flatter than these other two cheeses, and it has a softish, elastic interior and a sweet flavor that reminds me of milk and honey.

Ossau Iraty, the Basque cheese made in the Pyrénées, is a rich, sheep's-milk poem. No matter how crumbly it is, as you savor it, it turns to cream. I usually like aged cheeses, but I prefer an adolescent Ossau Iraty because of its tender creaminess.

Cantal is another noted mountain cheese, also from the rugged Auvergne. It's tall, fat, and round, and when it's young, it is slightly rubbery and very creamy. As it ages, its crust becomes thick and craggy and mousey brown. Myth has it that this big, crumbly cheese is the precursor to cheddar.

Here's the tale. In the very distant past (many hundreds of years ago), Auvergnat masons were brought to Scotland to build walls. Their work done, they made their way home. But not all returned to their volcanic mountains. Some settled in southern England near the town of Cheddar, and there did what they knew to do—built walls, kept cattle, made cheese.

Cantal has three mountain cousins, Salers, Salers Tradition, and Laguiole. I could never quite distinguish among them, no matter how often I tasted them. It turns out that I'm not the only one who doesn't quite understand the differences among these cheeses.

The story of Cantal clearly demonstrates the importance of cheese to the French. Cantal can be made with milk from any cow, including one called the Salers, which is the traditional breed of the Auvergne. Salers has an A.O.P. Unlike most A.O.P.s, it doesn't specify what sort of milk must go into the Salers, which is usually made with a variety of cows' milks, but rarely if ever with milk from the Salers cow. Then there is the Salers Tradition, which must be made in a specific geographical area only with milk from the Salers cow.

Certain Cantal are made exclusively with milk from the Salers, but because they're not made in the appropriate geographical region, they cannot be called Salers Tradition. (If the cheese maker wants to set his cheese apart, he can label it "Cantal made with milk from the Salers.")

Needless to say, those in the French cheese business, and in the Auvergne cheese industry, continue to trip over all this nomenclature. The riddle will one day be solved, so that everyone knows exactly what he or she is making or buying, because there are people in the dairy industry and in the government puzzling it out.

As if further proof was needed, this dairy drama demonstrates that cheese in France is no small thing. Officially, there are more than four hundred cheeses produced in France. The unofficial number is closer to 1,600, when you take into account all the tiny farms producing tiny amounts of—mostly—tiny cheeses. De Gaulle thought he had it bad trying to govern a country that produced 246 varieties of cheeses in the 1940s. He had no idea.

I've given you some hints about how to create your own cheese platter. But now I want to introduce the idea of The Perfect Cheese. When I find one—a particularly creamy Vacherin, a slice of Brie that oozes just the right way and smells like heaven, a perfectly aged Camembert that smells of pasture and seaside, a wedge of Roquefort Carles that promises its unique creamy tang, or a buttery slab of Salers Tradition that evokes fresh butter, toasted hazelnuts, and Auvergnat farms, I serve it alone. Tasting one perfect cheese comes close to a religious experience.

While I understand the simple craving for French cheeses that leads us all to haunt American supermarket cheese sections in search of them, I truly believe that French cheese is best in France. But I understand that we cannot all go to France every time we want French cheese, which is why I want to assist you in your cheese choices elsewhere.

Many French cheeses are exported to the United States and arrive there in tip-top condition. Many, however, do not.

Any pasteurized milk cheese from France can be imported into the United States, whereas only raw milk cheeses that are aged more than sixty days can be, which amounts to a handful of hard, mountain cheeses and some blue cheeses like Roquefort. I normally don't counsel eating pasteurized milk cheeses, though—they are universally mild and have a tendency to be flavorless. My advice is to seek out French cheeses that are made with raw milk. These have to have been aged for sixty days or more, which precludes cheeses like Brie, Camembert, and other soft, bloomy cheeses. It includes all the glorious mountain cheeses.

My advice? Seek out the raw milk cheeses of France (www.fro mages.com). Then, go beyond that and look for cheeses with the name Hervé Mons on their label. He is the best known *affineur*, cheese ager, in France. He has devoted his life to perfecting the development, aging, and exportation of cheeses, and he has an exclusive with Whole Foods. Some of the cheeses he exports are made with pasteurized milk, notably his Camembert. It's very, very good.

And then again, you may want to think local the next time you're planning a cheese tray. American cheeses, some made with raw milk, are popping up all over. They are good to exquisite.

Whichever cheeses you decide to serve, less is more. Five is an optimal number—more risks overwhelming.

ESSENTIAL BREAD

Bread is vital to the cheese course. Here are some suggestions.

- Baguette—a must
- Bread with dried fruit and/or nuts
- Rye bread (without caraway)
- Sourdough
- Spelt bread

Putting anything other than cheese on the cheese tray is not very French. That said, a beautiful bunch of grapes or a few ripe figs in the autumn, when they're fresh from the vine or tree, is a beautiful touch. Crackers are not advised (unless you've run out of bread).

Though cheese is ceremoniously eaten after the French meal, it is eaten at many other moments and in many other guises as well. I still have memories of my first sandwich in Paris a hundred years ago. It was fat slices of Camembert on a baguette that had first been slathered with an ample amount of butter. I ate it in the Tuileries on a chilly day, and it remains one of my favorite food memories.

Gruyère and Comté are often used in sandwiches, too, the kind you buy at the bakery or train stations. Ends of cheese from the cheese platter are set on pastry, drowned with custard, and baked into quiche; cheese is melted over bacon and potatoes, sprinkled on toasts that are floated in soup; layered with vegetables and baked into a gratin; melted into cream to make a luscious sauce.

WINE AND CHEESE

While conventional wisdom says that red wine goes with cheese, truly gorgeous pairings say otherwise. White is the wine for cheese. White wine can be everything—rigorous and flinty, light and aromatic, floral and tender, sweet and buttery. It can have hints of hazelnuts and caramel, nuts and herbs, and any number of other subtle aromas that make it the right wine for cheese. Red wine, while it can be sumptuous, is more difficult to combine with cheese as the tannins in it tend to fight, rather than enhance. And yes, it is all right to transition from the red wine of the main course to white, contrary to *idées recues*, popular opinion.

FRENCH CHEESE

ORGANIZATION OF FRENCH CHEESE

French cheese is divided into eight groups. It helps to know what they are.

The eight groups are:

- ♦ Fresh cheeses—like fromage frais (basically, cheese curds that can be either chunky or smooth), cheeses that are just a few days old.
- ♦ Soft, bloomy rind cheeses—like Camembert, Brie, Coulommiers, and Neufchâtel. These cheeses are

somewhat elastic, ranging from firm when they are unripened, to tender when they are fully ripened. These cheeses take on an aroma of ammonia when they are overripe, which is pleasing to some.

♦ Soft, washed-rind cheese—like Livarot, Maroilles, Pont l'Évêque, and Époisses, these cheeses are washed with anything from naturally colored brine to beer, wine, or even tea. The longer these cheeses are aged, the more intense their aroma.

♦ Pressed cheeses, uncooked and cooked—St. Nectaire, Cantal, Salers, Laguiole, and Morbier are among the uncooked pressed cheeses.

♦ Blue or "parsleyed" cheeses—these cheeses can be made with cow, sheep, or goat milk. Penicillium is injected into them.

♦ Cooked, pressed cheeses—these are mountain cheeses that can age for up to many years. The milk is heated, then curdled and pressed into a mold. Once out of the mold they are salted—sometimes by being floated in a salt brine—then carefully aged. Comté, Beaufort, Gruyère, Abondance, and Emmenthal are all members of this family of cheese.

♦ Goat cheese—these are small cheeses, because goats give up to just two liters of milk per day. They range from very soft and wet to elastic and creamy to extremely hard. They offer a wide panoply of flavors, and those that have aged to a firm hardness can be used in place of Parmigiano Reggiano.

♦ Fromage fondu—there is a ninth category called *fromage fondu*, which aren't really cheeses, but a cheese product made from melted cheese and other ingredients, including whey, powdered milk, and other substances. These are low-priced dairy products, and often used industrially. They count, however, as a "family" of cheese.

RAW VERSUS PASTEURIZED MILK FOR CHEESE

What's the difference between a cheese made with raw milk and one made with the pasteurized version? The world.

Raw milk is complete. It is filled with life, enzymes, and bacteria. It has all the potential for the nuances of flavor it needs to develop into a perfectly ripe and gloriously flavored cheese, if it is properly aged.

Generally, raw milk is transformed into cheese within hours of it being taken from the animal, minimizing risk of contamination. It is kept in a temperature-controlled environment and checked many times a day so that wild yeasts and bacteria that will help it age and develop flavor are correctly doing their job. Most cheeses follow a similar process:

The milk—often still warm from the animal—is curdled with rennet.

Sometimes the milk is heated.

The milk sits for twenty-four hours, until the curds form.

Depending on the cheese, the curds might be cut, drained, and whipped, or drained and scooped into molds. Those that are cut generally sit another twenty-four hours before being put into a mold.

The cheese stays in the mold until it drains enough to hold the shape of the mold (for goat cheese, this might be twenty-four hours; for Salers Tradition, it might be several days).

Depending on the cheese, once it is removed from the mold it might be washed, rinsed, brined, turned, tapped, and/or shifted until it is aged to perfection.

When carefully aged, a raw milk cheese will offer the fullness of its flavor, aided and abetted by wild yeasts that settle into the cheese and ferment into flavor.

When milk is pasteurized it loses vitality and most of its potential for developing flavor. While some pasteurized milk cheese can develop rich flavor—round, orange Mimolette comes to mind, with its hazelnutty flavor when it's many months old— it will never have the flavor it might have achieved were the milk alone.

But what about dangerous bacteria in raw milk? There aren't systematically "dangerous" bacteria in raw milk. There may be dangerous bacteria in anything if it is contaminated, but this can happen as readily with pasteurized as with raw or any other kind of milk. Raw milk cheese is actually safer than that made with pasteurized milk. If a "bad" bacteria or contaminant falls on a raw milk cheese that is vital and bursting with life, the "good" bacteria in the raw milk will fight off the "bad" bacteria. If a "bad" bacteria falls on pasteurized cheese, which has been robbed of most of its "good" bacteria, nothing puts up a fight and the "bad" goes wild.

Today, there is a process called thermalization, which results in a milk that lies somewhere between raw and pasteurized. It has become acceptable even to proponents of raw milk cheese, as the process leaves some useful bacteria intact. (Milk is pasteurized at about 161°F / 72°C; it is thermalized at about 113°F / 45°C; it comes from the cow at about 98°F / 37°C.)

A PANOPLY OF FRENCH CHEESE,
FOR YOUR TASTING PLEASURE

Each Saturday morning I approach the cheese truck at my market with anticipation. What will I choose? What will I discover?

I know I'll find Camembert, Livarot, Neufchâtel, and Pont l'Évêque, which I refer to as the "Queens of Norman cheese." They'll be there in every stage of ripeness, for every palate, ready to be purchased whole, by the half, by the quarter (except the Neufchâtel, which is heart shaped). All of them are made with milk from the Norman cow, a black-spotted animal that is small and gives a relatively small amount of milk, which is extremely rich and creamy. Each cheese is made slightly differently, and while the texture is similar, each offers a different shade of flavor.

Alongside these will be the fat Pavé d'Auge, another Norman standby with a particularly mild flavor. Depending on the week, there will be cheeses from around the hexagon—gooey, rust-colored, and funky-smelling Époisses from Burgundy, the most consistently exquisite Brie de Melun, which threatens to run all over the other cheeses; a tender, almost fruity Abbaye de Citeaux made by the monks of Citeaux, which is a winter-only indulgence; pure white Ossau Iraty made in the Basque country with sheep's milk. There is a variety of fat, flat rounds of Tomme, generally young mountain cheeses that offer variations on a creamy theme. Tommes, which include raclette, are as good to eat as they are delicious melted over . . . anything.

There is always a selection of goat cheeses. Some of these come dusted with ash, which used to come from the bottom of the cauldron used for heating and curdling the milk over a wood fire. That ash hindered the aging process, and the vegetable ash used today—now purchased from the pharmacy because it has to be sterile—does the same thing.

Others are pure white, and along with their "ashed" cousins, they come in fanciful shapes that are sometimes astounding. One of my favorites is a flat round that is dusted with ash and marked with the Occitane cross. Called Cathare, it is a study in mild creaminess when young, aging into a rich tang. Some are shaped like a keg, some like a short log, some are rolled into a sort of lumpy ball shape, others look like a big Hershey's kiss. There are flat rounds, and Camembert-shaped goat cheeses, other small "dots" that are called *boutons de culottes*, trouser buttons, and a very famous small, fat round called *crottin*, or dropping (as in manure). There is one goat cheese, called Valençay, that always makes me smile. It was once shaped like a pyramid, but today it has no point. According to legend, Talleyrand, a wily French diplomat on whose estate the cheese was made, had his cheesemakers lop off the top when Napoleon returned from an unsuccessful campaign in Egypt, because he was concerned the pyramid shape would cause offense.

Then there are sheep's-milk cheeses, which are much fewer in number than either cow's- or goat's-milk cheeses. Their rarity belies their gorgeous flavors, all of which are founded in the richness of the milk. Aside from my true love, Ossau Iraty, and its cousin, Agour, is the silken Perail, a small disc made with sheep's milk when there isn't enough milk to make Roquefort; Lingot de la Ginestarie, a rare, creamy cheese from the Midi Pyrénées; Corsica also produces many sheep's milk cheeses, including Brocciu, which is aged with a fern frond pressed into it, and Brin d'Amour, which has herbs of the *maquis*, or local landscape, pressed into it, with a predominance of rosemary and savory.

These cheeses are staples at my market, depending on the season. Each week features something new and different, too, which might be an interloper from Italy—last week it was taleggio—a rare and sharp Gouda with cumin from Holland, or even a beef tallow–wrapped cheddar from England.

BLUE CHEESE QUICHE
{ QUICHE AU FROMAGE BLEU }

This is a classic quiche recipe, and quiche is a classic supper for the French family. It ends up being a perfect way to use up pieces of cheese from the end-of-meal cheese tray.

I know when I have bits and pieces, I love to grate and mix them into this glorious custard. Sometimes I use Camembert, which I slice rather than grate; sometimes Comté, sometimes blue, as here. Cheese is a must for a quiche, but you can also do as the French do and add some smoked salmon with onions, or a touch of bacon, to make quiche Lorraine. Really, the possibilities are endless. The best quiche is, to me, the simplest. For wine, try a Loire Valley white, such as a Cour-Cheverny from Domaine des Huards.

I call for blue cheese here, because I always have bits of blue cheese left over and we love it in a quiche. But of course, use the leftover cheese you have (or buy cheese specifically for this quiche—it's delicious!).

1 recipe On Rue Tatin's Tender Tart Pastry (page 207)

2 large shallots, minced

6 large eggs

⅔ cup (160ml) heavy cream or crème fraîche

1 cup (250ml) milk (preferably whole)

Fine sea salt and freshly ground black pepper

6 ounces (180g) blue cheese, such as Roquefort (or the cheese of your preference)

1. Roll out the pastry to fit a 10½-inch (26.25cm) glass or metal pie plate (not one with a removable bottom). Crimp the edges, poke the bottom all over with a fork or the tip of a sharp knife, and place the pastry in the freezer for 30 minutes and up to several hours, or in the refrigerator overnight.

2. Preheat the oven to 425°F (220°C). Position a rack in the bottom third.

3. Line the pastry with aluminum foil and pastry weights or dried beans, and bake until the pastry is golden at the edges, about 15 minutes.

Remove from the oven and remove the aluminum foil and pastry weights. Return the pastry to the oven to bake until the bottom is golden, 5 minutes more. Remove from the oven, sprinkle the shallots over the pastry, and set aside. Reduce the oven temperature to 375°F (190°C) and carefully move a rack to the center.

4. In a medium bowl, whisk together the eggs, cream, and the milk until thoroughly blended. Season lightly with salt and generously with pepper, then add the cheese and stir until it is blended. Turn the mixture into the prebaked pastry, and arrange the cheese evenly over the bottom of the pastry. Sprinkle the top with nutmeg (if using), and bake until the filling is golden, puffed, and completely baked through, 30 to 35 minutes. To test for doneness, shake the quiche—if it is solid without a pool of uncooked filling in the center, it is done. You may also stick a sharp knife blade into the center of the filling, and if it comes out clean, the quiche is baked through.

5. Remove the quiche from the oven, then serve.

SERVES 6 TO 8

MAMIE'S TARTIFLETTE
{ LA TARTIFLETTE DE MAMIE }

No one can resist this delectable combination of potatoes, melted cheese, and air-cured meats. It's a perfect winter supper, accompanied by a crisp, green salad. It's the kind of dish Mamie made on those nights when it was already dark at five, the rain or snow was coming down outside, the fire was burning in the fireplace. If you make this, use whatever hard cheese (cheddar, Gruyère, Comté . . .) you have on hand—it's a great way to use leftovers.

To thinly slice the cheese, make sure it is chilled, and use a cheese slicer that results in almost paper-thin slices.

Serve this with an Arbois red, or an Arbois Chardonnay.

NOTE: *This is a great dish to serve to a large group; just multiply the ingredients.*

1½ pounds (750g) small waxy/starchy potatoes, such as Yukon Gold, scrubbed

2 teaspoons coarse sea salt

½ pound (250g) soft mountain cheese, such as raclette or a young Comté, thinly sliced

½ pound (250g) air-cured ham or a mix of air-cured sausages, thinly sliced

½ cup (120g) small pickled onions

½ cup (120g) cornichons

1. Preheat the oven to 450°F (230°C) and position a rack in the center.
2. Place the potatoes in a medium pot with the salt and add water to cover. Bring the water to a boil over medium-high heat, then reduce the heat to keep the water boiling gently and cook until the potatoes are just tender throughout, about 15 minutes. Drain the potatoes and transfer them to a 10 by 12-inch (25 by 30cm) baking dish.
3. Layer the slices of cheese as evenly as possible over the potatoes. Bake until the cheese is bubbling and slightly golden, 15 to 20 minutes.
4. Serve the potatoes and cheese with the air-cured meats, the onions, and the cornichons on the side.

SERVES 4

A QUICK WEEKNIGHT SOUFFLÉ WITH CHEESE AND CHICKEN

{ UN SOUFFLÉ RAPIDE POUR MILIEU DE LA SEMAINE, AU FROMAGE ET POULET }

This is a lovely and very traditional dish that uses up leftovers (cheese and chicken) in a truly French way! It is quick to put together the day you want to serve it. You can also make the béchamel the night before and heat it slightly before finishing the soufflé. A truly perfectly baked French soufflé is slightly runny in the center, and this is how it is best. But if the idea of a runny soufflé doesn't appeal, add five extra minutes of cooking time! Serve a simple white here. I like the whites from Gaillac, near Toulouse.

3 tablespons unsalted butter, plus more for the baking
    dish

1 tablespoon grated hard cheese (Parmigiano Reggiano
    works well here), for the baking dish

½ cup (125ml) whole milk

½ cup (125ml) non-ultra-pasteurized heavy cream

1 large clove garlic, green germ removed, minced

3 tablespoons all-purpose flour

Fine sea salt and freshly ground black pepper

4 large egg yolks

⅔ cup (85g) cooked chicken, diced

5 large egg whites

¾ cup (45g) grated Parmigiano Reggiano or Gruyère or
    other leftover cheese

1. Preheat the oven to 425°F (220°C) and position a rack in the center.
   Thickly butter a 1½-quart (1.5L) soufflé dish and dust it with the grated
   cheese.

2. In a small saucepan, heat the milk and the cream together over medium
   heat, and keep hot.

3. Melt the 3 tablespoons of butter in a medium saucepan over medium
   heat. Add the garlic, stir, and cook for 1 minute. Whisk in the flour and
   cook for at least 2 minutes, to remove the taste of the flour from the
   mixture. Whisk in the hot milk and cream mixture and cook, whisking
   continuously, until the mixture thickens, 2 to 4 minutes. Season generously with salt and pepper, remove from the heat, and whisk in the egg
   yolks. Mix in the chicken, and keep warm.

4. Whisk the egg whites with a pinch of salt until they hold stiff points.
   Be careful not to overmix them—you don't want them to be grainy.

5. Fold one-third of the egg whites into the warm béchamel mixture.
   Fold in all but 1 tablespoon of the cheese, then fold in the remaining
   egg whites. Gently pour the mixture into the prepared soufflé mold.
   Using the back of your thumbnail, make an indentation all the
   way around the edge of the soufflé. You will have some of the soufflé
   mixture on your thumb, gently shake it into the center of the soufflé,

then sprinkle the top of the soufflé with the reserved 1 tablespoon cheese.

6. Bake until the soufflé is golden and puffed, about 20 minutes (or 25 minutes, if you want the soufflé cooked all the way through). Remove from the oven and serve immediately.

SERVES 4 TO 6

CHAPTER 7

Indispensable Dessert

I WAS JUST READING THE RESULTS OF A POLL THAT
asked the French about their favorite desserts. Big winners were
crêpes, *Île Flottante* (floating island), *mousse au chocolat*, and *tarte
aux pommes* (apple tart). But the top dessert? *Fondant au chocolat*
(molten chocolate cake—see page 131).

I love living in a country where I read the results of a national
poll on dessert, then go to someone's home the very same night and
eat the dessert that came out on top.

This happened at Sophie's, not because she'd read the poll but
because she's part of the trend. Sophie is the most efficient person I
know. She worked at her very busy job all day, came home, got the
kids ready for bed, and fed them dinner (pasta and Gruyère, grated
carrot salad, sweet yogurt and fruit). But here we all were a couple
of hours later after a simple meal of tapenade and crudités, salmon

with cinnamon and green beans, salad, and cheese, lounging at the dinner table. Sophie got up to get dessert and returned with molten chocolate cakes. I almost started laughing. Instead, I asked for the recipe.

There were eight guests at the dinner party, and fourteen small cakes. We meandered through dessert, sipping on a rich, smooth Languedoc which Sophie's husband, Jean, had poured to go with the cakes. Sophie offered coffee and it was then that I noticed all the cakes were gone. There was no embarrassment. No one said, "Oh no, I ate too much." Instead, there was satisfaction and a feeling of well-being, and many compliments to the chef.

Yet it's funny. If you ask a French person whether or not they like dessert, the answer is often a diffident *"Pas spécialement,"* not really. I just chalk it up to the duality of the French personality that has them drinking red wine, eating foie gras, and rarely gaining weight or getting heart disease. On the one hand, they say they don't like dessert, but set molten chocolate cakes in front of them and they'll eat two.

This complete lack of complex about indulging in delicious dessert became obvious to me early on in my French career, when I was interviewing for the job of chef at a *salon de thé* in Paris. The owner had invited me to her country home for lunch, to sample the type of meal she wanted me to prepare. We were four at the table. Dessert was a big fruit tart with gorgeous golden pastry. Our host cut it in quarters and served each person their share. I surreptitiously glanced at the other diners, who were happily devouring their entire piece, so I did, too. It occurred to me then that while so many in this world try to hide their love of sweets and desserts, the French are standing atop the Eiffel Tower proclaiming their sweet addiction to the world.

Like specialty food shops, hilltop villages, and hidden court-yards, dessert is part of France's soul, and it has been around a long time. When the order of the French meal was first created in the seventeenth century, dessert—which comes from the word *desservir*, to clear—was in fact a signal to move to an anteroom and enjoy a selection of sweets, from cakes and sorbets to dried fruits and bonbons, candies.

Whether it is from this early tradition of finishing a meal with sweets, or perhaps from France's colonization of countries producing sugarcane, the French have a serious sweet tooth. They eat dessert at every meal, they sugar their water and milk, they load up their coffee and tea, to the tune of about fifty-five pounds of sugar per capita, and there isn't a shred of guilt associated with it. (In the United States, we guiltily consume much more than the French, about seventy-six pounds of sugar per capita, but research suggests much of it is hidden in the form of soft drinks and processed foods, not enjoyed in desserts like molten chocolate cake.)

In fact, the French think that sugar develops intelligence. This particular belief may have roots in a sixties ad campaign created by the sugar beet industry of northern France, that referred to *le sucre d'intelligence*, the sugar of intelligence. One of the ads included this phrase: "Sugar, it's the shortest route to energy. Muscles, brain, and nerves need a rest from the stress put upon them, and not only does sugar wipe out fatigue, but it feeds the nerve cells." Questionable research behind these claims, perhaps, but it contributed to what was already a national obsession.

Whether or not sugar contributes to intelligence, it clearly contributes to pleasure. Which means that in France, dessert isn't a guilty pleasure any more than a croissant stuffed with chocolate is at breakfast, a macaron is at *goûter*, or snack time, a cream-draped tart is after supper. These all enter into what is simply a French food group.

When I first met Edith, she had four young children, a hungry coal-burning furnace in a broken-down old home, a traveling husband. This meant simple meals. She always fed the kids first, and dinner was often a bowl of vegetable soup followed by a big mound of steaming pasta topped with cheese. Dessert was plain yogurt loaded up with sugar. For the adults? There was usually something freshly baked—a cake, a tart, a pudding—which she had somehow made between bedtime and dinner. It's not that she didn't want her children to eat freshly baked dessert; it's that they simply preferred sweetened yogurt.

Today her kids have families of their own, and Edith has more time to make dessert, which she does regularly. She has many favorites and she's just slightly obsessive so that whatever is her favorite dessert of the moment will be on the menu for weeks at a time. I taste many of Edith's creations since her house is on the way to the train station, where I go often, and it's also at the end of a bike path between her village and my town. We meet over coffee, and there is always something sweet on the side.

During one of Edith's dessert obsessions we had chestnut cake for several weeks, which I loved. But it could be anything. Her banana cake is a favorite, an apple clafoutis–like cake is another. Sometimes she serves fresh cheese drowned in maple syrup, or a thin chocolate cake that uses ground almonds instead of flour. Edith makes profiteroles at the drop of a hat because it's Bernard's favorite, and she turns every last one of her summer red currants into a zippy little sorbet. I've never seen Edith turn away from a dessert, and she is the kind of hostess who, if there are four guests, cuts the tart into four pieces. Even if she is just serving coffee, there is always at least a square of semisweet chocolate to go along with it.

Marie Boivin, a sixth-grade math teacher, a woman so full of life and verve she creates a colorful vibration when she walks in the room, is the heart of my monthly wine-tasting group. Her clothes are outlandishly cheerful, her laughter rises to the ceiling, she lives life to the fullest. Naturally, Marie is a gourmande who, with her partner, Claude, loves to eat and cook. "I've always worked full time, and I've always cooked, even when the kids were little," she said. "There is nothing hard about peeling a few carrots and popping them in water to cook, making a flan and putting it in the oven, roasting pork, or sautéing a steak or two."

When it comes to dessert, Marie has one fallback. "Tarts," she said. "I'm not a baker, but anyone can make a tart."

Marie is right and wrong. She's right because anyone *can* make a tart. But she's wrong because not everyone makes a good tart. A good tart is one with crisp pastry that tastes of butter and toasty flour; whatever it is filled with must be just the right amount of sweet, and the pastry must be baked all the way through. While a tart is quick and easy to put together, and it can bake during dinner to be served warm, the careful baker makes sure to either pre-bake the pastry, or bake the tart on the bottom of the oven, so the pastry bakes faster than the filling.

"Bread pudding [page 229] is another of my secrets," she said. "And sometimes I make cakes. I like to make pound cake, but that has to be done the night before." Whatever the simple dessert might be, for Marie it is the indispensable period at the end of the sentence.

As for Eloise, a single mother of three and inveterate cook, she cannot envision a meal without dessert. "If I don't have time, it's yogurt and sugar," she said. "But if I'm cooking, it's a real dessert." Eloise is the keeper of her family recipes, including dessert. Among her favorites is her grandmother's *gâteau cocotte* (page 41) that she varies with cubes of pear or apple, chocolate pieces, spices. Another is *biscuit rouler au Nutella*, a light vanilla cake rolled around a filling of Nutella. "It's my kids' favorite," she said.

Eloise leaves no stone unturned in her search to find good ingredients. She uses the local specialty of dried prunes in many desserts, sometimes soaking them first in water and rum. A farm near her raises kiwis, and another apples, which she combines in a sweet fruit salad that she'll serve with madeleines. For Nutella, she relies on the local organic food cooperative, which carries a healthier alternative. "It's like Nutella without palm oil," her son, Cyprien, chirped, licking some off a spoon.

The importance of dessert cannot be underestimated; sometimes meals feel like a prelude. Take the case of my friend Michel Amsalem. He's a professional *chef patissier*, and his pastry shop was *the* destination for all the years I've lived here, until he sold it a year ago (to everyone's chagrin but his own!). Now, he's thrilled to work for a colleague until he retires, filling shelves with his signature, classically prepared desserts. Dinner at the house Michel shares with his wife, Chantal, falls into the category of "prelude to dessert." The food is always delicious because Chantal is a good cook, but I think every guest is just waiting to see what's coming for dessert.

What sets Michel's cakes apart is his creativity with flavor and texture, and his sensitivity. For instance, he loves to make cakes that reflect the personalities of his friends. One year for my birthday he created a sumptuous chocolate and ginger cake with a delicately crunchy praline layer. "It's surprising, like your jokes," he said. "You never quite know when to expect them." He liked it so much it became a staple at the bakery, called "La Suzanne." Bernard's cake combines passion fruit and chocolate, reflecting his passion for every subject. Edith's is lemon filled with raspberries, because she's so colorful, and his wife Chantal's is a blend of nuts and crisp butter pastry, because she's no-nonsense.

According to Michel, the French palate has changed. "People want desserts that are less sweet than they were," he said. "They want to taste flavors more, not sugar. They're asking for more subtlety in dessert, less masquerading."

Naturally, having a professional baker as a friend tends to be intimidating, but Michel loves everything. He's eternally curious, too, and never above asking for a recipe. That is why my chocolate chip cookies wound up in his pastry case every day.

Betty is such a great cook, but she's not a dessert fan so she is likely to buy dessert. This is its own kind of thrill, because when people buy desserts they buy fancy ones, and I just love seeing what they've chosen. Not long ago we had dinner at Betty and Louis's, and Betty pulled out a *galette des rois*, king's cake, an almond cream and puff pastry cake that is "in season" for about six weeks in January and February. It's made to celebrate the gift of the Magi, and hidden inside each one is a *fève,* or porcelain figurine.

Over the centuries, the *fèves*, which literally translated means bean, began as a dry bean, then was a coin, then a flat disc of porcelain, and then miniature religious figurines. Now, it can be anything from teeny Limoges-style coffee cups (I still have one I got in a *galette*) to a fanciful painted cowboy boot to a cat with golden eyes.

Betty warmed up the *galette*, served up six shattering pieces, and "somehow" got the *fève*. I'm not saying she cheats. Betty is the most proper, correct, and elegant person I know. Yet, she has this thing about *fèves* that means the universe provides; I've never been to a *galette* event without her getting the *fève*.

I confess to a many-year fixation on *fèves* myself. Who wouldn't

fixate on these miniature works of art that come in one of the dream-
iest pastries ever invented?

When the kids were small, I'd buy several *galettes* each season from the patisserie with the best *fèves*, just to get the collection (they come in series, very clever on the part of the French
pastry industry). I did it for the kids, of course, who loved finding
ing the *fèves*. They kept them on a small shelf with miniature
cubbyholes, that was set where it caught the afternoon light. One
day I was exclaiming over the cute little *fève* that Fiona had just
won (the slinky cat with golden eyes). "You can have it, Mom," she
said. She was six; I was forty-nine. I backed off my *fève* obsession
after that.

And then there are Alain and Philippe—excellent cooks both—
who simply adore old-fashioned, sweet, cream-laden, baroque-style
desserts that they get from a favorite patisserie in Rouen. I already
love going to their house for lunch, because the meal is like sifting
through an Easter basket—there is just one thrill after another until
that moment of dessert, which always comes early in the evening
since lunch is languorous. Philippe brings forth whatever he's purchased. It is always fanciful and frothy. Lately, his choices have tended toward cream, meringue, and hazelnut or walnut confections, the
kind that when you put a bite in your mouth, it disappears in a delicate, sweet haze.

Buying dessert is a very French pastime, the proof being all the
gorgeous cakes and pastries available in every pastry shop in the
land. I love watching people buy pastries and cakes, and I love even
more the creative ways that pastry shops have of anchoring pastries
inside their boxes. At Patisserie de Rêves in Paris, their boxes are
lined with thin Styrofoam, into which they stick fanciful pink skew-
ers to keep pastries stable. I once bought pastries at Jacques Genin,

one of Paris's finest patissiers/chocolatiers, which were put into a box and into a bag. I walked out the door and stopped to chat with someone on the street. Mr. Genin walked by, adjusted the bag on my arm so the box inside was sitting straight, doffed his cap, and went on his way. "That is service," I thought. At other shops they section off boxes with pieces of shiny gold cardboard, creating little corrals for cakes, tarts, or individual pastries.

And then it's fun to watch people carefully carry their pastries to their cars, the Métro, or simply down the street. Live bombs aren't treated more delicately.

The moral to this sweet tale? Make dessert, then enjoy it. You'll feel French, and you'll feel happy.

MICHEL'S MOELLEUX AU CHOCOLAT

{ GÂTEAU MOELLEUX AU CHOCOLAT MICHEL }

This recipe is from Michel Amsalem, a professional patissier who loves to fool around in his home kitchen making cakes that taste like heaven. We spent a lot of time discussing moelleux *and he tested this recipe on his customers before calling me to share it. It's delicious.*

While the recipe calls for two types of chocolate, you can also use just one semisweet or bittersweet chocolate that is 60% to 65% cacao. The margin of baking time is large—the shorter time results in an almost runny center for the cake; the longer time gives a more solid, but still very soft interior. Either way, the cake is luscious! If baking the cake for a shorter time, when you cut each piece, work fast to move it to an individual plate. While I prefer to bake this as one cake, you may prefer to bake it in ramekins. For 10 ramekins filled nearly to the top with batter, the baking time will be 15 to 18 minutes.

7½ tablespoons (112g) unsalted butter, plus more for the pan

½ cup (75g) all-purpose flour, plus more for the pan

Large pinch of fine sea salt

10 ounces (300g) chocolate, finely chopped (use 5 ounces each of 52% cacao and 70% cacao, or 10 ounces of 60% to 65% semisweet or bittersweet chocolate)

6 large eggs

1 cup plus 2 tablespoons (225g) vanilla sugar

2 to 3 tablespoons confectioners' sugar

Edible flowers, such as pansies, primroses, and forget-me-nots, for garnish (optional)

1. Preheat the oven to 350°F (180°C) and position a rack in the center. Butter and flour a 9½-inch (22.5cm) springform pan or eight ramekins.

2. Sift together the ½ cup of flour and the salt onto a piece of waxed paper or parchment paper.

3. In a small, heavy-bottomed pan, melt the 7½ tablespoons of butter over medium heat. Place the chocolate in a large, heatproof bowl. When the butter is melted, pour it over the chocolate and whisk until the chocolate has melted into the butter.

4. In another large bowl, whisk the eggs with the vanilla sugar just until thoroughly combined—do not whisk them to a pale yellow. Whisk in the chocolate mixture, then quickly whisk in the flour mixture. Pour the mixture into the prepared pan, set the pan on a rimmed baking sheet, and bake until the edges of the cake are baked but the center is still soft and tender, 30 to 40 minutes.

5. Remove the cake from the oven and let cool on a wire rack for 10 minutes before removing it from the pan and transferring it to a serving platter. Let it cool to lukewarm. Dust the cake with the confectioners' sugar and garnish with the flowers, if desired.

SERVES 6 TO 8

EDITH'S PROFITEROLES
{ PROFITEROLES D'EDITH }

Edith, my dear friend who paints by day and keeps a huge household going the rest of the time, runs constantly. She is always creating gorgeous paintings, working in the garden, building a wall, driving to Alsace to pick up the vintage tiles she bought on eBay, calling the pool repairman, sewing exquisite silk scarves, or making red currant sorbet, and yet she manages to put a beautiful meal on the table. Profiteroles are often dessert. If Edith has time to make this dessert (she makes the ice cream, too), then anyone does.

I suggest buying your favorite artisanal ice cream, or making either the speculoos or vanilla ice cream (pages 263 and 202). The recipe calls for 2 pints, but it depends on how much or little you want to fill the choux (small puffy pastry shells).

Serve the profiteroles topped with sliced, toasted almonds and—if desired—a sprinkling of fleur de sel.

FOR THE CHOUX PASTRY:

> 1¼ cups (170g) all-purpose flour
>
> Zest of 1 lemon, preferably organic, minced
>
> ½ cup (125ml) whole milk
>
> 1 teaspoon fine sea salt
>
> 7 tablespoons (105g) unsalted butter, cut into thin slices
>
> ½ cup (125ml) water
>
> 4 large eggs

FOR THE CHOCOLATE SAUCE:

> 10 ounces (300g) semisweet chocolate (I suggest Lindt brand), coarsely chopped
>
> 6 tablespoons (90ml) non-ultra-pasteurized heavy cream

> 2 pints (1L) ice cream of your choice
>
> ½ cup (75g) sliced almonds, lightly toasted, for garnish (optional)
>
> Fleur de sel, for garnish (optional)

1. To make the choux pastry, preheat the oven to 350°F (180°C) and position a rack in the center. Line two baking sheets with parchment paper.

2. In a medium bowl, mix the flour and the lemon zest together and set aside.

3. Put the milk, salt, butter, and the water in a medium saucepan over medium heat. When the butter has melted, remove the pan from the heat and add the flour and lemon zest all at once, mixing with a wooden spoon until the dough forms a ball and comes away from the sides of the pan. Continue mixing for 1 minute to dry out the dough just a bit.

4. Remove the pan from the heat and beat in the eggs, one at a time, until combined.

5. Either form the choux using two teaspoons, or spoon the batter into a pastry bag fitted with a ½-inch (1.25cm) tip, and pipe out the choux (you should get 30), leaving about 1½ inches (3.75cm) between each one. Bake until they are puffed and golden, 25 to 30 minutes. (The baking time will vary depending on your oven.) Remove them from the oven.

6. To make the chocolate sauce, while the choux are baking, place the chocolate and 6 tablespoons (90ml) water in a small, heavy saucepan over medium heat. When the water simmers, whisk the mixture until the chocolate melts. Whisk in the cream, and keep the sauce warm.

7. To serve, set three choux pastries on a dessert plate, and cut each in half horizontally. Place a scoop of ice cream on the bottom of each choux pastry, and cover the ice cream with the top of the choux pastry. Spoon a generous amount of chocolate sauce over each choux. Garnish with toasted almonds and fleur de sel, if desired.

SERVES 10 (MAKES 30 CHOUX PASTRIES, WHICH CAN BE FROZEN)

CARAMELIZED ORANGES

{ ORANGES CARAMELISÉES }

A classic dessert from Eloise, this one shines and crackles with caramel! Serve it alone, or with crisp Norman sablés, *sand cookies.*

FOR THE ORANGES:

> 4 pounds (2kg) oranges, preferably organic, zest removed in strips and julienned
>
> ¾ cup (150g) sugar, for candying the zest
>
> ¾ cup (180ml) water
>
> 2 tablespoons (30g) light brown sugar

FOR THE CARAMEL:

> ½ cup (100g) vanilla sugar
>
> 2 tablespoons hot water

1. Bring a small pot of water to a boil and blanch the zest. Drain and pat dry. Repeat the blanching process and pat the zest dry. Set aside.

2. Bring the sugar and the water to a boil in a small, heavy-bottomed saucepan over medium heat, stirring occasionally until the sugar has dissolved. Add the orange zest, bring the syrup to a boil, and cook until the zest is translucent, about 8 minutes. Using tongs or a slotted spoon, transfer the zest to a plate and let cool.

3. Remove the pith from the two zested oranges, as well as the pith and skin from the remaining oranges. Slice the oranges into ¼-inch-thick (6mm) slices, and reserve any juice.

4. Cover the bottom of a 1½-quart (1.5L) serving dish or attractive soufflé dish with the first layer of oranges, and sprinkle them lightly with the brown sugar. Repeat, sprinkling equal amounts of sugar over each layer of the oranges except for the last layer. Pour the reserved juice over the oranges. Set aside.

5. To make the caramel, combine the vanilla sugar and the hot water in a small saucepan and heat it over medium heat, rolling the pan so the

mixture caramelizes evenly. Don't be tempted to stir it once it is bubbling—it will gradually turn golden—you are looking for a deep golden color. The minute it is deep golden remove it from the heat and pour it evenly over the oranges. Let the oranges sit until the caramel has cooled and hardened, then cover and refrigerate for at least 2 hours.

6. Remove from the refrigerator, sprinkle the candied orange zest over the caramel, and serve immediately.

SERVES 6 TO 8

KINGS' CAKE WITH APPLES
{ GALETTE DES ROIS AUX POMMES }

Fève *literally means "bean," but it is used to describe the tiny porcelain figurines that go inside the* galette des rois. *You can use what you like—a dry bean or a coin, like the monks who invented the* galette *did, or a little figurine. Be sure to warn your guests that there is something hard hidden inside the* galette, *so no one bites down on it unawares.*

I love to serve Champagne with this dessert.

NOTE: *If you have frozen puff pastry, remember to remove it from the freezer at least 20 minutes before you plan to use it, so that you can roll it out. If you cannot find almond flour, grind ½ cup (80g) almonds to a fine powder in a food processor with 2 tablespoons of the vanilla sugar called for in the almond cream.*

1 pound (500g) puff pastry

FOR THE ALMOND CREAM:

4 tablespoons (60g) unsalted butter, at room temperature

⅓ cup (65g) vanilla sugar

1 large egg

1 tablespoon all-purpose flour

1 teaspoon pure vanilla extract

4 or 5 drops bitter almond extract, or as desired

½ cup (75g) finely ground almonds (also called almond flour)

FOR THE EGG WASH:

1 egg

2 teaspoons water

FOR THE APPLES:

1 tablespoon unsalted butter

3 medium apples (about 13 ounces; 400g), peeled, cored, and very thinly sliced

1. Roll out the puff pastry to a very thin (⅛-inch / 3mm) rectangle. Cut out one 10-inch (25cm) round and one 10½-inch (26.25cm) round. Place them on a baking sheet and refrigerate for 30 minutes. Reserve the scraps for another use.

2. To make the almond cream, in a medium bowl, whisk the butter with the sugar until it is soft and well combined. (If you've used some of the sugar to grind whole almonds into almond flour, whisk in the remaining sugar with the butter.) Whisk in the egg until the mixture is light, then whisk in the all-purpose flour, vanilla extract, and almond extract until thoroughly combined.

3. Stir in the almond flour gently until combined.

4. To make the egg wash, in a small bowl, whisk together the egg and the water. Set aside.

5. To make the apples, while the pastry is chilling, melt the butter in a large skillet over medium heat. When the butter is frothing, add the apples and stir, coating them with the butter. Cook, stirring and shaking the pan, until the apples are golden and almost tender throughout, 7 to 10 minutes. Remove from the heat.

6. Preheat the oven to 425°F (220°C) and position a rack in the center.

7. Assemble the *galette*: Remove the pastry rounds from the refrigerator. Place the cream in the center of the smaller round, and spread it out, leaving it thicker in the center, until it is about 2½ inches (6.5cm)

from the edge of the pastry. Cover the almond cream with the apple slices, in a single layer. If you're going to place a *fève* in the *galette*, now is the time. Top with the second round of pastry, lining up the edges with the bottom round of pastry.

8. Brush the *galette* with the egg wash, then, using the blade of a very sharp knife, score the top of the *galette*, going nearly all the way through the pastry. Using the back of a knife blade (the dull edge), press it into the edges of the *galette* at regular intervals to make a scalloped edge. This helps the pastry rise evenly.

9. Bake the *galette* until it is golden and puffed, and baked all the way through, 25 to 30 minutes. Remove from the oven and let cool for 20 minutes before serving.

SERVES 6 TO 8

CHOCOLATE AND RASPBERRY TART
{ TARTE AU CHOCOLAT ET AUX FRAMBOISES }

Baptiste Bourdon, my favorite market gardener near Louviers, invites us occasionally for a sumptuous meal. He served this rich little jewel after dinner one night, and everyone asked for more. You'll make it often, it's so delicious and easy.

You can garnish this chocolate tart with ripe pears in winter (I like to sauté them in a bit of butter and lemon first), with strawberries, raspberries, or the berry or fruit of your choice.

1 recipe Sweet Pie Pastry (page 208)
8 ounces (250g) semisweet (about 52% cacao) chocolate, diced
6 tablespoons (90ml) water
½ cup (125ml) non-ultra-pasteurized heavy cream
3 cups (180g) raspberries
1 tablespoon confectioners' sugar

1. Preheat the oven to 375°F (190°C).

2. Roll out the pastry to fit a 10½-inch (26.25cm) tart pan with a removable bottom. Line the pastry with aluminum foil and pastry weights. When the oven is hot, bake the pastry until the edges are golden, about 15 minutes. Remove the foil and the weights and continue baking until the bottom of the pastry is just golden, 5 minutes more. Remove from the oven and let cool on a wire rack.

3. While the pastry is baking, place the chocolate and the water in a small, heavy-bottomed saucepan over medium heat. As the chocolate melts, whisk it so it doesn't stick to the bottom of the pan. When the chocolate has melted, remove it from the heat and whisk in the cream. Pour the chocolate into the prebaked pastry shell, urging it toward the edges without spreading it until it is evenly distributed in the pastry shell.

4. When the chocolate has "set," arrange the raspberries on top, close enough together that you cannot see any chocolate. Just before serving, dust the tart with the confectioners' sugar.

SERVES 8 TO 10

CHAPTER 8

Le Petit Déjeuner— Breakfast *à la Française*

HERE IS THE BEAUTY OF FRENCH BREAKFAST. WHETHER the morning be rushed or staid, time is given to it just as it is to every other meal. Even on a weekday morning, breakfast gets its specific moment. Someone gets the coffee made and the bread sliced, someone else pulls out the accompaniments, then everyone sits down together. There is a big basket of fresh or toasted bread on the table, but no plates because, somehow, the French psyche doesn't mind crumbs and even the occasional drip of jam on the tablecloth. There won't be a napkin and there isn't much conversation; breakfast is focused. It's about waking up, a quick but rich moment to gently emerge into the day, fueled by coffee and chocolate, toasted bread, and the luxury of butter and jam.

"But what about croissants?" you ask. What's really happening at breakfast time in most households is that toasters are working overtime. The French buy their bread one day and toast whatever is leftover for breakfast the next. Croissants are considered special, and they're also the original fast food—you eat them for special occasions and for those desperate moments when you're starving and there wasn't time to make toast.

When I first arrived in France thirty years ago, I, too, labored under the illusion that every French breakfast included a delicate croissant and café au lait. My first morning, fresh off the plane from Seattle, I made a beeline for a patisserie, stopping at the first one on my path. I was fortunate in my ignorance, because it happened to be Ladurée near the Madeleine, already a cherished spot yet hardly the commercial success it is today. I walked in, my small suitcase in my hand on this, my first visit to Paris. Waitresses were dressed then as now, in serviceable black dresses with frilly little aprons. I sat down, tucked my bag under the table, and ordered my vision of the typical French breakfast, a croissant and a café au lait—I didn't even know then that the French term for milky coffee is *café crème*.

My vision became real. I'll never forget that croissant, with its perfect touch of sweetness, its shower of crumbs that fell down my front and onto the table. Naturally, I was mortified, looking around to see if I'd created an international incident, if anyone had noticed. I observed that everyone else in this hushed spot was delicately dunking his or her croissant into their *crèmes*, so I followed suit. It was a revelation, and I thought at the time that croissants should come with instructions. One dip, no more crumbs.

I finished up that croissant and timidly requested another *crème* with, this time, a *pain au chocolat*. Thus began a love affair that has lasted. *Pain au chocolat* is still my favorite morning pastry; dipped into good, black coffee with a jot of foamed milk, it is the height of perfection.

Over the next weeks and months I tried everything from my neighborhood patisserie, which was in the 9th arrondissement and has long since disappeared. *Pain au raisin*, I found, was much more filling than croissant, which came in handy some days, but the blend of yeast dough, pastry cream, and rum-soaked raisins has never been my favorite. Brioche, though, is another story. My first taste of morning brioche was the start of yet another love affair. I could—and often do—drown in the pillowy, buttery goodness of this fine and rich bread, which is more aptly referred to as cake. ("Let them eat cake," supposedly said by Marie-Antoinette to the starving French peasantry, was in reference to brioche.)

Those gorgeous, golden, shattery pastries that sit on patisserie and boulangerie shelves, which are called *viennoiseries* because they were based on Viennese pastries and popularized by a Viennese baker in Paris, don't go to waste, but they are not the stuff of the everyday French breakfast. As my friend Michel Amsalem, a professional pastry chef and baker, said, laughing, "I spend my time making croissants and *pains au chocolats*, but sometimes I wonder who eats them all. My coworkers might eat one or two but I never do. I like my toast and jam."

Michel's wife, Chantal, who spent her time serving customers at the boulangerie the couple owned, definitely knew where they went. "Weekends," she said, her hand on her perfectly clad hip. "Weekends are the big moment for *viennoiseries*. People have time then, and *viennoiseries* deserve a little extra time."

Chantal, who resembles Isabelle Adjani right down to the burgundy-colored hair and those beautiful lips, wasn't born to be a *boulangère*, baker's wife—she has her degree in pharmaceutical preparation—but she took to it avidly when she married Michel. She got to know her customers' tastes, spoiling them just a little, advising Michel on what and how much to make. "We had a business to run and our public to take care of," she said. She always exercised her particular brand of seduction as she sold Michel's wares, which included batting her eyelashes and perhaps tucking an extra croissant in someone's bag. "Knowing what the customer wants, and how to serve them, is just good business," she said.

Nadège, another *boulangère* who dresses to the nines ("Is it a prerequisite for the role?" I ask myself), is married to Fréderic Bénard (Frédo), whose pastries would kill anyone's resolve to eat fewer of them. Nadège has a degree in English, but, like Chantal, she fell in love with a pastry chef who wanted his own shop. When you do that, you become the *boulangère*. She knows her customers so well she often acts as confidante or therapist, listening to their stories as she leans gracefully over the cash register, concern in her gorgeous hazel eyes. This can mean a long wait, but Frédo's work makes it worthwhile.

Frédo and Nadège's bakery is in the heart of our town of eighteen thousand, right on everyone's path to school or work. "Children whose parents didn't have time to make breakfast eat croissants and *pains au chocolats*," she says. "People going to the office who didn't eat at home, or who want to eat breakfast with their colleagues get them, and so do retirees."

Wednesday mornings are big, too, because little children don't have school that day. "Moms come in with their kids and get them a croissant or *chouquettes*," Nadège says, referring to sugary, golden little choux pastries.

Nadège and Frédo live upstairs from the boulangerie, and they enjoy meals in a small kitchen right behind the shop. Unlike at Michel and Chantal's, where their in-shop breakfast included toasted, grain-filled bread, butter, and jam, *viennoiseries* are often on the menu for the young couple and their four children. "Mistakes," Nadège said with a laugh. "We eat the mistakes."

The scene at their morning tables is typically French. There are big bowls of strong coffee on the cloth-covered table for the adults, equal-size bowls of hot chocolate made with either Banania, a uniquely French chocolate drink thickened with powdered banana and barley, or another powdered chocolate, for the children. An increasing number of the French drink flavored teas, but as my friend Sophie put it, "Tea is like colored water, if you ask me!" She wouldn't be caught dead with a liquid in her morning bowl that smelled like peaches, or raspberries, or black currants. "Give me coffee, the blacker the better," she said.

There is a big pat of butter—usually lightly salted—jars of jam—sometimes homemade—and usually a jar of honey. There is a tin holding sugar cubes—they go by twos and threes into both coffee and hot chocolate—and the toaster is nearby. In some families—like Eloise's—toast is grilled on a flat, old-fashioned "toaster" that has holes in it and is set right over the gas flame. "We prefer toast on this little thing," she said, even though she has an electric toaster. "It's more homey."

Many families also put breakfast cereals on the table. The variety never ceases to amaze me. It's almost as extensive as in the United States. There are a few uniquely French brands, like Jordans, with its muesli-style cereals whose labels promise environmentally correct production methods, locally grown cereals, and no genetically modified grains. The rest most of us have seen before, with brand names of Nestlé and Kellogg's, though there is one big difference. They're all sweetened. There are no plain Cheerios or cornflakes. Everything is coated in sugar.

There is one unsweetened cereal created in Australia that is called Weetabix. It contains little sugar and bears a strong resemblance to hay in both flavor and texture. The company produces a chocolate cereal called Weetos, which is slightly sweetened and tastes like vitamins. I wonder how they retain shelf space with all the sweet competition.

I sometimes wonder if the French have a different metabolic system from others, because they start the day with so much sugar yet seem to get a lot done. That mid-morning drop after an early sugar high either doesn't happen or it gets taken care of by the chocolate bar in the desk drawer that one of my friends, Benedicte, always nibbles on when she is tired. I'm not sure if that is just her or if every French person has an emergency chocolate bar somewhere nearby.

Nathalie is a breakfast bread and butter eater, though she acknowledges that cereal makes a welcome change for her boys. "They don't eat it every day; it's a treat," she said.

Edith, devoted as she is to plain, healthy, organic food, took to buying cereal once her children became adolescents. "It's not that I stopped caring," she said. "It's just that I figured if I gave in on that and the worst thing they did was eat sweet breakfast cereal, then I was a lucky mother!"

When Betty's sons, who are now in their late thirties, were growing up, they ate cereal, though they much preferred morning crêpes. "I made them the night before," she said, laughing. "Even I wouldn't get up and make them in the morning." She'd reheat them, and the boys would slather them with butter and fill them with sugar or jam. These, they dunked in their child's version of café au lait, which was made with Ricoré, an instant blend of coffee and chicory powder they stirred into hot milk. "That's such an old-fashioned breakfast," Betty said. "But they just loved it. It gave them the adult coffee experience."

French yogurt, as common for breakfast as it is for dessert, deserves a chapter of its own. The varieties appear endless, each more creamily delicious than the next one. Sweetened with vanilla, with chunky fruit in the bottom, with caramel syrup on the top, organic, low fat, high fat, sheep's milk or goats' milk, the choice just continues to expand.

In my lovely little town of Louviers, there is a patissierie or boulangerie on just about every corner. Just for fun, I decided to do a brioche tasting and went to ten of them, returning home laden with brioche ("laden" is a euphemism—brioche doesn't weigh much). We tasted all ten (the leftovers were toasted for several subsequent breakfasts) and the surprising best came from a bakery where I rarely go. It was just the right level of butteriness, the right edge of sweetness, the perfect level of weight and tenderness. It remains my local benchmark for brioche.

Recently, bakers began making miniature *viennoiseries*. This is a move I've championed, because it takes the decision-making out of breakfast, for you can have one of each.

Edith and I sometimes exercise this choice when we meet for coffee and pastries early Saturday mornings before the market. She goes to the bakery, I go to the café, where the owner is busily straightening chairs, the music and coffee machine are turned on, the lights a beacon in the early morning. We have our regular table; he knows our drinks and starts to prepare my *double exprès* and Edith's *double crème*. Nathalie often joins us, riding up on her bicycle, hair flying, in time to order a quick *double exprès* before going off to the office, where she'll be inundated by patients.

This particular café is like many in the countryside. There is no basket of *viennoiseries* on the counter, so they tolerate pastries from the bakery next door, and the ensuing crumbs on the table. It's the price of doing business.

Often Edith buys a big brioche and sets it in the center of the table, and we tear off hunks as we "remake the world," which is how the French describe conversation among good friends. Sometimes, though, she'll go the mini-viennoiserie route with a focus on her favorites, *chausson aux pommes*, puff pastry folded over apple compote, or *pain aux raisins* and mine, *pain au chocolat*.

No matter how often I have them, *viennoiseries* remain a treat for me. I love the Saturday-morning indulgences where, if I've met Edith, I've had my breakfast by eight (there are always leftovers, which I bring home for Fiona). Otherwise, my last market stop is Nadège's bakery, where the line can snake out the door. I wait my turn for two croissants and two *pains au chocolats*, and head home, where I'll make a giant bowl of coffee in my sturdy little Francis Francis espresso machine, and a big bowl of hot chocolate for Fiona, who loves it made with squares of semisweet chocolate melted into farm-fresh milk. Then we share breakfast surrounded by market produce.

After a French breakfast, once everyone has gone on their way, the lingering peace remains. I love walking into a French home at that moment. There is the scent of toasted bread, the underlying aroma of butter and the tempting perfume of coffee. Bowls—which are, somehow, always pretty, rarely color coordinated, filled with personality as each belongs solely to its owner—are right where they were left, there is that messy scatter of crumbs on the table. The tableau speaks of warmth, comfort, and togetherness.

BANANIA

At the turn of the twentieth century, French journalist and entrepreneur Pierre-François Lardet sat on the shore of Lake Managua, in Nicaragua, sipping a tasty local beverage made with powdered banana, crushed grains, cacao, and sugar. Seduced by its flavor, he re-created it on his return to France, eventually marketing it under the name Banania, a name created by his equally entrepreneurial wife, Blanche.

It hit the market at a time when France was at the height of its colonial wealth, and both bananas and cacao were considered luxury products. The powder was immediately popular, made more so during World War I when Mr. Lardet shipped a trainload of the powder to French soldiers on the front. These included Senegalese shooters (infantry from Senegal who were particularly skilled with rifles) universally admired for their courage and joyful kindness. The smiling face of a Senegalese soon decorated the Banania box, and the drink—which was also a cereal—became a breakfast fixture, promising nutrition to a war-torn population.

The French affection for Banania has never waned, its production never faltered. Today it includes wheat flour and malt, and honey as well as sugar. There are many versions of it now—some with the smiling Senegalese, some without. Banania takes up a large share of the powdered chocolate shelf in the supermarket, and the French breakfast table, where children daily dip their *tartine au beurre* into a bowl of steaming hot chocolate.

HOMEMADE HOT CHOCOLATE
{ CHOCOLATE CHAUD FAIT MAISON }

I make this on the coldest winter mornings, and pour it, steaming, into a warmed bowl. It is perfect for sipping and dipping. A bowl of sugar sits on the table for bringing this to the appropriate sweetness.

> 1 ounce (30g) semisweet chocolate (I use 70% cacao), broken into squares
> 1¼ cups (185ml) whole milk
> Drizzle of pure vanilla extract (optional)

1. Place the chocolate and the milk in a small, heavy-bottomed saucepan over medium heat. Heat the milk, whisking, until the chocolate has melted into it. Remove it from the heat right before it begins to boil, and whisk in the vanilla. Naturally, you'll find your perfect ratio of chocolate to milk; this is mine!

SERVES 1

APPLE SLIPPERS
{ CHAUSSONS AUX POMMES }

These are a beautiful breakfast or snack pastry, filled in France with plain, highly sweetened apple compote. They're a standard breakfast or snack pastry, and absolutely delicious. I like to make them with the Apple and Pear Compote (page 288)!

> 1 pound (500g) puff pastry
> 1 cup (250ml) Apple and Pear Compote (page 288)

FOR THE EGG WASH:

> 1 large egg
> 2 teaspoons water

1. Preheat the oven to 400°F (200°C) and position a rack in the center.

2. Cut out 8 circles of puff pastry measuring about 5 inches (12.5cm) in diameter. Roll out the circles to make ovals that measure about 7 by 5 inches (17.5 by 12.5cm).

3. On the lower third of each oval, place 2 tablespoons of compote. Whisk together the egg and the water in a small bowl and brush some of this egg wash around the bottom edge of the ovals, then bring the top edge up and over the compote, to form a half oval. Gently but firmly press the edges of the pastry together, without completely mashing the edges or they won't puff.

5. Brush the top of each *chausson* with the egg wash, then, using a very sharp knife, make three or four slashes in the top of each *chausson*.

6. Bake until the *chaussons* are golden and the pastry is completely puffed, about 20 minutes. Remove from the oven and let cool for 10 minutes before serving. The filling may still be very hot, so warn your guests.

MAKES 8 *CHAUSSONS*

CRÊPES

Do as Betty does and make these the night before, then serve them for breakfast, heated in the oven first. A warm crêpe is a good crêpe. Serve them with the filling(s) of your choice. My children's favorites: home-made red currant jelly, Nutella (homemade, of course!), lightly salted butter, and vanilla sugar or brown sugar.

NOTE: *This is a sweet crêpe recipe, destined for dessert. If you want to turn these into savory crêpes, just omit the sugar and provide savory fill-ings such as grated cheese, thinly sliced ham, or . . .*

    1¼ cups (190g) all-purpose flour

    ¾ teaspoon fine sea salt

    2½ cups (635ml) whole milk

    1 tablespoon vanilla sugar (optional)

    3 large eggs

    2 to 3 tablespoons clarified butter

1. Sift the flour and the salt together into a bowl, and make a well in the center. Add 1¼ cups (310ml) of the milk and all the vanilla sugar, and gradually whisk in the flour. Add the eggs one at a time, whisking just until they are blended. Whisk in the remaining milk. Let sit for 30 minutes, to allow the flour to expand and absorb the liquid.

2. Heat a 10½-inch (26.5cm) crêpe pan (nonstick is fine) over medium-high heat. Brush the pan with some of the clarified butter, and, using a ¼-cup (60ml) measure, pour the batter into the center of the pan. Quickly turn and shake the pan until the batter coats the bottom. Let cook until the crêpe is golden and beginning to curl at the edges, about 1½ minutes. If the crêpe is cooking too quickly and getting close to burned on the bottom, reduce the heat slightly. Take the edge of the crêpe in your fingers, or lift it using a wooden or plastic spatula, and gently pull the crêpe up. Turn it over and continue cooking until the other side of the crêpe is lightly golden, 30 seconds. Transfer the crêpe to a plate and keep warm in a very low oven, covered with a cotton tea towel, or serve directly from the pan. Repeat with the remaining butter and batter.

MAKES 14 CRÊPES

CHAPTER 9

The Delights of
French Bread

I NEVER, EVER GET OVER THE THRILL—OR PRIVILEGE—
of living within minutes of four boulangeries, each of which has
fresh bread on the shelves throughout the day.

I have my favorite, of course. It's called Aux Blés d'Or, At the
Golden Wheat, and the taste of their *rétrodor* or *fagotine*, both versions of baguette, are visions of yeasty loveliness. But when Aux
Blés d'Or (which is Frédo and Nadège's shop) is closed on their single day of rest, Sunday—"How can they do this?" I sometimes ask
myself—I go to the competition. Thanks to one of the more intel-
ligible French laws, there must be one boulangerie open in each
neighborhood every day. I consider myself extremely lucky, because
each of my local bakeries makes at least one fabulous loaf, so we are
never without great bread.

I walk to the boulangerie once a day, sometimes more, and the pleasure of emerging with a baguette in my hand, rounding the corner, and tearing off the *quignon*, end, to chew on, is indescribable. But I'll try to describe it anyway. It is complete good fortune, laced with indulgence, crowned by the feeling of being absolutely spoiled. After all, a team of bakers has been up since three A.M. baking for *me*. They've prepared the dough in their big, flour-dusted mixers, weighed and shaped it by hand, tucked it into thick, rising cloths, slit it with a razor blade and then slid it into the blistering oven when it's just the right level of airiness. All of that so that I can enjoy the paradisiacal pleasure of crust and crumb between my teeth. If I ever for one second think I'm in the wrong place, the heel of a baguette brings me back to my senses.

There is something so reassuring about walking into the warm and yeasty-smelling world of the boulangerie every day, and being part of the lively tableau it represents. The scene changes little. The sparkling glass cases on one side are always filled with fresh and artful cakes, tarts, and individual pastries. On the other side are the savory offerings, from quiche studded with smoked salmon or sprinkled with herbes de Provence, to baguette sandwiches wrapped with colorful raffia. Behind it all, on tall, wooden shelves, is the glorious tableau of French breads.

My bread preference is always baguette style, because I'm more of a crust than crumb person. It is also the bread the French do best. The baguette is everywhere, from the back of a bicycle (sometimes mine), where it balances the length of the journey from boulangerie to home, to the stroller, where it is tucked next to baby. It might be clenched under the arm by the briefcase-carrying monsieur who stops by the boulangerie on the way home from work, sitting on the backseat of the car leaving its trace of crumbs, or simply held by its brown square of paper, which the server has deftly twisted around its middle.

Most of the people I know are bread connoisseurs. Nathalie and Arnaud get bread at Aux Blés d'Or, because they like the same baguette I do. With their three boys, they eat lots of bread. Edith, on the other hand, true to her rebel spirit, prefers dense loaves of organic whole wheat bread, which she will drive miles to procure. She also loves the yard-long loaves from the market that look like huge paving stones and have a gorgeous, creamy interior. She buys three at a time, and I'm sure half of one is eaten by the time she gets home.

Nadine, a dear friend who happens to be Edith's sister-in-law and lives on a farm about fifteen minutes from Louviers, cannot fathom a meal without bread. She and her husband, Christian, travel frequently, and she isn't always able to get to the boulangerie before a meal. "I always keep baguettes in my freezer," she said. "We have to have our bread."

Philippe and Alain, friends who live in a manor house between Louviers and Rouen, are not just bread lovers, they are bread devourers. Philippe is a florist in Rouen, and he has his favorite bakery there. Every weekend, before he closes up his shop, he buys enough loaves of chewy crisp sourdough bread studded with walnuts, or figs, or hazelnuts, to last them for several days.

Chantal and Michel's story is amusing. Michel, the baker, loves to add corn flour or poppy seeds to his white-flour loaves. He might mix in some nuts or seeds, too. At home, though, the bread on the table is whole wheat organic bread from our local organic grocery store. "Chantal has to eat organic," he says, shaking his head with a laugh. "I eat my bread at work; we eat her bread at home."

The yeasty French bread world begs to be explored, day after day. Bakers offer an array of loaves, either of their own creation, or those of the mill who supplies them with flour.

In the case of Frédo at Aux Blés d'Or, he buys flour from a nearby mill that is milled from local wheat. When he signed up with this mill for regular flour deliveries he got the right to make their signature baguette, which is the *rétrodor*. He is the only baker in Louviers with that right, because if all the bakers could make it, it would cease to be special. As it is, the *rétrodor* is a gorgeous, golden, very special loaf with a tender interior, made with a certain grade of flour that adapts well to long, slow fermentation. It's yeasty and almost a bit sweet, with a bouncy, almost creamy texture. Those who love it line up outside Aux Blés d'Or on a daily basis.

Rétrodor is part of a family of breads called *baguette de tradition*, traditional baguettes. They have individual names like *rétrodor, parisse, banette, florian*. They're brands, and they have what is called a *cahier des charges*, or bill of specifications, that means if you see these names in a boulangerie window, you know you'll find a great baguette inside.

Millers began the development of these *baguettes de tradition* after a steady decline in bread quality that began during World War II, when bread was made with everything from ashes to buckwheat flour. By the 1970s, bread was in a sorry state in the cities of France, and the number of small country bakers was slowly diminishing.

During the 1980s, mills began investing in research to develop recipes that would use more of their high-quality flour and would result in a baguette that was like those prewar—with a crisp crust, an almost creamy interior filled with holes and flavor, a springy texture, and some keeping quality.

Today, bakers sign a contract with a mill that delivers flour on a regular basis. As part of their agreement, the mill supplies recipes to the baker, along with the blend of flour needed to make the recipe. *Baguette de tradition* is just one result—there is a whole panoply of other breads based on recipes that millers have created, flour blends that they deliver, and loaves that the baker executes.

The *baguette de tradition* is protected by law so the French bread consumer can buy with confidence. The first article of the law stipulates that only bread baked at the boulangerie can be sold at the boulangerie, a response to the increasing number of *boulangers* who, until the law was passed in 1993, bought frozen loaves, thawed them out to bake, and sold them as their own. The second article of the law stipulates that breads with the word *tradition* in their description can contain just four ingredients—flour, salt, water, yeast—and they must be made according to traditional methods. This means that the dough is mixed together gently, left to rise for many hours, then baked.

The law ensures a certain quality standard, but bread is only as good as its baker. A *rétrodor* will always be tasty, but in the hands of a baker like Frédo, it can be out of this world.

This young man with his soft, sleepy look (no doubt a result of getting up each morning at three) has a gift with dough. He uses the recipe supplied by his miller, but he adds his brand of calm to the whole operation. He bakes the *rétrodor* twice a day, and there is never any left by early evening. He also bakes many other loaves inspired by the mill that supplies his flour—there is the *fagotine*, which looks like a baguette with pointy ends that contains a bit of whole wheat flour and some powdered sourdough to give it a tang; a loaf-shaped dark bread studded with grains called *hastings*; *pain de campagne*, country bread with some rye flour; *baguette* rolled in sesame seeds (so delicious), and another that is black with poppy seeds. Every few months, there's a new loaf on the shelf, the result of the miller's research.

"When I'm not so busy," said Frédo, who is the father of four young children as well as the owner of his bakery and its chief baker and pastry chef, "I want to make my own sourdough breads. That day will come."

The difference between *baguettes de tradition*, which are solid and gorgeously crisp of crust and wheaty of flavor, and a regular baguette that shatters when you tear off a piece is huge. An ordinary baguette is to the *tradition* what Wonder Bread is to a good, homemade loaf. The ordinary baguette has its own *cahier des charges*, which stipulates that it can contain up to seventy-seven different ingredients, including additives like fava bean flour and ascorbic acid (for keeping quality), liquid yeast, fats, and oils. Not all ordinary baguettes contain these, but many do.

The price of the ordinary baguette is protected by law to ensure that the French don't rise up and revolt, as they did during the Revolution, when most people couldn't afford to buy bread. A regular baguette, which weighs 200g (about 6.5 ounces), costs 96 centimes; a baguette *tradition*, which weighs about 300g (10 ounces), generally costs 1.20 euro.

As Frédo said, "You pay more for better bread, which takes up a lot more of my time. It's simply the price of quality."

Bread is present at every meal, from breakfast through lunch, into snack, and at supper. It is essential for helping get food on a fork, for eating with salad to balance the vinaigrette, and for using as a prop with cheese. Bread is also essential for sopping up sauce, a common practice.

I learned, much to my chagrin, however, that sopping—or *saucer*, as it is called—is not a polite occupation. I was at a very lovely restaurant with my friend Eloise, the mother of three small children and a primary school teacher, several years ago. I'd already lived in France for more than a decade, and I was an experienced *sauceuse,* sauce mopper-upper, a practice I'd copied from my French friends. We were enjoying our meal, which included lamb with a rich and creamy sauce. After I'd finished the dish, I took a piece of bread from the basket and began to sop up the sauce. Eloise, horrified, quickly looked around her, leaned over, and whispered, "Susan, you cannot do that!"

I ate my deliciously sauced piece of bread. *"Pardon?"*

"Susan, it isn't dignified, it just isn't done," she said. "It isn't classy, nor is it polite." She was truly shocked, and so was I. For at least two decades I'd happily sauced my plate in all manner of situations, and with all manner of people who were doing the same. No one had ever said a word.

"Anyone raised with dignity knows not to sauce," Eloise said in her worst, perfect-person manner. Then she started laughing. "Okay, we all like to sauce, just not in public. But if you have to do it, at least put the bread on your fork and take a little sauce, but not all of it."

It turns out that saucing the plate is an insult to the hostess, because it implies there wasn't enough food on the plate. It is the American equivalent to licking a plate. Since I learned that, I have stopped saucing in public.

Now that I am sensitive to the saucing issue, I can say that between what is proper and what is done lies a huge gulf. At any given time in any given restaurant, someone is saucing a plate with a piece of ever-present bread. I can assure you, though, that person will never be me.

There are other French protocols around bread that I learned on my visits to French farms. I remember my friend Danie Dubois, who raises geese and makes the finest foie gras in all of France, lifting up a huge, round loaf of sourdough bread and holding it against her chest. She took the foot-long bread knife, which was as sharp as a razor, and cut plank-size slices, using the wicked knife and slicing toward her chest. The first time I saw her do this I tried to stop her. "Oh, Susan," she said. "This is simply how we slice our bread here. It's less dangerous to others this way." I didn't want to point out how it looked as though she was putting her own life in jeopardy.

In Brittany, I learned that a fresh loaf is always blessed with the sign of the cross before being sliced. And in the Pays Basque, a loaf is never set on its back once from the oven, but always with the slash marks in view because doing otherwise is a sign of disrespect. In Normandy, a big country loaf is kept for a day before being sliced, because it needs to "ripen" to be digestible. And on farms throughout the land, a small wooden "cage" often hangs from the ceiling. In the old days, that cage held bread away from the rats. Loaves were baked once a month, so for ten days to two weeks people had "fresh" bread; after that, the bread was hard and had to be softened in either warm milk, or broth, or a mixture of eggs and milk, or even wine. Not a crumb was thrown away.

It used to be that every tiny village had a bakery. The baker would fire up the oven once a week or once a month, depending on need, and bake enough bread to supply the village. It took hours for the wood-fired oven to heat up to the degree necessary to bake bread—around 500°F (260° C)—and the bread took about an hour to bake, yet the oven would stay hot for hours. Villagers brought their roasts and gratins, their tarts and their cakes to bake in the residual heat. Most of the village wood-fired ovens that are still standing rest unused except for special festivals when they might be pressed into service. Then, people flock to watch the bread being baked, then buy a loaf or two.

Today, times are easier. Villagers, or those who live on isolated farms, now come to larger towns like mine where there is a boulangerie on every street corner.

The boulangerie generally closes its doors around seven thirty P.M. If you've forgotten to buy bread and slide in then, as I occasionally do, there isn't much on the shelf. According to statistics, each French person consumes at least half a baguette a day. According to my observation, I'd say they consume twice that. When bread is as good as it is today, one baguette goes down like a trick.

You may want to try to bake your own French bread, and I don't blame you. There is nothing quite like fresh bread to make life perfect. That said, I'll warn you right now that producing a loaf of bread that resembles the beautiful loaves on the French boulangerie shelves is a challenge indeed. But, I've included several recipes in this chapter, and the rest is up to you!

Here are a few tips:

■ Less is more, both in amounts of yeast and flour, and in kneading. For the sourdough bread, you want the dough to be more batter than bread dough. That means it's a bit sticky to work with, so have plenty of flour on hand to dust your hands, the work surface, and whatever mold you use to bake it.

■ For yeast dough, you want it to be soft, too. And you want to use less yeast than you think is necessary. My rule of thumb is 1 rounded teaspoon yeast for up to 6 cups flour. Then, I let the dough sit so that the yeast has time to do its work, without pressure.

▪ Salt is important, but since it retards the action of yeast, I always add it after I've let the yeast sit with the water and flour for a bit, to give the yeast a chance to show what it can do.

▪ Start bread in a hot oven so the crust develops. You can turn it down after ten minutes. Your loaf is ready when you knock on it and it sounds hollow.

A VISIT TO THE LOCAL BAKERY

To be in a bakery kitchen, or *laboratoire* as it is called, is to enter a flour-dusted world. Official garb is white shirt, white pants, white shoes, white apron tied around an often-ample waist. Flour, which is flicked onto counters where loaves are shaped, poured into mixing bowls, and dusted onto risen loaves, sifts onto everything, including eyebrows and lashes, giving the kitchen an otherworldly dream quality.

Breads that have risen for hours are slid into long, low ovens, then shifted around with long-handled wooden spatulas called *pelles*; a baker has to be deft and graceful to work a *pelle* in what can be a confined environment.

If you are in a boulangerie's *laboratoire* at three A.M. you're likely to feel as though you're in a real-time movie. The bakers move around slowly, waking up as they switch on the oven; check rising; measure the water, yeast, and flour into huge mixers in preparation for the loaves they'll make today. They may have had coffee at home, but there's a pot brewing somewhere, sending the toasty aroma into the kitchen to aid the waking-up process.

Loaves that have been left overnight in a rising cupboard are pulled out and, as soon as the oven is hot, slashed with a *lame*, a razor blade fit on a handle, so steam escapes during baking, allowing the loaf to rise evenly.

Since the baguette is the basis of the boulangerie's wares, there are many series of them baked throughout the day. At one boulangerie in my town, a batch goes in the oven every three hours so a warm loaf is always waiting. There is another reason for the frequent baking of the baguette. An ordinary baguette—which can be delicious if made by a good baker—doesn't last more than three hours once out of the oven. Because it is flour, water, salt, air, and a bundle of additives that encourage it to rise and bake quickly, it dries out at the drop of a hat. So, baking every three hours is what the French would call *astucieuse*, clever. It isn't just about bread, but about fresh bread.

While the breads bake, brioche is being mixed up, a gorgeous golden blend of butter, eggs, sugar, and flour. Loaves of sourdough bread that have risen all night are checked with a gentle pat, to see how much longer they need to rise, and the accoutrements for making tarts, quiches, sandwiches, and all the other elements that compose the offerings in a boulangerie, are brought forth.

Most bakeries also make morning pastries, *viennoiseries*, and a selection of desserts. Bakers can be pastry chefs, and pastry chefs can be bakers. You can always tell when you walk into a bakery where the strength lies. A *boulanger*'s shop will offer decent tarts, cakes, and pastries, but his breads will be made and baked to golden perfection. A *patissier*'s bread will be just fine, but the cakes, tarts, and pastries will be exceptional.

Many of the varieties of breads in the French boulangerie have been around forever, like fat, oval *pain de campagne,* country bread, that is made with white and some rye flour; the oversized baguette that is called simply *pain* and weighs exactly twice what a baguette weighs; the white sandwich loaf that is called *pain de mie* (which literally translates as crumb bread, because it has very little crust and lots of crumb), the *boule*, a round loaf that can be made with many different types of flour.

There is also *pain au levain*, sourdough bread that was traditionally baked into a huge round called a *miche*; *ficelle*, string, a very thin loaf that weighs exactly half the weight of a baguette; and *pain Viennois*, a tender white loaf shaped like a baguette that contains flour, sugar, milk, butter, and occasionally chocolate chips, and was the first bread in France to be made with yeast, in 1840, when others were all still made with sourdough starter.

There are more types of breads that grace the shelves of the French boulangerie, many of them regional specialties. In cities there are bakers known for their breads packed with olives or dried cherries or flavored with curry or herbs. In Normandy, including my town of Louviers, *pain brié* is our local bread. Compact, made with white flour and a touch of butter, it was favored by fishermen and sailors because of its long keeping quality. In southern climes, *fougasse* is found in most boulangeries. A lovely, flat yeast bread that is cut right through, with cuts that are about 1½ inches long so that it bakes into a beautiful pattern, its origins appear to be Italian, though one can never be sure. Among all the stories that are told of the *fougasse*, the one I prefer says the baker used it as a way to test the temperature of his wood oven. He rolled out a piece of dough until it was flat, slashed it in several places so it would rise evenly, and baked it; the result pleased so much it became a staple in bakeries along the Mediterranean.

Whatever the bread, if made fresh by a good baker, it is more than the staff of life—it is the pleasure that awaits, every single day of the week.

THE DAILY LOAF

The following are just a few breads—of various sizes, flours, shapes—found in the French boulangerie.

Baguette: This is the standard loaf of French bread, and there are specific criteria to its shape and content. The baguette weighs 8 ounces (250g) and is about 30 inches (75cm) long. It is made from flour, water, salt, and yeast, though it can contain a percentage of fava or soybean flour, malt, gluten, sourdough powder, or vitamin C. Traditionally, the baguette was made with white flour. Today it is made with all sorts of flours and has everything from grains to olives added to it. Since the French revolution when the people cried out for affordable bread, the price of baguette has been regulated. Today, the cost is 90 centimes (about $1.20). There are many "brand-name" baguettes made with different types of flours, which can be sold at a higher price. They include *rétrodor*, *parisse*, *banette*, *tradition*, *campagrain*, *buchéron*. These breads are generally made according to traditional methods. Since 1993, all bread sold in boulangeries must be mixed, shaped, and baked on the premises.

Baguette au levain: Sourdough baguette. Many of the *baguettes tradition* are sourdough as well.

Boule: ball, or round loaf, either small or large

Chapeau: small, round loaf topped with a chapeau, or hat

Couronne: ring-shaped loaf

Epi: like a baguette, only cut at regular intervals so that when baked, it looks like wheat stalk

Le Fer à Cheval: horseshoe-shaped loaf

Ficelle: a thin loaf that weighs exactly half that of a baguette

Fougasse: a flat, rectangular, lacy bread made of baguette dough; can be filled with onions, herbs, spices, cheese, olives, bacon. Can be made of puff pastry.

Miche: large, round, country-style loaf

Pain bio: bread made with organic flour

Pain bis: made with flour that is less refined than white flour

Pain de campagne: made with white flour and a percentage (up to 50 percent) of rye flour

Pain au céréales: made with white flour and a variety of cereals like rye, oat, barley, buckwheat

Pain complet: made entirely with whole wheat flour

Pain de fantaisie: any bread other than baguette

Pain aux graines: anything *aux grains*; includes seeds like sunflower and flax

Pain au levain: any bread made with sourdough and a longer rising time

Pain de mie: rectangular white sandwich loaf that is nearly all *mie*, or crumb, and very little crust. It is made for durability and is used for, among other things, sandwiches, croutons, toast points.

Pain aux noix and *pain aux noisettes*: bread, most often rye or wheat, filled with walnuts or hazelnuts

Pain polka: bread that is slashed in a crisscross (like the steps of a polka!) pattern; usually a large country loaf cut in this pattern

Pain aux raisins: most often rye or wheat bread studded with raisins

Pain de seigle: bread made from ⅔ rye flour and ⅓ white flour

Pain de son: a "health bread"; recommended to help digestion, it contains a percentage of wheat germ

Pain viennois: shaped like a baguette, this tender, white flour loaf was the first bread in France to be made with yeast, in 1840. It usually contains flour, sugar, powdered milk, water, and yeast.

CHANTAL'S FILLET OF PORK WITH HONEY

Chantal Amsalem prepares this quick dish often, and serves it with Belgian endives. She loves the sweet-and-sour aspect of the pork, and the ease with which it goes together. I love this with tarragon, though use the herbs that you have at hand. Once you've made this with pork, you'll find that you will use the same preparation for chicken, fresh tuna, veal . . . the options are many!

Serve this with the seared endive and braised asparagus (pages 262 and 14), serving one endive per person, and three or four asparagus spears arranged nicely alongside the endive.

Try a chilled white Burgundy with this dish.

½ cup (5g) fresh herbs, including tarragon and flat-leaf parsley, minced

1 clove garlic, green germ removed, minced

1 tablespoon extra-virgin olive oil

1 pound (500g) fillet of pork, cut in ¾-inch-thick (1.95cm) slices

Fine sea salt and freshly ground black pepper

2 tablespoons freshly squeezed lemon juice

2 tablespoons mild floral honey

Fleur de sel

1. Cover herbs and garlic with a small bowl.

2. Heat the oil in a large, heavy bottomed skillet over medium-high heat. When the oil is hot but not smoking, add the pork slices and cook until they turn golden, 3 to 4 minutes. Season the pork with salt and pepper, turn the pork slices, and cook until they are golden, about 3 minutes. Add the lemon juice and shake the pan, then turn the pork slices. Reduce the heat to medium, drizzle the honey over the pork, and shake the pan so the honey melts into the pork. Strew the herbs and garlic over the pork, turn the slices, and cook, shaking the pan, until the garlic just begins to turn golden and is very fragrant, and the pork is just slightly pink in the center, 1 to 2 minutes.

3. Transfer the pork to a warmed serving platter. Pour any juices over it, and scrape any garlic and herbs from the pan onto the pork. Season with fleur de sel and serve.

SERVES 4

VIENNESE BREAD
{ PAIN VIENNOIS }

Sweet, tender, delicious! This bread is great for breakfast or for afternoon snack. I slice off a length, slice that in half, and use it to make a semisweet chocolate "sandwich." Miam!

FOR THE BREAD:

> 1 cup (250ml) whole milk
>
> 1 teaspoon baker's yeast (SAF brand is best, but Fleischmann's active dry is fine)
>
> 2 tablespoons sugar
>
> 1 teaspoon fine sea salt
>
> 2¼ to 2½ cups (325 to 360g) all-purpose flour
>
> 2 tablespoons unsalted butter, melted

FOR THE GLAZE:

> 2 teaspoons unsalted butter, melted
>
> 1 teaspoon milk

1. To make the bread, scald the milk in a small saucepan over medium heat, just until it has tiny bubbles around the edge. Remove from the heat and transfer to a bowl or to the bowl of a stand mixer. When the milk is slightly cooled (test it on the inside of your wrist—when you can't feel the heat of the milk, it is the perfect temperature), stir in the yeast and the sugar. Let sit until some of the yeast has bubbled up to the top of the milk (this means the yeast has proofed). Add the salt, stir, and slowly add half the flour, then the melted butter. Add up to 1¼ cups (187g) of the remaining flour to form a fairly thick dough. If the dough is still soft and very sticky, add additional flour, 1 tablespoon at a time, until you get a dough that is firm, but not stiff.

2. Turn out the dough onto a lightly floured work surface and knead by hand for 5 minutes. If you are using a stand mixer, fit it with the paddle and knead the dough on the lowest speed for 5 minutes.

3. Form the dough into a ball, return to the bowl, cover with a tea towel, and let rise in a warm spot (68 to 70°F / 20 to 21°C) until doubled in bulk, about 1½ hours.

4. Preheat the oven to 375°F (190°C) and position a rack in the center.

5. To make the glaze, melt the butter and the milk together, whisk them together, and keep warm.

6. Punch down the dough and form it into a baguette shape measuring 18 by 3 inches (45 by 7.5cm). Let it rise until it is about one-third larger, about 30 minutes, then brush the loaf with the glaze and bake until the loaf is golden and baked through, about 25 minutes.

7. Remove from the oven, brush the loaf again with the glaze, and let cool before slicing.

MAKES ONE 18 BY 3-INCH (45 BY 7.5CM) LOAF

CURRY DATE BREAD
{ PAIN AU CURRY ET AUX DATTES }

I had a bread like this from Kayser bakery in Paris and thought perhaps I'd died and gone to heaven. It was golden yellow, lightly spicy, elastic the way bread should be, and punctuated by gorgeous, sweet dates. It's a bit hard to figure out where in a meal this sort of bread might go; it's really a small meal in and of itself. I like to make this and serve it warm from the oven, with air-cured ham, sheep's-milk cheese, and a great glass of Languedoc red.

NOTE: *The amount of flour you use will vary greatly on the brand of flour and the climate. When the air is dry, more flour is needed.*

3 cups (750ml) very warm water (about 115°F / 46°C)

1 teaspoon dry yeast, preferably SAF or Fleischmann's

5 to 6 cups (750 to 900g) unbleached all-purpose flour, plus more for dusting

Scant 1 tablespoon fine sea salt

2½ tablespoons curry powder (page 172)

1 cup (about 200g) dates, pitted and cut into large dice

1. Place the warm water in a bowl or in the bowl of a stand mixer. Add the yeast and 1 cup (150g) of the flour and stir. Let sit until the yeast bubbles to the surface, about 15 minutes. Stir in the salt and the curry powder, then gradually add the flour, mixing slowly, until you have a

dough that is thick but soft. Continue to mix or knead until the dough is elastic and still somewhat sticky, yet it doesn't stick to your fingers, adding additional flour if necessary. Be careful not to add too much flour—you don't want the dough to be hard or tough. This will take up to 10 minutes in a mixer, or by hand.

2. Form the dough into a ball, dust it with flour, and let it rise in the bowl in a warm spot (68 to 70°F / 20 to 21°C) until it has doubled in bulk. Punch it down and knead in the dates. Let the bread sit for about 30 minutes.

3. Punch down the dough and form it into a ball. Dust a 10-inch (25cm) cake pan or Dutch oven heavily with either flour or semolina, and place the dough in the pan. Dust the top of the bread with flour, cover loosely with a cotton tea towel, and let rise in a warm spot until the loaf is about one-third larger, 30 to 45 minutes. Gently poke the side of the loaf—if an indentation remains, your loaf is ready to bake; if it springs back, it needs more time.

4. While the dough is rising, preheat the oven to 425°F / 220°C.

5. When the dough is ready to bake, slash the top with a very sharp knife, about ¼ inch (6mm) deep, in whatever pattern you like—do slash it at least three times, though. Bake until it is golden and sounds hollow when you tap it on the bottom, about 35 minutes. Remove the bread from the oven and turn it out immediately onto a wire rack.

MAKES 1 LARGE, DELICIOUS LOAF

CURRY POWDER

{ CURRY }

Make this in small batches and use it up, or make it in a larger quantity and keep it in an airtight container in a cool, dark place. Once you've made this curry powder, you may want to adapt the recipe to your own taste or simply make a variety of powders for a variety of dishes.

2 small, dried hot peppers
1 tablespoon coriander seed
1 generous tablespoon cumin seed
½ teaspoon red mustard seed
½ teaspoon yellow mustard seed
1 generous teaspoon fennel seed
10 cardamom seeds
2 whole cloves
½ teaspoon ground ginger
¾ teaspoon turmeric

1. Place everything but the ginger and the turmeric in a small skillet over medium heat and toast until you can smell the seeds and they begin to turn golden. This will take just a few minutes, so be vigilant!
2. Transfer the seeds to a bowl to cool, and then grind them to a fine powder in a spice grinder.
3. In a small bowl, mix all the ingredients so that your powder is homogeneous. Use it up, or store it carefully!

MAKES ABOUT ⅓ CUP CURRY POWDER

CHAPTER 10

A Dozen
Great French Techniques

ASK ANY FRENCH COOK ABOUT COOKING TECHNIQUES, and she or he will deny that they have any in their repertoire. They aren't lying. They just don't realize that included in being born French is an instinctive understanding of certain cooking techniques.

It's more than that, of course. Simple cooking techniques are passed down through generations.

Here's an example: When my dear and funny friend Sophie gets home from work with her wicker basket of produce (she drives by a farm on the way and stops if she has time), she has a plan to serve crudités with mayonnaise as a first course. There is no mayonnaise in the basket, nor in her refrigerator. She'll just make some for the evening meal.

Sophie grew up watching her grandmother and her mother

make mayonnaise. To her, it's second nature. She could buy some, of course—there are at least three brands at the supermarket. "Why would I buy it?" she asks, rhetorically. "It takes five minutes to make and mine is better than anything at the store."

Sophie's grandmother learned to make mayonnaise from her mother, who learned to make it from her mother. You get the idea. There are many stories about the origins of mayonnaise, but the following is my favorite: According to legend, the origin of mayonnaise says it has been around since the eighteenth century, when the Duc de Richelieu captured the port of Mahón, in Minorca. To celebrate, his chef invented a sauce (but of course, what else would he do?!) that he called "Mahonnaise." So it's possible that Sophie's relatives have been teaching the techniques of mayonnaise making for a great many generations.

In any case, mayonnaise in the hands of most French cooks—including Sophie's—is child's play. It takes just minutes to whisk together an egg yolk, some Dijon mustard, some vinegar or lemon juice, and some salt. It takes just another few minutes to slowly add vegetable oil—not olive oil, it's too unstable—until the mixture is nice and thick. At that point it pays to whisk in some olive oil, for a veneer of flavor.

TECHNIQUE #1:
EMULSIFYING (FOR A COLD SAUCE):
MAKING MAYONNAISE, WITH SOPHIE'S TIPS

"It doesn't matter about the temperature of the ingredients—my mustard is usually cold since I keep it in the fridge," she says. "The secret is to add the oil slowly, slowly, slowly. The other secret is to whisk it by hand, not in a blender. It's more tender that way."

- In a bowl, whisk together 1 tablespoon of the acid—
  whether it's vinegar, lemon juice, or a blend of the two—
  1 large pinch salt, and 1 teaspoon Dijon mustard.
- Whisk in an egg yolk or a whole egg (a whole egg makes
  a slightly lighter textured and colored mayonnaise).
- While whisking, add 1 cup (250ml) oil in a very fine
  stream; continue whisking until the mixture gets quite
  thick. Then, you can add the oil a bit more quickly but
  still gradually. When you've added all the oil, whisk in
  2 to 3 tablespoons extra-virgin olive oil to finish it off.

When Sophie serves mayonnaise as a dip for shellfish, she adds
lemon zest. If it's for crudités, she'll add tarragon and black pepper.
For a sandwich, she mixes in some minced garlic. The possibilities
are almost endless.

ANOTHER EMULSIFICATION:
FABULOUS VINAIGRETTE, WITH SUSAN'S TIPS

Making vinaigrette is similar to making mayonnaise, though without the quantity of oil, and without the egg or egg yolk. I think a vinaigrette is one of the best sauces ever, for drizzling on everything
from steamed vegetables to roasted chicken, not to mention lettuce
leaves. I make them all the time, and here are my best tips:

- Dice 1 shallot.
- Place it in a bowl with 1 tablespoon of either vinegar or
  lemon juice. Whisk in a big pinch of salt, and 1 generous
  teaspoon Dijon-style mustard.
- While whisking quickly, slowly pour in the oil of your
  choice—¼ cup (60ml) will suffice. You can use any oil in

a vinaigrette because you're not trying to get an emulsion that will keep for several days, but an emulsion that will be used immediately to dress anything from lettuce leaves to a freshly steamed fish fillet. My favorites are extra-virgin olive oil and hazelnut oil (preferably from the Leblanc family, in Burgundy).

TECHNIQUE #2:
EMULSIFYING (FOR A HOT SAUCE):
MAKING BEURRE BLANC, WITH BAPTISTE'S TIPS

Beurre blanc is the sauce that makes people dream about the food they ate in France. Another emulsion, it's a bit *démodé*, or old-fashioned, but that doesn't mean it's any less exquisite. Because it's delicate and loaded with butter, it's not part of the quick-and-lean cuisine of today. But cooks like Baptiste make it for saucing fish or occasionally vegetables, like fresh-from-the-ground asparagus.

- In a small saucepan, reduce ¼ cup (60ml) vinegar (or use half vinegar and half lemon juice) and 1 diced shallot until there is just enough liquid left to keep the shallots moist (about 2 teaspoons).
- Add 1 tablespoon crème fraîche, which will prevent the beurre blanc from separating.
- Once the cream is hot, whisk in 6 ounces (12 tablespoons) cubed cold butter, piece by piece, so that it emulsifies (thickens) into the hot mixture instead of melting. You work on and off the heat and push the butter around in the cream so the butter doesn't really melt, but incorporates into the sauce.
- You can make beurre blanc without crème fraîche but the

cream is a safety net that prevents the butter from melting into oiliness.

Once the beurre blanc is made, use it immediately. Some say you can keep it warm in a bain-marie, or a water bath—if the water bath is lukewarm, this works. If it gets too hot, the sauce will "break" and become oily. If the beurre blanc does "break" and turn oily, whisk in either a small ice cube or a couple teaspoons of water to cool it down. The best revenge, though, is to use it immediately. (This means whatever you use it on has to be cooked, ideally before you prepare the beurre blanc. It's a lot easier to keep vegetables or even a fish fillet warm than it is to keep a beurre blanc on hold.)

TECHNIQUE #3:
CARAMELIZING: MAKING CARAMEL, WITH BETTY'S TIPS

Caramel is another preparation the French cook is practically born knowing how to make. They don't consider it intimidating or difficult at all. Take Betty—she likes to keep her cooking very simple, particularly when it comes to dessert. But she will make caramel with her eyes closed, and one of her standby desserts is crème caramel. "It's so easy," she said.

I didn't believe my French friends when they said they made caramel and it was easy. When I learned to make caramel as a cooking apprentice, the process was full of mines and time bombs. I trembled before I began, paid very careful attention, brushed down the sides of the pan with water to keep the sugar from crystallizing, and didn't touch it beyond that. Despite my care and attention, boom! Half the time I ended up with sugar crystals and no caramel.

As I began to taste caramelized desserts at my French friends' homes and talked with them about making caramel, I decided to be like them and unlearn what I'd learned. After all, they just put sugar and water in a pan and let it turn golden. That was it. And that's what I do now, and it works every time.

So what's the difference between what I learned as an apprentice and what I practice now? Confidence, something all French cooks have in abundance.

- ◆ Have your mold(s) ready near the stove.
- ◆ Place the sugar in a saucepan and add a bit of water (1 scant tablespoon per ¼ cup / 50g sugar, or enough just to moisten the sugar)—this helps the sugar melt evenly. Let the water completely moisten the sugar before putting the pan over the heat.
- ◆ Don't have the heat under the pan too hot. If the caramel seems to be heating too fast at the edges, reduce the heat under the pan and lift up the pan to cool it down, swirling it as you do.
- ◆ Always swirl, never stir.
- ◆ When the caramel begins to turn golden, watch it like a hawk, swirling it in the pan so it colors evenly, for it can go from golden to burnt in a second. Special tip from Betty: Make caramel dark brown—it has more flavor that way.
- ◆ When the caramel is the color she wants it, Betty pours it into her crème caramel mold, swirls it around to cover the bottom and as much of the sides as it will cover before it hardens, and the job is done.
- ◆ To clean the pan, she lets it cool, adds water to it, and brings it to a boil. The residual caramel that is stuck to the pan melts away.

- Once the caramel is off the heat, you can add many things to it:
  - Whisk in some warm water—it will bubble up violently, but don't be concerned. When it calms, you will have caramel syrup.
  - Whisk in heavy cream—you'll get the violent bubbling, but again, don't worry and keep whisking. Then, whisk in some salt and/or salted butter. Pretty soon, you'll have salted caramel sauce.
  - Whisk in some heavy cream, then some diced semisweet chocolate, and voilà! Caramel chocolate sauce.
- Keep going . . .

TECHNIQUE #4:
BRAISING, WITH EDITH'S TIPS

Braising is one of the most common techniques in the French kitchen. It basically means cooking in a bit of liquid, and it's a fail-safe technique that produces lusciously moist and tender foods, from vegetables to seafood to poultry to meat. Edith is big on braising—when I first met her and she was vegetarian, every meal included some combination of braised vegetable. She's an expert.

- If braising meat or poultry, brown or sear it first, in either oil, or oil and butter. Searing creates caramelized juices that will add to the flavor of the dish.
- If using onions, add them to the pan once the seared meat or poultry is out of it. The moisture from the onions will help lift the caramelized juices off the bottom of the pan.

Stir the onions, scraping the juices up from the bottom of the pan, and cook until they are soft.

♦ Add liquid—wine, water, or broth—to moisten the ingredients and further lift the caramelized juices. You may need to do some more scraping to get all the juices from the bottom of the pan. (For one chicken, you might add 2 cups; 500ml liquid.) Return the meat and its juices to the pan, then add herbs, salt and pepper, a bit of olive oil, and whatever other flavors you want the dish to have.

♦ Bring the liquid to a boil, reduce the heat so it is simmering, cover, and cook until the meat or poultry is tender throughout, checking once in a while to make sure there is enough liquid to keep the ingredients moist and that the liquid is not boiling.

When braising just vegetables, like asparagus or endives, the protocol is a bit different. You don't brown the vegetables first, but last.

♦ Put the vegetables in a pan with olive oil, some water (¼ cup; 60 ml to about 1 pound; 500g vegetables), salt, pepper, herbs, garlic, onions, whatever other flavors you want to include.

♦ Bring the water to a boil, reduce the heat so it is simmering, cover, and cook, shaking the pan from time to time, until the liquid is mostly evaporated (yes, it will generally evaporate unless there is a vacuum seal on the lid).

♦ Remove the lid, increase the heat, and let the vegetables brown, shaking the pan from time to time.

Braising does not produce crisp vegetables, but the French don't care for crisp vegetables, unless they are raw. "Vegetables taste better when they're cooked all the way through," Edith says. "That's just how it is." She's right—vegetables cooked all the way through to complete tenderness (not mushiness) offer the fullness of their flavor.

TECHNIQUE #5:
REDUCTION, WITH DANIE'S TIPS

An indispensable technique in the French kitchen often comes into play when meat or poultry has been braised (and at other moments as well). It's called reduction. Danie often makes sauces for her dishes by reducing pan juices. Here is how she does it.

Let's say you've braised veal in white wine and herbs; the veal is cooked, and you want to make a sauce with the cooking juices.

- Remove the veal from the pan, increase the heat under the liquid to medium-high, and boil until the liquid has reduced by however much you think is necessary to make a nice sauce—usually you'll need about ¾ cup (185ml).
- By reducing the pan juices you've concentrated their flavor, which will make for a richer sauce.
- Once the cooking juices are reduced, you can add butter or cream or simply leave them as they are.

I reduce many liquids. For example, sometimes I braise or boil vegetables like squash or beets in water. When they're tender, I remove them from the liquid and make a reduction with it:

- Set the pan with the liquid over medium-high heat and bring to a boil. Cook until the liquid has reduced almost to a syrup. When the liquid first begins to boil, you don't need to hover over it. As it gets thicker, though, you do, because the sweet liquid can burn in an instant.

+ Once the liquid is the thickness you want, season it, stir in a piece or two of cold butter, and voilà! A beautiful sauce is made.

You can reduce 1 cup (250ml) fruit juice—apple, orange, pomegranate—into a syrup. With or without the addition of butter, reduced fruit juice makes a full, fruity-flavored, and very elegant sauce for duck, chicken, or fish.

TECHNIQUE #6:
SAUTÉING, WITH SUSAN'S TIPS

Sautéing is a quintessential French technique that everyone does all the time without even thinking about it. The word *sauter* means "to jump"; the idea is to keep the ingredients "jumping" in a hot pan so they cook through yet get nice and golden on the outside.

+ Put oil—usually a blend of peanut or canola and olive oil, because this mixture has a higher smoke point than plain olive oil—in a pan. (If you're a Norman cook who understands exactly how to heat butter so it stays golden without burning, you can use butter—but you can't let the heat under the pan get too high!)
+ When the oil is hot but not smoking, add thinly sliced ingredients—onions, mushrooms, precooked potatoes, cherry tomatoes, cherries, thinly sliced asparagus, thinly sliced fish, poultry, or meat—and cook, stirring and shaking the pan.
+ When the ingredients are golden and tender, your sauté is ready to eat.

TECHNIQUE #7:
MAKING CONFIT (FOR VEGETABLES) OR MELTING,
WITH NATHALIE'S TIPS

Melting—some call it *confit*—is a similar alchemy to making caramel, for ingredients slow-cook with a bit of liquid for a very long
time until they thicken, their sugar concentrates and caramelizes,
their flavor intensifies and becomes extraordinarily delicious. The
Bretons *confit* onions—it is a very good way to keep them—and
the resulting marmalade, so thick it is almost a paste, goes into soups,
stews, on bread, and in pastry. Because Nathalie is a Breton cook,
she has the knack for melting, especially onions.

♦ Melting begins with butter (2 to 3 tablespoons butter to
   2 pounds onions, for example), in a heavy-bottomed skillet.

♦ When the butter foams, add the ingredient to be
   melted—thinly sliced onions, let's say—season with salt
   and pepper, and cook over very low heat, stirring
   occasionally, until the onions have turned a brick-red
   color and are thick. This may take an hour; you'll wind
   up with onions that look like marmalade, and you'll find
   one million ways to use them.

♦ You can make marmalade with shallots, a combination of
   shallots, garlic, and onions, apples, pears, root vegetables . . .
   Experiment and have fun, and watch that marmalade as
   it begins to get thick and caramelize.

TECHNIQUE #7A:
MAKING CONFIT (FOR MEATS AND POULTRY),
WITH DANIE'S TIPS

Confit of meat and poultry is a wonder of the culinary world. *Confit*, in this case, means cooked gently in fat. It's a cooking process primarily from the southwest of France, where Danie comes from. She makes *confit* of goose legs and thighs by slowly cooking them in goose fat. She stores them completely submerged in goose fat, and when she wants a quick (gourmet) meal, she scrapes off most of the fat and puts the *confit* in the oven to heat and crisp. She cooks lentils, or sautés potatoes to go alongside. The result is *oh la la*.

Here is Danie's basic process for making *confit*:

- ◆ Rub meat or poultry (with its skin) with salt, herbs like thyme and bay leaf, and lots of pepper. Place the meat or poultry in a dish in a single layer, cover, and refrigerate it overnight, or for a couple of days, depending on the quantity and thickness. The salt extracts moisture, so you may need to drain the meat a couple of times. The more liquid is extracted, the longer the *confit* will keep.

- ◆ Rub off the salt mixture. Place the meat or poultry in a heavy stockpot, and cover it with goose or duck fat. You can use lard, too, but poultry fat is much tastier. Put the stockpot over medium heat and when bubbles come up from the bottom of the pan and the fat is hot, keep it just at a simmer for about 3 hours. The fat shouldn't get too hot or the meat or poultry will fry. What you want to encourage is molecular exchange; the meat or poultry (which has been flavored with the herbs and pepper) absorbs the flavorful fat, and the fat plumps it up.

- When the meat is cooked, let it cool in the fat. Transfer it to jars or containers, cover it entirely with fat, and refrigerate. It will keep for several months.
- When you want to use it, scrape away the excess fat (keep it for frying potatoes) and brown the meat or poultry in a heavy skillet until it is hot throughout and crisp on the outside. Then, prepare yourself for paradise.

TECHNIQUE #8:
CRÈME ANGLAISE, WITH EDITH'S TIPS

Making crème anglaise is a great technique to have up your sleeve. It is the basis of the very best ice creams, it can be flavored or thickened to dress up a tart, a cake, or fresh fruit and berries, and it's very impressive to serve. Edith is the best ice-cream maker I know. Here are her crème anglaise tips:

- Heat whole milk with a vanilla bean—vanilla makes almost any sauce better. (For more intense vanilla flavor, slit the bean down its length, scrape out the seeds, and add those to the milk, too. When you're finished with the bean, rinse and let it dry, then put it in your sugar to make vanilla sugar.)
- Use 5 to 10 egg yolks per quart/liter of milk for crème anglaise, depending on how thick you want the sauce or how smooth you want the ice cream. (Freeze the egg whites for another purpose, like marshmallows.) Five yolks gives a loose sauce and a slightly crystalized ice cream; 10 gives a very thick, rich version of both.
- Whisk together the yolks with 1¼ cups (250g) sugar until they are fluffy and pale yellow, then whisk in the hot milk. Leave the vanilla bean in the mixture when you

turn it back in the pan to cook so it can keep giving flavor to the crème anglaise.

♦ Set a sieve over a bowl next to the stove.

♦ Work over low heat, stirring the crème anglaise (with a heatproof silicone spatula) in a figure-eight motion—this allows it to move all over the bottom of the pan and cook evenly.

♦ If, after 5 minutes, your crème anglaise isn't thickening, do as Edith does and raise the heat slightly, along with your vigilance.

♦ The crème anglaise will thicken quickly, and when you feel the spatula glide easily across the bottom of the pan and sense resistance in the mixture that tells you it is thick—pour the crème anglaise through the sieve into the bowl to catch any possible solid particles.

♦ You now have a sauce for dessert or, once chilled, to churn into ice cream. You can, by the way, infuse a crème anglaise with may things instead of or in addition to vanilla—try cinnamon sticks, coffee beans, citrus zests (organic), tea, cherry pits (they'll give an almond flavor) . . .

TECHNIQUE #9:
ROASTING, WITH ASTRID'S TIPS

Roasting done by a French cook results in the most gorgeous poultry and meat. (Oddly, the French cook doesn't roast vegetables, though the French eater does love to eat them!) The French cook has the skill to produce a moist, golden, crisp, subtly scented roast chicken; a succulent roast rib of beef; a startlingly good roast duck. Astrid, a friend in Gaillac who owns a vineyard and loves to roast poultry and meats, shares some of her secrets here.

♦ To roast meats and poultry, you can either salt beforehand, or not. Salting before does allow the meat and poultry to absorb salt more easily, but it can also lead to meat that is too salty. Salting afterward gives just a veneer of salt, which often is all that is necessary. Astrid is, by the way, a post-roasting salter.

♦ Make sure whatever you are roasting is at room temperature. (Don't worry, neither meat nor fowl will putrefy if left unrefrigerated for an hour or two before roasting.) This allows for even roasting and a tender result.

♦ An oven temperature of 450°F (220°C) is ideal. At this temperature, meat seizes. The outside of the meat becomes temptingly golden and develops that irresistible roasted flavor.

♦ Less is more for roasting at high temperatures, though, because meat or poultry can dry out. Check whatever you are roasting after 20 minutes, and if it isn't cooked to your liking, check it again at 10-minute intervals.

♦ Meat, when properly roasted, should have the same texture when you press on it as the muscle between thumb and forefinger when the hand is relaxed. This means the meat is rosy (its interior temperature will be about 130°F / 55°C); if you like it more done, that's too bad because it will be dry, but just roast it longer—it will feel harder and less springy. If you like it truly *bleu*, or almost raw, then it will feel soft (and it will turn many away, because they will think it's raw). The French like their meat between *bleu* and rosy.

♦ For chicken, make sure it is at room temperature before roasting.

- Spread some butter between the breast skin and meat (be careful not to tear the skin). Slide in some herbs, too, and stuff the bird with a lemon that is cut in half and the herbs of your choice (for added flavor and moisture).
- Truss the bird so it makes a nice packet that roasts evenly.
- When it's roasted, remove it from the oven and flip it onto its breast so the juices from the interior run into the breast meat, making it moist.
- Let all meat rest for at least 20 minutes before serving, so it can relax from the heat, and the juices can reabsorb.

TECHNIQUE #10:
PASTRY, WITH DANIE'S TIPS
FOR MAKING PÂTE BRISÉE

The French cook is an expert at certain types of pastry. Included in this category is pâte brisée, a buttery-crisp pastry that is used for tarts and *tourtes* (covered tarts), turnovers, and pockets. Danie Dubois deftly makes pâte brisée nearly every day of her life. Every time it is perfectly golden, and it shatters like puff pastry when baked.

Danie is speedy in the kitchen, her hands often a blur, particularly when she's making pastry. She doesn't use machines; it's all done by hand. She has two golden rules: Work fast, and use chilled butter. By working fast, she barely touches the flour so the gluten doesn't develop and her pastry is tender; by using chilled butter she mixes it thoroughly with the other ingredients, without melting it into them.

- Danie mixes 1½ cups (225g) flour with ½ teaspoon salt; then, with her favorite little paring knife that is worn to needle-thin, she shaves 12 to 18 tablespoons (180 to 270g) of chilled, unsalted butter over the mix, depending on the texture she's looking for. More butter means more flakiness.

♦ With her fingertips, she quickly rubs it all together until it looks like chunky cornmeal.

♦ She adds quite a bit of water—about ⅓ cup (85ml)—to the mix, incorporating it with a fork or her fingertips. This results in a very pliable pastry that she pats into a flat round then lets sit for an hour at room temperature, covered with an upturned bowl. The whole mixing process takes her 5 minutes.

♦ She never refrigerates the pastry at this point, because if she did, it would be impossible to roll out.

♦ Once the pastry is rolled out and fitted into a mold or tart pan, Danie either freezes it for 30 minutes or refrigerates it for 1 hour before baking. Her method results in pastry that is shattery crisp.

NOTE: Danie has been much of my inspiration for making pastry. I do what she does, only I do it in a food processor. Why? Because I have hot hands and when I try to mix pastry by hand the way she does, the butter melts. The food processor method works perfectly, has been blessed by Danie, and is on page 207.

TECHNIQUE #11:
PASTRY, WITH CHEF JORANT'S TIPS
FOR MAKING PÂTE SUCRÉE

Pâte sucrée, or sweet pie pastry, is another fundamental French pastry. It's the sweet, crisp, cookielike dough that when baked into a tart shell holds pastry cream and berries, creamy chocolate, and various combinations of these.

I doff my pâte sucrée hat to Albert Jorant, pastry instructor at Ecole de Cuisine la Varenne in Paris, where I was an apprentice for a year. I had the good fortune to work on a project one-on-one with Chef Jorant, and he taught me his secret tips for making perfect pâte sucrée (among other things).

- Make the pastry by hand, not in a food processor. It's more efficient, the result more tender. (Okay, you may use a food processor—see page 208.)
- Put the flour on the work surface and make a well.
- Put room-temperature butter, egg yolks, salt, and sugar in the well, and mix them all together with your fingertips (which are cool).
- Gradually mix the flour into the wet ingredients using your fingertips until you have a crumbly mess on your hands.
- Using the heel of your hand, press out the crumbly mess, as though you were smearing it on the surface. This mixes the wet into the dry ingredients and is a technique called *fraiser*, to knead with the palm of the hand.
- Gather back the dough and smear it against the surface again. Do this as many times as necessary (probably no more than three times), until the mixture is smooth and homogenous, working quickly and with a light hand. You do not want to grind the ingredients into the work surface, but use the work surface as support.
- You can roll or pat out the pastry into a tart shell. You'll probably have scraps. Roll these into a sausage shape, roll the sausage of dough in sugar, cover with plastic wrap, and refrigerate. When the pastry is hard, cut it into rounds and bake them, to serve as cookies.

♦ Prebake the tart shell and fill it with custard and fruit, chocolate cream, or anything else you can think of.

TECHNIQUE #12:
BAKING, WITH CHEF JORANT'S TIPS FOR
CAKES AND COOKIES

I learned to make more than pâte sucrée under the tutelage of Chef Jorant. He showed me how to make all sorts of desserts. He was professionally trained, but his favorite desserts were simple ones, as are mine. He had some golden rules, which I will share with you here.

♦ Always add salt to any batter. Salt lifts flavor.

♦ When a recipe calls for egg whites beaten into a stiff point, whisk instead into a soft point (unless making meringues, when you've added sugar). Egg whites beaten into stiff points are hard to incorporate into other ingredients, and they can make your pastry dry.

♦ Folding is the best way to combine ingredients. It is gentle, and makes for tender cakes and cookies.

♦ Bake things hotter than you think you should—375°F to 425°F (190°C to 220°C).

♦ Always heat the oven 25 degrees F hotter than the recipe calls for, as the temperature will fall that much when you open the door and put a cool pan into the oven.

♦ Bake cakes less than you think you should. Your finger, when you press it into the top of a cake, should leave a slight indentation.

♦ You can make puff pastry, but there is no real reason to do so. Store-bought puff pastry, if made with real butter, is excellent and easy.

These are my top twelve cooking techniques. Use them—they'll develop your inner French cook, making you even better than you already are!

——— COLD EMULSION ———

MAYONNAISE

All cooks I know in France make their own mayonnaise. For the French cook, making mayonnaise is a bit like getting out of bed in the morning— you just do it, without really thinking about it. It's easy, it tastes great, you can make it taste exactly the way you like it.

Lately I've heard cooks talk about making mayonnaise with a whole egg, rather than egg yolks. I tried it and loved it because it's slightly lighter in density than regular, egg yolk mayonnaise. So here is the recipe. It makes quite a bit, and it's tough to make a smaller amount because you can't really halve an egg. The mayonnaise will keep for at least a week in the refrigerator (the safe estimate), and actually longer (up to three weeks—the true estimate), so you can use it as you would regular mayonnaise.

Once you have your mayonnaise, you can add things to it like capers, lemon zest, diced dill pickles, onions . . . It goes everywhere any other mayonnaise will go!

NOTE: *There are many myths wrapped around mayonnaise. One of the most current is that all the ingredients need to be at the same temperature. This is not true. What is true is that you must add the oil very slowly to the rest of the ingredients. You may make mayonnaise in a blender or food processor, but it will not be as tender as mayonnaise made by hand.*

 1 teaspoon sea salt
 1 teaspoon Dijon-style mustard
 1 tablespoon white wine vinegar
 1 large egg

2¾ cups (690ml) untoasted peanut oil

¼ cup (60ml) fine quality extra-virgin olive oil

1. Place a wet towel under a medium-size, nonreactive bowl to keep it from sliding around. Then, place the salt, mustard, and vinegar in the bowl and whisk them together.
2. Whisk in the egg until it is thoroughly combined with the other ingredients, then *very slowly* and in a fine stream, whisk in the oils. The mixture will thicken as you whisk. You may stop adding oil when it gets to the thickness you desire.

MAKES ABOUT 3 CUPS (750ML)

——— HOT EMULSION ———

FISH FILLET IN PARCHMENT WITH BUTTER SAUCE

{ FILLET AU BEURRE BLANC EN PAPILLOTE, SAUCE BEURRE BLANC }

This is a simple, infallible way to cook fish so that it emerges tender and moist. I call for white fish fillets here—you can use any member of the cod family, red snapper, halibut, or petrale sole. Serve this with a white Sancerre.

6 (4-ounce; 120g) white fish fillets, such as lingcod, cod, grouper, or red snapper, bones removed

Fine sea salt and freshly ground white pepper

3 teaspoons fresh lemon thyme or English thyme leaves

2 tablespoons (30ml) white wine vinegar

2 tablespoons (30ml) dry white wine or lemon juice

1 large shallot, finely minced

12 tablespoons (6 ounces; 180g) unsalted butter, cut into 16 pieces and chilled

1. Rinse the fillets under cold running water, pat dry, and refrigerate until just before using.

2. Preheat the oven to 450°F (230°C). Place a rack in the center of the oven.

3. Cut parchment paper into six 12 by 8-inch (30 by 20 cm) pieces. Place a fillet on the upper half of one of the pieces of parchment paper, lightly season it with salt and white pepper, and sprinkle each fillet with an equal amount of thyme leaves. Fold the lower half of the paper over the fish so the edges meet at the top. Make a small fold all the way around the edges of the paper to form a pocket, pressing firmly on the folds so that they stay closed. Set the packets on a baking sheet and bake until the parchment packets are puffed and golden, 10 to 12 minutes.

4. While the fish is cooking, combine the vinegar, wine, and shallots in a small, heavy-bottomed saucepan and bring to a boil over medium heat. Boil until the liquid has reduced to about 1 tablespoon. Remove the saucepan from the heat and immediately whisk in two pieces of the chilled butter, pushing the butter around in the pan. As the butter softens and emulsifies into the liquid, whisk in another piece and set the saucepan back over low heat. Continue to whisk in pieces of butter, working on and off the heat, until all of the butter has emulsified into the liquid and the sauce is thick. Immediately remove from the heat and season to taste with salt and white pepper.

5. Remove the packets from the oven, slice through the top of the parchment, and let the fish sit just for a minute while it releases liquid. Then, transfer each fillet to a warmed dinner plate. Nap (this is a technique where you put the sauce in a spoon, then tip the spoon so the edge touches whatever you are napping, and the sauce pours out slowly and covers the food evenly) each fillet generously with butter sauce. Place any excess butter sauce in a pitcher, to serve alongside.

SERVES 6

——— MAKING CARAMEL ———

CRÈME CARAMEL

Old-fashioned and impressive, crème caramel is the dessert that makes everyone sigh just a little bit, because it reminds them of their childhood, their favorite aunt, their mamie, their mother. It's loaded with nostalgia and . . . it tastes so very, very good! You'll be surprised how easy it is to make and how happy it will make your guests. Be sure to make it the morning of the evening you plan to serve it, because it needs time to cool, then chill slightly.

¾ cup (150g) granulated sugar
1 vanilla bean, split lengthwise, seeds scraped out
1 quart (1L) whole milk
6 large eggs
1 cup (200g) vanilla sugar

1. Preheat the oven to 350°F (180°C).
2. Fill a large baking pan one-third with water and place it in the oven. Set a 6-cup (1.5L) soufflé dish near the burner where you'll make the caramel.
3. Place the granulated sugar and 3 tablespoons water in a heavy-bottomed saucepan over medium heat. Stir so the sugar is completely moistened. Cook, swirling the pan occasionally as the sugar bubbles, until the caramel is deep gold, about 10 minutes. Don't be tempted to stir the caramel—let it bubble along by itself, swirling the pan from time to time. When the caramel is at the desired color, pour it into the soufflé dish. Swirl the caramel around in the dish so it climbs up the sides by about 2 inches (10cm). Don't be concerned if the caramel hardens before you can swirl it. Set aside.
4. To make the custard, first slit the vanilla bean down its length, then scrape out the seeds. Place the milk, vanilla seeds, and vanilla bean in a medium saucepan over medium heat and heat until tiny bubbles form at the edges of the milk. Remove from the heat and let cool to lukewarm.
5. In a large bowl, whisk together the eggs and the vanilla sugar until they are thoroughly combined—they don't need to be pale yellow, just

thoroughly blended. Remove the vanilla bean from the warm milk, then whisk the milk into the egg mixture. Strain this mixture over the caramel in the soufflé dish.

6. When the oven is ready, carefully set the crème caramel in the baking pan of hot water. (The water should come up about one-third the height of the baking dish. If you need to add more water, boil and add it now.) Bake until the crème caramel is set, about 1 hour. Check the crème caramel after about 50 minutes—it may look as though it is boiling, but don't worry. To test for doneness, insert a sharp knife into the center of the crème caramel—if it comes out clean, the crème caramel is ready.

7. Remove the crème caramel from the oven, remove it from the pan holding the water, and let it cool to room temperature. (This will take at least 2 hours, possibly more. You can't really rush this step.) You can serve it at room temperature, or chill and serve it chilled. (If it is chilled, it is likely to remove from the mold in one fairly solid piece. If you remove it from the mold at room temperature, it may crack, though will still be lovely.) To remove it from the mold, run a knife around the edge of the crème caramel, set a large, shallow serving dish on top of the mold and flip it. Tap the mold to loosen the crème caramel, which will drop out of the mold. You can re-chill the crème caramel or serve it immediately.

SERVES 8

—— BRAISING ——

EDITH'S RABBIT WITH DRIED PLUMS
{ LAPIN AUX PRUNEAUX D'EDITH }

If you cannot find rabbit, use chicken in this succulent recipe!

Serve this along with the special potatoes that Edith makes (see page 283).

2 tablespoons extra-virgin olive oil

1 medium rabbit (about 3 pounds; 1.5kg), cut in serving pieces, or one 3½- to 4-pound (1.75 to 2kg) chicken, cut into serving pieces

Fine sea salt and freshly ground black pepper

2 fresh bay leaves (from the *Laurus nobilis*) or dried imported bay leaves

20 sprigs fresh thyme

4 medium onions (4 ounces; 120g each), halved and very thinly sliced

1 cup (250ml) dry white wine, such as Sauvignon Blanc

8 ounces (250g) pitted dried plums

¼ cup (60ml) water

Several sprigs fresh flat-leaf parsley, for garnish

1. Heat the oil in a large stockpot over medium-high heat. When the oil is hot, brown the rabbit on both sides, seasoning each side with salt and pepper. This should take about 8 minutes.

2. Tie the bay leaves and the thyme together with kitchen string.

3. Remove the rabbit from the pan and add the onions. Stir, season with salt and pepper, and cook, stirring and scraping the bottom of the pan to release the browned cooking juices, until the onions are translucent and tender, 10 to 12 minutes. Return the rabbit and any juices it has given up to the pan, stir, then pour in all the wine and ¼ cup (60ml) water. Scrape up any remaining juices from the bottom of the pan. Add the herbs and the plums, pushing them down into the liquid. Bring the liquid to boil, reduce the heat so the liquid is at a lively simmer, and cook, covered, until the rabbit is cooked through, about 35 minutes, turning the pieces at least twice during the cooking time.

4. Remove the rabbit from the pan. Raise the heat under the pan so the cooking juices are boiling, and cook until they are quite thick, 8 to 10 minutes. Return the rabbit to the sauce with any juices it has given up. Turn each piece of rabbit so it is coated with sauce and warmed through, which will just take a matter of minutes.

5. To serve, remove the herbs from the pan, adjust the seasoning, and transfer the rabbit to a shallow serving dish. Spoon the sauce over it all and garnish with the parsley. Serve immediately.

SERVES 4 TO 6

—— REDUCTION ——

DUCK BREAST WITH ORANGE SYRUP
{ MAGRET DE CANARD AU SIROP D'ORANGE }

I suggest a richly flavored red, such as Minervois from Domaine de Bar-roubio.

1 cup (250ml) freshly squeezed orange juice

2 (13-ounce; 390g) fattened duck breasts, skin scored almost to the meat with a sharp knife

1 tablespoon unsalted butter, cut into 4 pieces and chilled

Fleur de sel

Freshly ground black pepper (optional)

Fresh herbs, for garnish (optional)

1. Place the orange juice in a medium, heavy-bottomed pan over medium heat. Bring to a lively simmer and cook until the juice is thickened to a syrup and has reduced by about two-thirds, for about 10 minutes. Check the juice frequently to be sure it isn't reducing too much. When the juice has reduced, remove it from the heat and set aside.

2. Heat a heavy skillet over medium heat. When it is hot but not smoking, place the duck breasts in it, skin-side down. Cover and cook until the skin is deep golden, about 8 minutes. Flip the duck breasts onto the meat side, then flip them immediately back onto the skin side.

3. Remove the duck breasts from the pan and drain off all the fat. Return the duck breasts to the pan, skin-side down. Continue cooking over low heat, covered, just until the meat is done on the outside, but is still very rare inside, an additional 5 to 6 minutes. Remove the duck breasts from the pan, and place them on a cutting board that will catch any juices that run from them. Season the duck breasts with salt and pepper (if using) and let rest for about 5 minutes.

4. To make the sauce, reheat the reduced orange juice over low heat. Quickly whisk in the butter, working on and off the heat so that it

emulsifies into the orange juice without melting, and thickens it slightly. Keep the sauce warm.

5. To serve, slice the duck breasts crosswise on an angle and arrange them in a rosette pattern just off-center on six to eight warm dinner plates. Drizzle the duck with the orange syrup, and drizzle the syrup around the edge of the plates as well. Garnish with herbs (if using) and serve immediately.

SERVES 6 TO 8

——— SAUTÉ ———

MUSHROOM RAGOÛT WITH SAGE ON TOAST

{ RAGOÛT DE CHAMPIGNONS À LA SAUGE SUR TOASTS }

When wild mushrooms are in season, this is the perfect way to prepare them. If you can't find wild mushrooms, you can use cultivated mushrooms, what the French call champignons de Paris. Whatever mushroom you use, you'll find that this dish goes particularly well with red meat, with roasted poultry, or with the duck breast on page 198. This is good with red or white wine. I like, though, to serve a red Gaillac with this.

FOR THE TOASTS:

    3 tablespoons duck or goose fat or extra-virgin olive oil

    6 slices best-quality white bread, cut about ½ inch (1.25cm) thick, cut into 4- to 5-inch (10 to 12.5cm) rounds

    1 clove garlic

FOR THE MUSHROOMS:

    3 tablespoons duck or goose fat or extra-virgin olive oil

    2 pounds (1kg) wild and cultivated mushrooms, trimmed, brushed clean, and cut into large pieces

Sea salt and freshly ground black pepper

2 cloves garlic, green germ removed, minced

10 fresh sage leaves, minced, plus more for garnish

Cheveux d'Ange peppers (hair-thin dried peppers from China), for garnish (optional)

1. Line a wire cooling rack with paper towels.

2. To make the toasts, heat the fat in a large, heavy skillet over medium-high heat. When it is hot but not smoking, add the rounds of bread and the garlic and cook until they are golden on both sides, about 5 minutes total. Don't walk away—they'll turn from gold to black quickly!

3. Remove the toasts from the pan and set them on the prepared cooling rack.

4. To make the mushrooms, melt 2 tablespoons of the fat in a heavy-bottomed skillet over medium heat. When the fat is hot but not smoking, add the mushrooms and stir until they are coated with the fat. Sprinkle them with a generous pinch of salt and toss them in the pan. Cook until they give up their liquid, about 3 minutes.

5. While the mushrooms are cooking, combine minced garlic and sage with 1 tablespoon of the fat.

6. Add the garlic and sage mixture to the mushrooms, toss, and continue cooking until the mushrooms are tender throughout, an additional 5 minutes. Season to taste with salt and black pepper and remove from the heat.

7. To serve, place the toasts on a serving platter, or in the center of six individual plates. Top with the mushrooms (use a ring mold if you have one). Garnish each with a sage leaf and peppers (if using). Serve immediately.

SERVES 6

—— CONFIT VEGETABLES ——

STEAK WITH MELTED ONIONS
{ STEAK AUX OIGNONS CONFITS }

I love to quickly sear flank steak for this recipe, which is so simple you'll do it with your eyes closed. Use the steak of your choice, though, and adjust the cooking time accordingly. As for the onions, you'll fall quickly, deeply in love. Nothing but a Pinot Noir from Burgundy will do here!

2 tablespoons unsalted butter

1½ pounds (750g) yellow onions, peeled and very thinly sliced

Fine sea salt and freshly ground black pepper

4 (5- to 7-ounce / 150- to 210g) steaks, the cut of your choice, at room temperature

Coarse sea salt (optional)

Flat-leaf parsley or fresh sage leaves, for garnish

1. Melt the butter in a large, heavy skillet over medium heat. When the butter is foaming, add the onions, season with fine salt and pepper, and stir so they are coated with butter. When they begin to sizzle and cook, reduce the heat to low, stir, cover, and cook until they are golden, about 20 minutes, stirring often so they don't stick. Once they are golden, continue to cook, stirring often, until they are thick and quite a dark brown color, an additional 20 minutes. Remove from the heat and reserve.

2. Heat a heavy skillet over medium heat until it is hot enough that a drop of water dances on the surface. Place the steaks in the pan, season with coarse salt, and cook for 2 minutes. Flip the steaks, season with fine salt and pepper, and cook until the steak is done to your liking. For those who like it rare, another 2 minutes will suffice; for medium, about 4 minutes will do the trick.

3. To serve, transfer each of the steaks to a warmed dinner plate. Top each steak with a mound of onions. Alternatively, place the onions in

the center of four warmed dinner plates, patting them into a thick round, and set the steak atop them. Season with coarse salt (if desired) and garnish with the herbs. Serve immediately.

SERVES 4

—— CRÈME ANGLAISE ——

VANILLA ICE CREAM
{ GLACE À LA VANILLE }

You'll never taste a better vanilla ice cream!

NOTE: *Keep vanilla beans in an airtight container out of the light. If they develop any imperfections, simply scrape and rinse them off, wash the jar, and air-dry the vanilla beans before returning them to the jar. Note, too, that when making the custard for ice cream, you must bring it very close to the curdling point in order for it to cook properly. The purpose of the sieve over the bowl is to strain out any beginnings of curdled custard.*

> 4 cups (1L) half-and-half
> 1 vanilla bean, split lengthwise
> 10 large egg yolks
> 1¼ cups (250g) vanilla sugar
> Small pinch of fine sea salt

1. Place the half-and-half in a large, heavy-bottomed saucepan. Scrape in the seeds from the vanilla bean and add the pod as well. Stir and scald over medium heat. Remove from the heat, cover, and infuse for 20 minutes.
2. In a large bowl, whisk the egg yolks with the sugar and the salt until they are pale yellow and light. Slowly whisk in the warm infused half-and-half with the vanilla bean, then return the mixture to the pan.
3. Set a sieve over a bowl.

4. Cook the custard mixture over medium heat, stirring continuously in a figure-eight pattern, until it feels thick and coats the back of the spoon and a line run through the custard on the back of the spoon stays clear. Strain the custard mixture into the waiting bowl. Remove the vanilla bean from the strainer, rinse and pat it dry, then return it to the custard.

5. Let the custard cool to room temperature, then refrigerate until it is chilled through. Transfer to an ice-cream maker and process into an ice cream according to the manufacturer's instructions.

MAKES 1 QUART (1L) ICE CREAM

——— ROASTING ———

SWEET BEET AND GOAT CHEESE TOWERS

{ TOURS DE BETTERAVES DOUX ET FROMAGE DE CHÈVRE }

In France where beets are sold precooked, this recipe comes together in a minute. I cook my own beets for this, though, preferring to use Chioggia— those beautiful beets with the white and pink rings—or golden beets, neither of which "bleed" into the goat cheese. Once you've made this the first time, you'll find yourself making it often. It's quick, easy, and beautiful to serve.

I always have a few ends of beets that don't quite slice perfectly. These I dice very small and add to the vinaigrette at the last minute. To complement the sweetness of the beets, try a dry Muscat Sec from Domaine de Barroubio.

Special equipment: mousse or pastry rings, generally about 3 inches (7.5cm) in diameter by 2 inches (5cm) in height. If you don't have these, make this and just enjoy the free-form shape! A mandoline is very handy for this recipe, too.

FOR THE BEETS:

> 3 large golden or Chioggia beets (1¾ pounds; 875g total weight), washed, unpeeled
> Coarse sea salt and freshly ground black pepper

FOR THE GOAT CHEESE:

> 7 ounces (210g) moist fresh goat cheese
> 2 small shallots, minced
> 1 clove garlic, green germ removed, minced
> Fine sea salt and freshly ground black pepper

FOR THE VINAIGRETTE:

> 1 tablespoon freshly squeezed lemon juice
> Pinch of fine sea salt
> 1 teaspoon Dijon-style mustard
> 1 small shallot, sliced paper-thin
> 1 teaspoon mild honey, such as lavender
> 1 tablespoon fresh tarragon leaves, minced
> ¼ cup (60ml) extra-virgin olive oil
> Freshly ground black pepper

FOR THE SALAD:

> 3 cups small arugula, watercress, or fresh flat-leaf parsley leaves
> Fleur de sel, for garnish (optional)

1. To make the beets, preheat the oven to 400°F (200°C).
2. Place the beets in a large, heavy baking pan. Add ½ cup (125ml) water, season lightly with salt and pepper, cover, and bake until the beets are tender, about 1½ hours. Remove from the oven and let cool thoroughly.
3. To make the goat cheese, while the beets are cooking, in a small bowl, mix the goat cheese with the shallots and the garlic. Season generously with salt and pepper.
4. To make the vinaigrette, place the lemon juice and salt in a small bowl. Add the mustard and the shallot and whisk together until

combined. Whisk in the honey. Add the tarragon mixture, and finally whisk in the oil. Season generously with pepper.

5. When the beets are cool, peel and trim them, then slice them very thin—about ⅛ inch (3mm) thick, using a mandoline, if possible, so the slices are uniform. Evenly divide the goat cheese among 30 of the beet slices, spreading it as evenly as you can and as close to the edges as you can. Stack the slices, pressing on them gently as you stack so they stick together and making sure the final layer is beet-side up, until you have six stacks of equal height. Using a mousse ring that is about 23 inches (7.5cm) in diameter, cut out even rounds from the stacks. Save the trimmings to feed the staff (!).

6. To serve, using an offset or other spatula, transfer the beet towers to the center of six salad plates. Place the greens in a small bowl and dress with half the vinaigrette, tossing thoroughly. Divide the greens among the plates, carefully placing them around the towers. Drizzle each tower with the remaining vinaigrette, garnish with fleur de sel and serve.

SERVES 6 AS A FIRST COURSE

ROAST APPLE AND PEAR CHICKEN
{ POULET RÔTI AUX POMMES ET POIRES }

This is an easy supper that takes a simple roast chicken and turns it into a feast. You can use either apple cider or white wine instead of water, and if you don't have apples, use all pears, or vice versa.

I recommend turning the chicken several times as it roasts, which results in a perfectly roasted chicken. If you don't have time to turn it, don't worry—you'll still have a gorgeous bird at the end of the roasting. I usually serve either hard cider from Loic Métrot, a local foie gras producer, or a white Burgundy from Domaine St Pancrace.

2 onions, cut lengthwise into eighths

3 fresh bay leaves (from the *Laurus nobilis*) or dried imported bay leaves

¾ cup (185ml) water, apple cider, or dry white wine, such as
Sauvignon Blanc

1 (3½- to 4-pound; 1.75- to 2kg) roasting chicken, with giblets

2 tablespoons unsalted butter, at room temperature

Sea salt and freshly ground black pepper

½ lemon

2 large, firm, and slightly tart apples, such as Cox's Orange Pippin
or Honeycrisp, peeled, cored, and cut into sixths

2 medium pears, such as Comice or William, peeled, cored, and
quartered lengthwise

1. Preheat the oven to 425°F (220°C) and position a rack in the center.

2. Place the onions and 2 of the bay leaves on the bottom of a roasting
pan. Add the liquid.

3. Remove the giblets from the cavity of the chicken, rub 1 tablespoon of the
butter inside the cavity, and season it generously with salt and pepper. Rub
the remaining 1 tablespoon butter on the breast meat under the skin (the
skin can tear easily, so be very gentle as you detach it from the meat). Add
the lemon half, the giblets, and the remaining bay leaf to the cavity and
truss the chicken. Place it in the roasting pan atop the onions, or on a rack
sitting in the pan above the onions. Roast for 15 minutes. (At this point, if
you don't have time to turn the chicken, don't be concerned—leave it to
roast for the entire hour without turning.) Sprinkle it all over with salt,
then roast for 10 minutes more. Turn it on its side and roast for 15 minutes
more. Turn it on the other side and roast for an additional 15 minutes.

4. Add the apples and pears to the pan, shaking the pan so they settle into
the cooking juices. Add additional water, if necessary, to keep the fruit
and onions moist. Turn the chicken on its back so the breast is up, season
it and the fruit with salt, and continue roasting until the juices run clear
when you pierce the leg and thigh joint, about 15 minutes more.

5. Transfer the chicken to a cutting board, placing it breast side down so
the juices run into the breast meat, and let it rest, uncovered, for at
least 20 minutes before carving.

6. Return the pan to the oven to continue roasting the fruit until it is
tender and beginning to turn golden, an additional 20 to 25 minutes.

Check the fruit from time to time and shake the pan, and add additional water, if necessary, to keep the fruit from burning to the bottom of the pan.

7. Carve the chicken and arrange it on a warmed serving platter. Cut the giblets into thin slices and arrange them on the platter. Squeeze the lemon half that was in the cavity over the chicken, through your fingers so you catch the seeds. Place the fruit and the onions around the chicken, and pour any pan juices over all.

SERVES 4 TO 6

——— PASTRY ———

ON RUE TATIN'S TENDER TART PASTRY
{ LA PÂTE BRISÉE D'ON RUE TATIN }

This is a perfect flaky, buttery pastry to use for sweet and savory creations. It is simple, fast, and absolutely no-fail.

1½ cups (225g) unbleached all-purpose flour

¼ teaspoon sea salt

12 tablespoons (180g) unsalted butter, cut into 12 pieces and chilled

5 to 6 tablespoons (75 to 90 ml) ice water

1. Place the flour and the salt in a food processor and process once to mix. Add the butter and process until the mixture resembles coarse meal. Add 5 tablespoons (⅓ cup; 75ml) of the ice water and pulse just until the pastry begins to hold together. If the pastry seems dry and dusty, add the remaining 1 tablespoon ice water.

2. Transfer the pastry from the food processor to your work surface and form it into a flat round. Let it rest on a work surface, covered with a bowl, for at least 30 minutes. The pastry can sit several hours at room

temperature, as long as the room isn't warmer than 68°F (20°C). The pastry is ready to use as desired.

MAKES ENOUGH FOR ONE 10½- TO 12½-INCH (26.5- TO 31.5CM) TART

PASTRY

SWEET PIE PASTRY
{ PÂTE SUCRÉE }

This pastry is the basis of those gorgeous fresh fruit tarts that decorate patisserie shelves throughout France. It bakes up crisp and golden, and you can fill it with pastry cream, dot it with raspberries, or use it for a chocolate tart, among other things. With the scraps, you can make buttery cookies that are delicious with coffee!

I recommend making this pastry by hand, but you can use a food processor, mixing the yolks, sugar, and butter together, then adding the flour and salt and pulsing just until the mixture is homogenous.

Roll out this pastry as far as you can, then roll it around the rolling pin to transfer it to a pie tin. If it breaks, gently press it together. Alternatively, you can simply press it into a tart tin. You don't have to worry about it being smooth—imperfections either bake out or are covered by the filling.

1¾ cups (230g) all-purpose flour
½ teaspoon fine sea salt
½ cup (100g) vanilla sugar
4 large egg yolks
8 tablespoons (125g) unsalted butter, at room temperature

1. Sift the flour onto a work surface and make a large well in the center. Place the salt, sugar, egg yolks, and the butter in the well and mix them with your fingers until they are thoroughly combined.
2. Gradually work in the flour with the fingertips of your hands, pulling flour from the sides into the butter mixture until large crumbs form.

Continue blending the pastry by cutting it into pieces with a dough scraper. You will think you've got a mess on your hands, but don't worry! It will all work out.

3. Gather the crumbs into a ball then continue to work it by pushing it away from you and against the work surface with the heel of your hand, gathering it up and pushing it out again until it is thoroughly combined. There is no need to let this pastry sit before rolling it out.

MAKES ENOUGH PASTRY FOR ONE 10½-INCH (26.5CM) TART

——— BAKING ———

TURNIP AND CREAM TART
{ TARTE AUX NAVETS À LA CRÈME }

Whoever thought the humble turnip could become sinfully delicious? You may be tempted to dress up this tart with more spices or herbs but DON'T! Try it this way—it's luxuriously, deliciously simple. I like to serve this with a white from the Pays d'Oc, from Domaine La Madura.

2 pounds (1kg) turnips, peeled and thinly sliced
1 recipe On Rue Tatin's Tender Tart Pastry (page 207)
Sea salt and freshly ground black pepper
Generous ¼ teaspoon freshly grated nutmeg
1 cup (250ml) crème fraîche

1. Preheat the oven to 425°F (220°C) and position a rack in the center.
2. Bring 3 cups water to a boil in the bottom half of a steamer. When the water is boiling, place the turnips in the steamer basket and steam until they are tender, about 15 minutes. Transfer the turnips to a wire cooling rack lined with a cotton towel, and spread them out in an even layer in as much as you can, so they "dry." You don't want the turnips too wet or too hot before you put them in the pastry.

3. Roll out the pastry into a round until it is about ⅛ inch (3mm) thick. Line a 10½-inch (26.5cm) tart pan with a removable bottom, leaving the edges of the pastry hanging over.

4. Arrange half the turnips in the pastry. Season generously with salt, pepper, and nutmeg, and pour over half the crème fraîche over the turnips. Repeat with the remaining ingredients. Fold the pastry up and over the turnips. Set the tart tin on a rimmed baking sheet and bake until the pastry is golden and baked through, 35 to 40 minutes. Remove from the oven and transfer to a wire cooling rack. Let cool for 10 minutes, remove the outer ring of the tart tin, and serve.

SERVES 6

—— BAKING ——

RHUBARB AND GINGER TART

{ TARTE À LA RHUBARBE ET AU GINGEMBRE }

This combination will send you to heaven. The sweet-tart of the rhubarb and the slight heat of the ginger are magic. There is one caveat to this recipe: If your rhubarb is green, the color could use a little brightening, so I suggest adding some strawberries to the rhubarb. Not too many—you want the filling to stay sweet-tart, not just sweet. Otherwise, garnish it with flower petals; no one will notice!

A tart like this ends up being a quick dessert. You can make the pastry yourself as suggested below, or you can use high-quality store-bought pastry (roll it out slightly so it falls over the edge of the tart pan); then you just need the filling. Try this combination, please, then go on to use whatever seasonal fruit you have!

1 recipe On Rue Tatin's Tender Tart Pastry (page 207)
¾ cup (150g) vanilla sugar

3 tablespoons instant tapioca

1 pound 9 ounces (800g) fresh rhubarb, trimmed and thinly
sliced crosswise (about 7 cups)

1 generous ounce (30g) candied ginger (to give 3 tablespoons
diced)

1 large egg, whisked with 1 teaspoon water

1. Preheat the oven to 425°F (220°C).

2. Roll out the pastry to fit a 9½-inch (23.75cm) tart pan with a removable
bottom. Line the tart pan with the pastry, leaving the edges of the
pastry hanging over.

3. Pour half the sugar into the bottom of the tart pan. Sprinkle 2 tablespoons of the tapioca over the sugar. Pour two-thirds of the rhubarb into
the tart pan, and spread it evenly over the pastry. Sprinkle with the
candied ginger, half the remaining sugar, and the tapioca. Top with the
remaining rhubarb, and sprinkle the remaining sugar over the rhubarb.
Shake the tart pan a bit so all the fruit settles into it. Bring the edges of
the pastry lightly over the fruit and toward the center of the pan, so that
the pastry almost covers the fruit.

4. Place the tart on a baking sheet. Brush the top lightly with the egg
glaze, then bake in the center of the oven until the pastry is golden
and the fruit is cooked through, about 50 minutes. Check the tart and
if it is browning too much, lightly place a piece of aluminum foil over
it, to protect it. You do want it to be deep golden.

5. Remove from the oven and let the tart sit for 10 minutes. Remove the
ring from the tart pan by setting the tart pan on an upturned bowl and
letting the ring fall away from the pan. Transfer the tart to a serving
platter and serve.

SERVES 8 (WELL, ACTUALLY, 4 CAN EAT IT EASILY!)

CHAPTER 11

Les Restes— Leftovers

THE FRENCH BY NATURE ARE ECONOMICAL.

You see it in everyday life, as they are always on the lookout for ways to save a *centime*, which often involves bending or getting around the rules. The notion of economy pervades the French kitchen, too, and the French cook wastes nothing, absolutely nothing. Most French cooks don't have to be economical, they just are. Take Edith. I've watched her rip through a big batch of imperfect apples from her trees that I might have relegated to the compost heap in my pre–French cooking life. She, however, ends up with just enough perfect apple flesh to make a clafoutis, that golden, custardy dessert that can be made with any fruit, even raisins.

This economy is a source of pride for the French cook. The first step is being a smart shopper, and for many this means going to the farm or the farmers' market. Every French cook I know recognizes that the produce they buy there will taste so much better and yield so little waste that it is well worth any effort and extra expense involved. Once they've turned these ingredients into a dish and eaten it, they contend with leftovers, often creating a dish that is even more delicious than the original.

And when I say more delicious than the original, I truly mean this. In the French cook's repertoire, there are few mashed-together fillings for overcooked vegetables, like the stuffed green peppers I remember eating at school as a child, or the rice casseroles of the sixties and seventies that tasted exactly like what they were—food no one had wanted the night before. No, the leftover in a French cook's hands is a precious ingredient to be turned into something exquisitely delicious.

Sophie makes a favorite dish with leftover chicken, of which she has a lot. "I love to roast chicken," she said. "It's easy, everyone loves it, I don't have to think much about it. And there are always leftovers." Sophie's mother was born in Tunisia, so her food always has an exotic edge. She makes these delicious little pastries that she calls *pastillettes*, which are based on the wonderful Tunisian dish called *pastilla*. *Pastilla* is a delicate mélange of pigeon and spices, dried fruits and nuts, the whole of it wrapped in crisp pastry and dusted with cinnamon and sugar; Sophie's miniatures are filled with chicken.

She blends the meat with spices, raisins, and herbs, tosses it all in a pan with egg to make a loose version of scrambled eggs, and wraps it in sheets of pastry called *feuilles de brick*, which resembles phyllo dough. These she bakes until they're golden, then dusts them with that haunting mix of confectioners' sugar and cinnamon. "Everyone loves them," she says. "And to be honest, sometimes I roast chicken just so I can make them!"

No amount of chicken goes unnoticed by Sophie. "I might have half a cup," she says. "But do I throw it away? *Mais non!* I can build an entire meal around it." She makes a fabulous soufflé, for instance. Her system is simple. She makes a thick béchamel that she flavors with bay leaf, then folds the chicken into that, along with egg yolks, grated cheese, and, finally, egg whites that she whisks by hand so they're not too stiff, but just right. The whole process takes her fifteen minutes. "I know, no one makes soufflé anymore, but they're fools. Soufflé is inexpensive, fast, and everyone loves it."

Once all the meat is off the chicken carcass, Sophie puts the carcass in a pan with onions, bay leaf, and carrots to make a broth for cooking pasta, or uses it as a base for a potage, or vegetable soup.

Chicken isn't the only leftover that turns into something gorgeous in Sophie's hands. In every French home there is always leftover cheese. It might be viewed as a problem, but not to a cook like Sophie. "Easy," Sophie said the other day as she and I sat down to eat one of her renowned quiches. "I had three different kinds of blue and I put them all in this quiche." It was scrumptious.

Virginie Lang works at home, managing her husband's construction business. She's one of those moms who can't imagine allowing her children to eat lunch at school, so when she's not working, she's cooking. She has it down to an art, never wasting a drop or a crumb. "I make tartines," she says. "They're my secret."

An open-faced sandwich, the tartine is a modern invention, which, in Virginie's hands, makes a filling, delicious dinner. She buys a big, round loaf of crusty bread that she has sliced at the bakery on a rattling machine that looks like it was invented by Rube Goldberg. She has on hand canned tomato sauce and never lacks for leftover cheeses. She'll have roasted bell peppers, which she makes or buys, smoked salmon, fresh goat cheese, a variety of vegetables great for slicing like cucumber, onion, carrots. She may have leftover mushrooms in cream, and she always has thin-sliced ham both boiled and air-cured, and salami-style sausages.

Then she layers whatever ingredients suit her fancy, using up cheeses as one of the layers and also to top them off. She puts the tartines in the oven and they emerge toasty, melty, and delicious. Virginie makes a green salad and calls it a meal. "The kids would eat these for every meal if I'd make them," she says.

Some cooks I know get prickly about the subject of food waste. Emmanuel Perret is a neighbor whose daughter, Elisa, is my daughter's classmate. When she's picking up or dropping off Elisa, she often prolongs her visit so we can talk about food. When the subject of leftovers comes up, it throws this fortyish woman with piercing eyes and curly black hair into a fit of pique. "I wouldn't dream of throwing away a leftover," she said. "It shouldn't be permitted." Happily, she admits to a knack with leftovers. "If I have some vegetables—let's say green beans and onions—I put them in a pastry shell, add some tomatoes and some more onions, a bit of crème fraîche and and we've got *tarte* for supper." She always has tuna on hand, and uses her leftover cheese with it to make a quick tuna *cake*, a savory bread, along with salad to feed her family for supper.

Then there are those who like the idea of leftovers so much that they create them. Emily Bertin is one. Instead of waiting to have leftovers, Emily "makes" leftovers by cooking a double batch of the same dish. She wants her family to eat home-cooked food, but she doesn't always have time during the week to prepare a meal. "I put half of whatever I've cooked in the freezer and that way we've always got a home-cooked meal," she said. "The dish isn't technically leftovers, but it's my leftovers."

Emily's signature dish is Moroccan tagine, a classic dish of the Maghreb that is rife with spices and floral perfumes. She makes

two types—chicken that she cooks with preserved lemons and olives, or lamb that she prepares with dried fruits and nuts. "My parents were raised in Morocco, so I ate lots of tagines when I was
growing up," she said. "My family loves it, too." Emilie gave me the
recipe for her tagines (see page 222), with the caveat: "If you're
going to do a tagine with preserved lemons and olives, do *not* add
dried fruit and nuts. It's either/or."

Leftovers save the lives of busy moms like Nathalie, whose med-
ical practice is growing at about the same speed as her three boys.
What saves her is Wednesday. "The boys are home from school, so I
run them around to their activities," she said, her frizzy hair flying
about as she nods and balances the big basket filled with vegetables
on the front of her bicycle. "But I also have time to cook." Her favorite dish is *hachis Parmentier,* which really should be the poster child
for French cuisine and its UNESCO cultural heritage status.

This dish that was born of leftover meat and mashed potatoes
is discussed, dissected, and improvised upon by everyone from
Marie, who teaches sixth-grade math, to a local chef who was just
awarded a Michelin star (his *hachis* is one-third butter, one-third
foie gras, and one-third duck, and not really made with leftovers!).
Nathalie's is one of the best, because she makes it with her cousin's
beef, which has first been simmered into a pot-au-feu. "Just in case
I don't have enough pot-au-feu, I add chicken or pork," she says. My
friend Danie Dubois, who raises geese and ducks, sometimes adds
leftover foie gras. Sophie's always includes duck, because Sophie
and her husband love duck, and a roast duck leaves ample leftovers.

Nathalie's other favorite haven for leftovers, which she shares
with Danie, is spaghetti Bolognaise (the French spelling of the Italian Bolognese). "I make it for the kids," says Nathalie. "At least
that's what I say. But I love it as much as they do!" "Bolognaise," as

it's referred to colloquially, is a basic tomato-based pasta sauce, which absorbs leftover pot-au-feu if *hachis Parmentier* isn't on the menu. She sautés onions and garlic, adds lots of parsley and tomatoes to make a sauce, then finally adds meat, cut or shredded into bite-size pieces. Danie makes her Bolognaise only with leftover lamb. "Susan, roast a leg of lamb so you can make my Bolognaise," Danie said. "You'll see that it's exquisite."

André-Louis Peissel is the father of my friend Eloise and is often her culinary inspiration, too. He loves to cook, in a rather old-fashioned way. Like Betty, he is not devoted to leftovers the way some French cooks are, because he feels that one should make the right amount the first time around. Yet he has one gold-standard leftover recipe. "Papa always makes rémoulade for leftover *gigot*, leg of lamb," Eloise said. "It's about the only leftover he serves." His sauce is very simple. He puts mustard in a bowl with an egg yolk and slowly whisks peanut oil into it until it is very thick. Then, he minces many shallots and folds them in. "My rémoulade is really just a vehicle for shallots," he says. "Cold *gigot* with rémoulade is one of the best dishes on earth." With that, he serves a salad.

Of all my friends, Danie, who lives in the dot-size Dordogne village of Peyrenègre, is the real queen of leftovers. She positively thrives on them. "And believe me," she says, "I don't waste a crumb, not a crumb. And I know how to make them delicious!"

Raised in one farm family and married into another, Danie is my true north when it comes to real French cooking. She loves being in the kitchen, she loves being at the table, she has a perfectly pitched palate so that her simple food has the most pure taste. Part of her passion for using leftovers creatively and deliciously has to do with her background. When Danie was first married she almost died of overwork. She was expected not just to mother her own children, but, because she lived with her in-laws, also to be their maid, chief cook, and housekeeper. Danie rejected this local tradition, because it left her dependent on her husband and his family, with no money or power of her own. So, she got herself two geese, raised and sold them, bought more, and little by little used the money she earned to build a small foie gras industry. Her skill was such that she made herself a name, and though she's kept her industry small and in the family—her son now runs it with her— she's one of the best-known producers of foie gras in her region.

Part of her economic strategy was using up leftovers. "I did it, and I still do it, naturally," she said. "My mother was economical and she taught me not to waste a scrap. I just do what she did."

Danie cooks for her large family, for guests at her bed-and-breakfast, for Hubert the postman, who stops by regularly for lunch, and for friends. She always has leftovers, and when it comes to using them, "Add potatoes" is her mantra. "It almost doesn't matter what the leftovers are. If you have potatoes, you can turn them into something wonderful." She adds potatoes and onions to leftover vegetables like zucchini, moistens them with some white wine, adds a bit of meat, then at the last, adds her secret weapon: a rich blend of goose fat, garlic, and parsley, or *hachis*, as the mixture is sometimes known. "*Hachis* makes the world go round," she says. "I've always got it in the refrigerator."

Danie keeps chickens, so she always has eggs on hand, too. "If I have leftover ratatouille, or Swiss chard, or even squash soup, I heat it up, crack eggs into it so they can poach, and voilà! A wonderful meal is born," she said.

The French are big pasta eaters, no doubt inspired by their Italian neighbors. That being said, the French cook's solution to leftover pasta is to turn it into a gratin—which involves adding quite a bit of butter and topping it off with cheese. The gratin, by its very buttery, cheesy nature, is a perfect way to use leftovers. Pasta also gets the sauce Bolognaise, sautéed vegetables, thick squash soup, and always, always, always lots of grated cheese.

We all know the importance of bread to the French, and it, too, fits into the French cook's repertoire for leftovers. Danie buys big, round loaves of sourdough country bread once a week and stores them, stacked on their sides, in a deep drawer built for the purpose. As the week wears on, the bread gets harder. She takes the hardest ends and cuts them into big cubes, which she rubs with garlic and uses to stuff a chicken. Or she'll slice a drying loaf, rub the slices with garlic, scrape fat from her home-cured ham onto them, and grill them under the broiler. "When I was growing up, this was our after-school feast," she said. "I still make it for my grandkids."

Marie Boivin, my sixth-grade math teacher friend, breaks up her leftover bread into small pieces that she soaks in milk. She adds sugar and vanilla, some raisins that she's soaked in rum, a few eggs, and some apples, mixes it all together, and bakes it, then serves it warm and sprinkled with sugar. "I can't give you quantities because I make it *au pif*, without thinking," she said. "It's one of our favorite winter *goûters*, snacks."

Fruit past its season ranks as a leftover in France. While one might be tempted to toss out autumn apples in March, when their skin is a bit wrinkled, their flesh a bit soft, the French cook figures out dozens of clever ways to use them. I've lived and cooked in France long enough that I'm now a French cook (not that I have *anything* against eating a simple, quick sandwich for Sunday lunch instead of sitting down for hours over a multicourse lunch!) and creatively using up excess fruit has become second nature to me. When my friends François and Marie-Hélène, Baptiste's parents, arrive every year with two huge crates of the most disgruntled- and delicious-looking apples I've ever seen, right at the height of apple season, I welcome them with joy (and just the slightest bit of panic because there are so many).

There must be six varieties in the crates, and neither François nor Marie-Hélène nor Baptiste can tell me their names, because the trees have been there for generations and the person who planted them is long gone. Some are the size of small pumpkins, with ruddy red skin. Others are raspberry red and butter yellow with soft flesh, and they look like they want to jump out of the crate and into your hand. Still others have a rough gold skin and bulges at the stem end. There is one tiny, tortured variety with deep folds in it, which tells me there were so many on the tree they were crowded for space. I can't wait to cook with them.

I store them outside under the eaves to stay cold. I always give some to Edith, who, though she has her own trees, never has enough apples, and to my friend Lena, who eats at least one apple a day and will do the same with these. Even after that I still have kilos left. Because I'm a French cook, I peel my apples because the peel is so tough it never breaks down. Then, I fold chunks into cakes, layer them in tarts, or toss them with sugar, spread them on rolled-out bread dough, and drizzle them with cream before baking. I make compote and juice, sauté them like a vegetable, poach them like pears, and candy them like plums.

As for leftovers in general, I love to turn them into a salad. It's simple. I take whatever meat or fish I have on hand, and occasionally potatoes or other vegetables—and sauté them in olive oil until they're golden and crisp—this takes a minute or two. Then, I add diced garlic, give the pan a shake or two, add some vinegar, and tip the ingredients atop a pre-dressed salad that I've peppered with avocado cubes, cherry tomato halves, and radish rounds. The combination of hot and crisp, cold and tangy is divine.

The economical nature of the French cook has given birth to a parallel cuisine in this marvelous country. Cooks throughout the hexagon are turning pot-au-feu into *hachis Parmentier*; sautéing leftover potatoes with bacon and tipping it into an omelet; soaking their bread in milk and either baking or frying it; spreading slices of bread with cheese and layering that with onions and tomatoes to create a sort of Frenchified pizza; blending all the forbidden foods like butter, cheese, and crème fraîche with pasta and turning it into something so good you cannot believe it exists. And all of these things are made with leftovers, from meals that were already created with thought and care. What a place, what a culture!

EMILIE'S SIMPLE TAGINE
{ TAGINE SIMPLE D'EMILIE }

Emilie Bertin makes this flavorful dish for her family often. It's a recipe from her mother, who was raised in Morocco, where tagine is part of the culinary landscape. It's something a bit different and appeals to palates of all ages. You may substitute lamb shoulder for the chicken and dried fruit for the olives and lemons. If using dried fruit, you can also include spices like cumin, cinnamon, and ginger. The method remains the same. A simple red is delicious here, such as a red from the Costières de Nîmes.

½ teaspoon lightly packed saffron threads

1 tablespoon freshly squeezed lemon juice

2 salted lemons (see Quick Salted Lemons on page 224)

2 tablespoons extra-virgin olive oil

4 chicken legs

4 chicken thighs

Sea salt and freshly ground black pepper

2 large onions (5 ounces; 150g each), thinly sliced

1 small bunch fresh cilantro

1 fresh bay leaf (from the *Laurus nobilis*) or dried imported bay leaf

10 sprigs fresh thyme

1 teaspoon piment d'Espelette or hot paprika, or as desired

¾ cup (3½ ounces; 105g) green olives, with pits

1. Preheat the oven to 350°F (180°C).

2. Crush the saffron in a mortar and pestle and place it in a small bowl. Cover it with the lemon juice and reserve. Drain the salted lemons and cut each quarter in half.

3. Heat the oil in a large, heavy Dutch oven over medium-high heat. Add as many pieces of the chicken as will fit in the pan without crowding, season lightly with salt and generously with pepper, and cook until the thighs are golden on the skin side, 4 to 5 minutes. Remove the thighs from the pan, turn the legs, season with salt and pepper, and continue to cook until they are browned on all sides, an additional 3 to 4 minutes.

4. Remove the chicken legs from the pan and add the onions. Reduce the heat to medium and cook, stirring them and scraping any caramelized juices off the bottom of the pan, until they are just softened, about 5 minutes. Season them lightly with salt and pepper, stir, return the chicken to the pan, then add 2 cups (500ml) water and finish scraping up any caramelized juices from the bottom of the pan. Add the saffron and lemon, the salted lemons, herbs, paprika (if using), and olives, and stir. Bring the liquid to a boil, increasing the heat under the pan if necessary, cover, and place the pot in the oven to cook for 1½ hours. Check the tagine once during cooking to turn the chicken, and shake the pot to make sure the chicken isn't sticking.

5. Remove the dish from the oven. Remove and discard the spices and herbs. Adjust the seasoning, and serve. Note: If you'd like the juices to be thicker, remove the chicken and keep it warm. Place the pot over medium-high heat and boil until it has reduced to your liking. Normally, the sauce in a tagine is quite thin.

SERVES 4 TO 8 (DEPENDING ON THE APPETITES)

QUICK SALTED LEMONS
{ CITRONS SALÉ FAÇON RAPIDE }

These are specifically for Emilie's Simple Tagine (page 222). Once you've used them in that recipe, though, and you discover how good they are, you're likely to find yourself using them in all sorts of recipes—a fish stew, a lamb ragoût. They're nice to have on hand, and will keep in the refrigerator for one month.

> ¼ cup (60g) coarse sea salt or kosher salt
> 4 medium lemons, preferably organic, washed and quartered, seeds removed

1. Combine 2 cups (500 ml) water and the salt in a medium saucepan and bring to a boil over medium-high heat, stirring occasionally. When the salt has dissolved, add the lemons and return to a boil, then reduce the heat so the liquid is simmering. Cook until the lemons are tender and the liquid has reduced to about ½ cup (125ml), about 20 minutes.

2. Remove from the heat and let cool. The lemons will keep in an airtight container in their liquid, refrigerated, for about 1 month.

MAKES 4 SALTED LEMONS

DEVILED EGGS À LA FRANÇAISE
{ OEUFS MIMOSA }

We might call these deviled eggs dressed up for a dance! They're a true blast from the French past, a recipe that was popular in the sixties and seventies but is back, in force! I got the idea from Dominique Léost, a history teacher in nearby Le Neubourg, who got the recipe from his mother. "It's a great and quick dish to make for the family, and guests love it, too!" he says.

These eggs, which are filled with a chicken mixture, are an original and refreshing way to use that little touch of luscious, leftover roast chicken. You might use any leftover meat or fish for this; let your imagination be your guide! Try a white Sancerre here.

NOTE: *Use eggs that are a few days old, as very fresh eggs are hard to peel. When pushing the egg yolks through the sieve you might think there are too many but don't stop! The idea is to present a sunny yellow plate with the eggs almost hiding underneath the egg yolk. Also, while recipes for homemade tapenade and mayonnaise are supplied, you may use store-bought versions.*

4 large eggs

1 tablespoon tapenade (see page 251)

2 tablespoons mayonnaise (see page 192)

1 small shallot, minced (to give 1 tablespoon)

1 scallion, white part only, minced (to give 1 tablespoon)

1 teaspoon freshly squeezed lemon juice

2 ounces (60g) cooked chicken breast, cut into ¼-inch (6mm) pieces

Fine sea salt and freshly ground black pepper

1 small bunch fresh chives

1. Place the eggs in cold water and bring to a boil. Boil for 10 minutes, then transfer them to a bowl of ice water. When the eggs are chilled, peel them.

2. While the eggs are cooking, place the tapenade, mayonnaise, shallot, scallion, and lemon juice in a small bowl and mix well. Add the chicken and mix, then season generously with salt and pepper.

3. Mince all but about 10 of the chives, and add them to the mixture. Taste and adjust the seasoning.

4. Slice the eggs in half, and gently remove and reserve the yolks. Fill the holes in the egg white halves with the chicken mixture, mounding it up so that you use it all. Place the eggs on a serving plate. Place the egg yolks in a fine-mesh sieve. Hold the sieve over the filled egg whites and push

the egg yolks with your fingers through the sieve so they rain atop the filled egg whites. Pretty soon, you'll see the mimosa part of this recipe!

5. Mince the reserved chives, and sprinkle them over the eggs. You may prepare these up to 2 hours in advance, or serve them immediately.

MAKES 8 EGGS

THE BEST-EVER DISH FOR WEDNESDAY NIGHT
{ HACHIS PARMENTIER }

Hachis Parmentier *is the French version of shepherd's pie, served in homes, in humble restaurants, in schools, and in starred establishments. It is, basically, leftovers from pot-au-feu or ragoût, sandwiched between layers of gorgeous mashed potatoes. A standing trend in French restaurants is to make it with freshly roasted duck, venison, or wild boar, which can make it even more delicious and delicate than it already is.*

If you don't have leftover meat, start with freshly ground beef and pork, making sure they aren't too lean. Note these mashed potatoes—they'll become your favorite!

I like a red from the Languedoc with this dish.

20 sprigs fresh thyme

3 fresh bay leaves (from the *Laurus nobilis*) or dried imported bay leaves

2 pounds (1kg) starchy potatoes, such as russets, peeled and cut into large chunks

Coarse sea salt

2 tablespoons extra-virgin olive oil or goose or duck fat

1 large (5-ounce / 150g) carrot, trimmed, peeled, and diced

1 large (5½-ounce / 165g) onion, diced

2 leeks, white parts only, rinsed well, trimmed, and diced

2 shallots, diced

Fine sea salt and freshly ground black pepper

5 cups cooked meat (from pot-au-feu, roast chicken, or beef),
shredded then coarsely chopped, or 1 pound (454g) medium-lean
ground beef and 4 ounces (125g) medium-lean ground pork

Scant ½ teaspoon ground allspice

½ cup (125ml) broth from pot-au-feu or beef stock

5 tablespoons (74g) unsalted butter

½ cup (125ml) heavy cream

2 large eggs

1. Preheat the oven to 425°F (225°C). Tie the thyme and two of the bay leaves together with kitchen string.
2. Place the potatoes in a large saucepan and add water to cover by 1 inch (2.5cm). Add 2 teaspoons salt and one of the bay leaves, bring to a boil, reduce the heat so the water is simmering merrily, and cook until the potatoes are tender throughout, about 20 minutes.
3. While the potatoes are cooking, heat the oil or fat in a large, heavy-bottomed skillet over medium heat. When the oil or fat is hot but not smoking, add the carrot, onions, leeks, and shallots, season with salt and pepper, and cook, stirring often, until the vegetables are nearly tender throughout, 10 to 15 minutes. Add the meat, breaking it up as you do, the tied bay leaves and thyme, and allspice. Stir, season with salt and pepper, and cook, stirring often, until the meat is nearly cooked through, about 15 minutes. Remove from the heat and stir in the broth. Stir well, scraping up any caramelized juices from the bottom of the pan. Taste and adjust the seasoning.
4. When the potatoes are cooked and while the meat is cooking, drain them, saving about ¼ cup (60ml) of the cooking liquid. Mash the potatoes until they are nearly smooth, then mash in half the butter until it is thoroughly mixed. Add the cream and the reserved cooking liquid, mix well, then add the eggs individually, mixing well after each addition. Generously season the potatoes with salt and pepper.
5. Place half the potatoes in a 8½ by 12-inch (21.25 by 30cm) baking dish and smooth them without packing them down. Remove the thyme and bay leaves. Add the meat and its cooking liquid, spreading it in an even

layer, then top with the remaining potatoes. Cut the remaining butter into small pieces and dot them around atop the potatoes. Bake in the center of the oven until the potatoes are slightly golden on top and the dish is thoroughly hot, about 20 minutes. Remove from the oven, let cool for about 10 minutes, and serve.

SERVES 4 TO 6

HOT TARTINES

OPEN SANDWICHES

{ TARTINES CHAUDES }

This is an easy recipe that makes use of leftovers, staples, any delicious things that you might think of to set on a thick slice of bread and bake in a hot oven! Try a red Anjou from Domaine de Montgilet.

3 large cloves garlic

Four ½-inch (1.25cm) thick slices bread, cut to about 6½ by 4 inches (16.25 by 10cm), toasted

Generous 1 tablespoon extra-virgin olive oil

4 ounces (120g) button or shiitake mushrooms, trimmed, brushed clean, and thinly sliced

Fine sea salt and freshly ground black pepper

6 ounces (180g) firm goat cheese, cut into very thin slices

About 6 tablespoons (89g) red bell peppers packed in oil (see page 249)

4 ounces (120g) Gruyère cheese, grated

Fresh flat-leaf parsley or basil, for garnish

1. Preheat the oven to 425°F (220°C). Line a baking sheet with aluminum foil.
2. Remove the green germ from 2 of the cloves of garlic, and mince these. Rub each slice of toast with the remaining clove of garlic.
3. Heat the oil in a medium skillet over medium heat. When it is hot, add the mushrooms and the minced garlic, season with salt, and sauté

until the mushrooms are tender, about 5 minutes. Remove from the heat, season with pepper, stir, and reserve.

4. Arrange the slices of toast on the baking sheet. Divide the goat cheese among the slices of toast, making sure it completely covers each one. Top with the mushrooms, and 1 generous tablespoon of the red peppers and garlic in oil mixture, then sprinkle with the grated cheese. Bake until the cheese has melted, about 10 minutes. Remove from the oven and garnish with the remaining bell peppers among the tartines, arranging them on top. Garnish each with an herb sprig and serve.

SERVES 4

MARIE'S BREAD AND APPLE CAKE
{ GÂTEAU AU PAIN ET AUX POMMES }

Marie Boivin makes this luscious dish with her leftover bread. It resembles bread pudding, except that it is almost more apple than bread. She likes to serve it warm from the oven for goûter, or snack time. "It's perfect then," she said the other day. "It's hearty and warming, like a fire in the fireplace on a freezing day." Marie might include a cup of raisins and some rum here. I like to add cinnamon to this (but then, I'm American!).

2 large eggs

3 cups (750ml) whole milk

Generous pinch of fine sea salt

½ cup (100g) vanilla sugar, plus 1 tablespoon

1 teaspoon pure vanilla extract

Zest from ½ lemon, minced (optional, but delicious)

8 ounces (250g) day-old bread, cut into 2-inch (5cm) pieces

3 medium (5-ounce; 150g each) apples

2 tablespoons unsalted butter

¼ teaspoon ground cinnamon (optional)

1. Preheat the oven to 375°F (190°C).

2. In a large bowl, whisk the eggs just until they are combined. Whisk in the milk until it is combined with the eggs, then whisk in the salt, ½ cup of the vanilla sugar, the vanilla extract, and the lemon zest (if using). Fold the bread into the custard mixture and let it soak for 20 to 25 minutes, folding it gently once or twice to ensure that all the bread cubes are evenly soaked in the custard mixture.

3. While the bread is soaking, peel, core, and dice the apples into 1-inch (2.5cm) cubes. During the last 5 minutes of the soaking time, place the butter into a 9 by 13-inch (23 by 33cm) baking dish, and place it in the oven to melt the butter.

4. Remove the baking dish from the oven and swirl the butter around so the bottom is covered. Fold the apples into the bread mixture, then pour the mixture into the baking pan. Mix the cinnamon (if using) and the reserved tablespoon of sugar in a small bowl, then sprinkle over the top of the bread and apple mixture.

5. Bake in the center of the oven until the mixture is golden on top and the custard is cooked, about 40 minutes. Remove from the oven and let cool for 10 minutes before serving.

SERVES 6 TO 8

FRENCH TOAST
{ PAIN PERDU }

A French cook will never *throw away a piece of bread. This means that every French cook has a repertoire of tasty recipes to use up day-old bread.* Pain perdu, *which translates as "lost bread" and which we call French toast, was born of this economy. Here, I gussy it up with brioche, but this recipes works perfectly with any bread. Make a double or triple batch, depending on how many guests you have.*

This makes a very quick breakfast or brunch dish. Serve it sprinkled with confectioners' sugar, and with Apple and Pear Compote (page 288) on the side.

1 large egg
1¼ cups (310ml) milk
1 teaspoon vanilla sugar
½ teaspoon pure vanilla extract
Pinch of fine sea salt
Ten ½-inch (1.25cm) slices day-old brioche or other bread
2 tablespoons unsalted butter
Confectioners' sugar, for dusting

1. Whisk together the egg, milk, vanilla sugar, vanilla extract, and salt in a large bowl.
2. Place as many slices of bread in the bowl as will fit, and let them soak until they are saturated but not falling apart, 3 to 4 minutes.
3. Melt the butter in a large skillet over medium heat. Transfer the soaked bread to the pan and cook until it is golden on one side, about 3 minutes. Turn, and cook until it is golden on the other side, 2 to 3 minutes. Transfer to a warmed serving platter. Continue soaking and sautéing the remaining brioche. When it is all cooked, sprinkle it with confectioners' sugar and serve.

SERVES 3 TO 4

CRISP CHICKEN AND SPICE POCKETS
{ PASTILLETTES AU POULET }

I'm always impressed by what my French friends make with leftovers. These crisp and tasty little pastillettes *are a perfect example. Sophie makes them, and they're based on the Tunisian* pastilla. *She loves this dish and invented this small version, which everyone loves and begs for when they go to her house for dinner. This reflects the way that cuisine from northern Africa has become mainstream in France.*

These are easy to put together, I promise. There are steps that make the recipe look long and complicated, but it is not! Try—you'll enjoy these hauntingly flavored, slightly exotic little packets and may want to serve them as a first course, or as a main course with steamed asparagus, or green beans, or even a tomato salad alongside.

In fact, they are so tasty you'll probably find yourself cooking chicken just so you can make them! I like to serve them with a spicy little wine from the Côtes du Rhône.

¼ cup (60ml) extra-virgin olive oil

1 large onion, diced

Fine sea salt and freshly ground black pepper

½ teaspoon ground cinnamon

Zest of ½ lemon, minced

2 teaspoons freshly squeezed lemon juice

¼ teaspoon saffron threads

3 cups cubed cooked chicken (from 2 leg/thigh pieces and 1 chicken breast)

1 cup (10g) gently packed fresh cilantro leaves, minced

3 large eggs

10 *feuilles de bricks* or leaves of phyllo dough, cut in half and kept covered so they stay pliable

3 to 5 tablespoons (45 to 75g) unsalted butter, melted

2 tablespoons almonds, lightly toasted and chopped

1 to 2 teaspoons orange flower water

1 tablespoon confectioners' sugar, for garnish

Generous ¼ teaspoon ground cinnamon, for garnish

1. Preheat the oven to 400°F (200°C).

2. Heat 3 tablespoons of the oil in a large, heavy-bottomed skillet over medium-high heat. Add the onions and mix so they are coated with the oil. Season with salt and pepper and cook until the onions are turning golden and are tender throughout, about 6 minutes. Remove half the onions from the pan and transfer to another skillet.

3. Add the cinnamon, lemon zest, lemon juice, and the saffron to the onions that have remained in the large skillet, stir, and add the chicken, cilantro, and ⅔ cup (85ml) water, and stir. When the water is

simmering, reduce the heat to low, cover the pan, and cook until the chicken has absorbed about half the water, stirring once just to make sure all is cooking evenly. This will take about 10 minutes.

4. While the chicken mixture is cooking, add the remaining 1 tablespoon oil to the skillet with the onions and place it over medium heat. Cook the onions, stirring occasionally, until they turn golden and crisp at the edges, about 10 minutes. Remove from the heat.

5. Whisk the eggs together in a small bowl. Season them lightly with salt and pepper.

6. When the chicken has absorbed most of the water, add the eggs and cook, stirring slowly but continuously, until they are scrambled but still very soft, just a minute or two. Remove from the heat and stir in the caramelized onions. Taste and adjust the seasoning.

7. To assemble the pastillas, brush a *feuille de brick* or two half-sheets of phyllo dough generously with butter. Place 3 generous tablespoons of the filling in the center of the pastry. Top with almonds and a generous drizzle of orange flower water. Bring the edge of the pastry over the filling from one side, then from the other, making a narrow packet. Brush the top with butter, then bring the ends toward the center, making a square and neatly enclosing the filling. Transfer the packet to a baking sheet, setting it folded side down. Brush lightly with butter. Repeat using all the filling and the pastry. You should have 10 packets.

8. Place the packets in the center of the oven, and bake until they are golden and crisp, which should take 25 to 30 minutes. While they are baking, sift together the confectioners' sugar and the cinnamon.

9. Remove the *pastillas* from the oven and sift the sugar and cinnamon mixture over them. Transfer them to a serving platter and serve immediately. (If you'd like to get fancy, place a star anise on the *pastillettes* before dusting with sugar, then remove it so you have a star design on top.)

MAKES 10 *PASTILLETTES*

ANDRÉ-LOUIS'S RÉMOULADE
{ LA REMOULADE D'ANDRÉ }

While André-Louis Peissel is not a devotee of leftovers, he is a devotee of this marvelous sauce, which he serves with leftover leg of lamb. He slices the lamb thin, then puts a dollop of rémoulade—which is really a simple mayonnaise studded with shallots—on his plate, and the marriage is made. I use André-Louis's rémoulade on sandwiches (if there is any leftover) and with cold chicken. It's easy to make and delicious to have on hand.

2 teaspoons Dijon-style mustard

1 large egg yolk

¾ cup (185ml) untoasted peanut or other neutral oil

3 shallots, diced

Fine sea salt

1. Place the mustard and the egg yolk in a medium bowl. Slowly whisk in the oil in a fine stream. The mixture will become quite thick. Fold in the shallots, then season to taste with salt.

MAKES ¾ CUP (177ML)

CHAPTER 12

L'épicerie

L'ÉPICERIE MEANS (SMALL, ENTICING, LITTLE) GRO-
cery in French. It also is a somewhat old-fashioned term for pantry.
In many ways, they are one and the same. In former times, every
village included an *épicerie* within walking distance so the typical
home cook didn't really need an extensive pantry. Today, as villages
melt into towns, and cities and distances and traffic increase, each
home has developed its own *épicerie*.

In the home *épicerie*, one finds the staples that allow the French
cook to pull a rabbit from a hat in record time, sometimes twice a
day. It's all part of the marvelous sense of organization the French
learn in school as they carefully line up their paragraphs, double-
underline key phrases in specific colors using a ruler to make sure
the lines are straight, and have color-coded *lutins*, or notebooks
with plastic pages, to keep papers in order. The French sense of

organization spills naturally into the home and kitchen. From there, it spreads to the *épicerie*.

Today's home *épicerie* includes the freezer, typically an upright model with drawers that hold premade pastry, fish, shrimp, the odd bag of frozen vegetables, a small tub of ice cream, a loaf of bread, and often herbs from the frozen food chain store Picard. (They are surprisingly flavorful, shaken out of cleverly designed boxes so they stay fresh.) Either the frozen food has been put up by the homemaker or brought in by the hunter (this is typical in the countryside—not too many urbanites have wild game in their freezers), or there are selections from the supermarket or Picard. A French freezer is never overstuffed, though, and it never seems to contain anything superfluous.

The *épicerie* also includes the *refrigerateur* or *frigo*, though I'm not always sure why. When I have occasion to peek into a French *frigo*, what I see are mostly empty shelves and doors. Oh, the *frigo* comes in handy for the occasional leftovers and bottles of white or rosé. There is likely a package of *lardons* (chunks of bacon), some grated Gruyère, maybe a jar of mustard, and a tub of crème fraîche. There is always butter, and there is often thin-sliced boiled ham, maybe some slices of air-cured ham, and smoked salmon, too. But that's about it. In France, the *frigo* bears no resemblance to the bulging American refrigerator. It serves as a holding area rather than a storage bin.

I'm not saying that French refrigerators don't hold carrots and lettuce and other fresh vegetables—they just don't hold them for very long. And most root vegetables are stored outside, or in a cool cellar. Shallots and garlic sit on baskets on the counter, or hang from rafters outside.

The *épicerie*, which includes all the makings of a meal except for fresh ingredients, is renewed regularly, so that everything in it is fresh; you won't find anything in there that has outlived its use-by date; nothing will stay in the freezer too long. This is Mamie's wisdom—she tolerated no waste and understood that having too much was just as bad as having nothing at all. In the French *épicerie*, it's all about rotation.

When I first came to France and spent a month as a cook at Edith and Bernard's, it took me a while to become accustomed to cooking out of the garden and from the market. I quickly got used to it, though, particularly when I tasted the flavors of everything, which were so intensely fresh. I also became used to the empty refrigerator, realizing how many things in my own American refrigerator had just sat there, waiting to be used (and never were used). I learned how fast fresh ingredients become un-fresh, which led me to understand why the French shop so often. I also learned that a carefully planned pantry is the key to wonderful meals. That, beyond all the cooking techniques I was learning at school, was the true start of my education in French cooking.

Not every French cook shops daily—that would be impossible. But built into every French cook's consciousness is the idea of shopping often. There isn't that notion of shopping in bulk and stuffing the refrigerator with big bags and boxes of ingredients. Some very busy cooks, or cooks who aren't entirely attuned to preciously delicious meals, resort to the *drive* that one of our local supermarkets built recently. They order ingredients online and drive through and pick them up. I've never heard anyone who uses the *drive* for fresh ingredients be entirely happy with what they find in their grocery bags, though. The *drive* is more of an emergency measure than anything else.

Edith, who shops almost daily, has one of my favorite pantries. It was fashioned when the house was remodeled to include a gorgeous veranda on the other side of the kitchen wall. The architect (her older brother, Christian) included space for cupboards in that wall, and the pantry is simply part of that space. The door to it, which is at the end of the kitchen, was originally an exterior door built several hundred years ago, and it's made of solid dark wood and garnished with heavy metal bolts and locks.

It opens to reveal what it has held since I've known it, all the makings for healthy, interesting meals—lentils, buckwheat groats, rice, couscous, pasta, all on the same shelf, along with several bags of flour and sugar. Below the "dry goods" shelf is one with spices, condiments, dried fruit, vanilla sugar, baking powder, chestnut puree, bars of semisweet chocolate, dried plums, blueberry jam, red currant jelly, and as many containers of lavender honey as the shelf will hold. Edith and Bernard have a house in Provence, and they return laden with lavender honey and olives. The olives, by the way, share shelf space with mustard, capers, cornichons, tuna, anchovies, and sardines. Then there is the floor of the pantry, for storing baskets of potatoes and onions.

Just for fun, a peek in Edith's refrigerator reveals a crisper drawer filled to bursting with lemons—she uses their juice in her salad dressings, to blend with water and drink, to add to a braise. The zest goes into her chestnut cake, her madeleines, her chocolate cake, her choux pastry. She's always got oranges for Bernard's early-morning orange juice, and butter for breakfast. There is usually a jar of jam or jelly, and a half-finished package of Provençale olives, which she throws into her endive salad or adds to pizza or just serves plain. There are several bottles of white and rosé, a handful of different beers, and lots of empty shelf space. The only time she'll have meat or fish in there—a rabbit, fat cod fillets, perhaps some ham—is if she's going to use it immediately. Rabbit with dried plums is on her winter menu often; the morning of the day she plans to serve it, she's at the market early to pick up the rabbit.

Eloise has a small pantry down the hall from her kitchen, where cans of tuna jostle cans of tomatoes and cans of garbanzo beans, stacked

SEA SALT, PARTICULARLY FLEUR DE SEL

In every French kitchen that I've ever set foot in, a container of fine, gray sea salt and one of coarse salt sit next to the stove. Fleur de sel is not far away.

When I speak of sea salt, I am referring to salt harvested in Guérande, on the southern coast of Brittany, because it is the best I've ever tasted (and I taste every sea salt I can get my hands on). There, in marshes built by the Romans, *paludiers*, salt rakers, channel sea water until it evaporates to just the right thickness, then they pull the salt from it to make pyramids on the dikes separating the marshes. When the salt has drained enough, they transfer it to wheelbarrows and take it to the salt house. There it is cleaned by having anything undesirable removed from it. Any salt that is inextricably mixed with plants or feathers is stored to use on icy roads in winter. The rest is ready to sell.

The salt comes from the water as coarse, gray salt. It's naturally coarse; it's gray from the twenty-seven minerals it contains. Some is then ground into fine sea salt; some is dried out so it can be put in tabletop salt grinders and not corrode them; some is left slightly damp.

Fleur de sel, the flower of the salt, is a whole different matter. This capricious salt forms on the top of the marsh when the east wind blows. This is so poetic, but there is also a reason for it—wind from the east is rare in western France. It is a dry wind (as opposed to that from the west, which is a wet wind), and when it blows over the salt marshes in Guérande it causes a very thin crust of sparkling salt to form on the surface of the water. This is painstakingly scraped off and put in pyramids on the dikes between marshes. When it first comes off the water, it is pale pink, like a mild sunset. Within about thirty minutes, the pink fades to leave pure white salt. It turns out that delicate pink color is from plankton that die and fade away.

The use of the gray salts becomes quickly instinctive, and it is hard to give rules. But I'll try. Coarse salt is good for using in pasta water, soups, bread dough, anything liquid; it's great thrown on meat and poultry right from the oven or the grill, on bread dough before it goes into the oven to be baked, basically anywhere you want a great, big crunch of mild salt. Fine salt is good for everything else, from pastry to sautéing to other general cooking. As for fleur de sel, it's a precious condiment. Sprinkle dishes with it right before you serve them, from the first course right through the salad course, and sometimes even into dessert (Michel's Moelleux au Chocolat on page 131 is fantastic with a little fleur de sel sprinkled on top).

by twos. Bags of pasta and couscous bump against flour, sugar, dried plums, raisins, and almond flour, because Eloise needs plenty of emergency rations on hand for her small children, and she loves to bake.

She takes her children "shopping" to two local farms once a month. The farmers at her first stop have adopted this lively young woman and her beautiful red-haired children. "They invited us to help with the grape harvest this year, and we got to eat with them all afterwards," Eloise said. "What a meal—it was all fresh ingredients from the farm."

There, Eloise stocks up on potatoes, onions, and kiwis (the farmer is one of the biggest kiwi growers in the area); at the second farm nearby, she buys her month's worth of apples, and dried plums, a local specialty. Each child emerges from this farm munching on a big apple, a gift from the farmer.

When they get home, Eloise organizes her purchases in the

pantry, which extends to an outbuilding behind her tall, old house. There, she has a small freezer, too, that holds bread, fish fillets, a chicken, some ground beef, and a variety of vegetables that she's prepared herself. "I've always got homemade choux pastry in there," she said. "And frozen berries, ice cream, and fruit coulis for an impromptu dessert."

Nadine lives in an old farmhouse that she and her husband, Christian, an architect, renovated to include a homey kitchen with a huge skylight that showers light on the sink area, and a small woodstove that makes it cozy. Next to the kitchen is a long, narrow, shelf- and counter-lined hallway that serves as a pantry; it connects the kitchen with a small outdoor area, which means it is cool year-round. In fact, in winter it's so cold that Nadine hardly uses her refrigerator. Christian is a recreational pilot, and he and Nadine often take a day to fly to a favorite spot in Brittany, or one on the other side of Normandy, or the Loire Valley. There, they'll stock up on the local specialties they've come to love, like pork pâtés and rillettes (similar to pâté), fish terrine, air-cured sausages of all sorts, including *andouillette*, which is made with tripe, liqueurs and bottles of wine. These riches sit on the pantry shelves, ready for Nadine to pull down and serve for aperitif.

The pantry includes a big freezer that has plenty of baguettes in it, along with fish fillets and meat, berries from Nadine's large garden, and sliced apples ready for a tart, from the trees sprinkled around their property. She also has wild mushrooms in there, because half their property is woods, home to morels, cèpes, and chanterelles. Their son and his family live in Bosnia, and Nadine and Christian visit regularly, returning with more wild mushrooms, usually dried, from the woods there. These make their way into sauces, soups, and tarts.

Sophie's pantry is walk-in, too, right off her small kitchen. Its shelves are bulging with pots and pans, bottles of special olive oil she buys when they go to Provence, balsamic and sherry vinegars, back-up jars of mustard and cornichons, tapenade, olives, anchovies, and roasted peppers for the impromptu pizzas she makes.

Sophie's pantry is a bit different than many of her cohorts because she travels so much. She has green tea from China in there, a special selection of toasted grains that she picked up in Ethiopia and which she serves with coffee; pistachio paste, thin rye crackers from Sweden, sweet pastries from Algeria. Her freezer includes bags of toasted nuts from Turkey, and hanging on her kitchen wall are strings of dried eggplant and peppers she picked up there also. "I'll never cook with them," she said. "But they're beautiful to look at." Her refrigerator holds crème fraîche and heavy cream, "Because I love sauces," she said, and at least three different nut oils and nut butters because Sophie is, among other things, a nut-aholic. "Nut oil makes everything taste more sophisticated," she said. "My favorite salad is endives with blue cheese and walnuts, with walnut oil . . . there's nothing better."

I love Betty's pantry, too, because she's an organized cook, always ready for anything. She and her husband, Louis, are newly retired, and they just moved into Betty's mother's beautiful old home about fifteen minutes from Louviers, in a charming little town on the banks of the Seine. They're becoming accustomed to a gentler life, which does not include daily shopping the way it used to when they both worked.

Beautiful brown eggs from Louis's chickens sit in a pretty, wrought-iron egg stand in Betty's kitchen—she's always got more than she can use, so a visitor to their house usually leaves with a half dozen. Her pantry around the corner is neatly organized with jars of pâté and boxes of nuts and crackers for aperitifs in one area, bags of pasta, couscous, semolina, flour, and sugar in another. She has little boxes of heavy cream that sit near canned cherries and peaches. "You never know when you'll need cream, and it never hurts to have fruit on hand," she said. Her refrigerator holds cheese and milk, carrots and lettuce. "I'm always prepared," she said. "Maybe I'm too prepared, but I like to be organized." Part of her organization includes a supply of English tea, which she drinks with milk.

Louis, who cooks as well, makes sure that there is always Spanish rice, garlic, saffron, and paprika in the pantry for his specialty, paella. He is also the wine expert of the family. He keeps at least one bottle of white and one of rosé in the *frigo*, for the unexpected guest. In his small wine room off the kitchen, he has a great selection, with a preference for Burgundies and Bordeaux.

Baptiste and his companion, Mathilde, are a bit the exceptions to the rule in that Baptiste sells his produce at four markets a week, coming home with fresh ingredients from each, including the region's finest eggs, bunches of hot watercress, crusty sourdough bread, farm-fresh cream and butter. His pantry are his fields, aside from the drawers where he keeps flour, sugar, and chocolate, for making mousse, or his special raspberry and chocolate tart (page 138). Because he doesn't have to worry about fresh ingredients, his real "pantry" focus is on wine, which he stores in a small, old building he outfitted as a wine cellar, and which sits behind his restored barn of a house. Baptiste loves to find unusual wines, and his cellar is an exemplary collection of small-production wines with a special focus on Burgundy, the Loire, and the Languedoc. He and his father make hard cider and *pommeau*—a special Norman aperitif made with cider and Calvados—which he keeps in his wine cellar to pull out for picnics and barbecues.

THE WINE CELLAR

Where I live, in Normandy, old houses have gorgeous wine cellars with vaulted stone ceilings. I've got one underneath my house. The temperature is constant (52°F / 11°C), and it's a great place to store wine, even if you're only storing it from one meal to the next.

When I first moved into my fifteenth-century house, I fell in love with the wine cellar. I hung up candlelabra and dried flower arrangements, put pretty baskets of fruits and vegetables on the rough floor, imagined many a tasting and dinner down in the cool, dark spot. When oenologue Hervé Lestage, my friend and colleague, first saw the cellar, he gasped. "Get everything out of here," he said, waving at the dried flowers and the fruit and vegetables. "They'll flavor the wines. Nothing can be down here."

I did as he said. And, in the end, I decided against tastings and dinners in the cellar because it's really quite small and full of bottles, and not so adapted to dining. What I have hosted there, though, have been many a Halloween party for small children where the candles throw shadows on the walls, the peeled grapes really do feel like eyeballs, and pistachio shells make great witchy fingernails.

In Normandy, Bordeaux is the traditional wine to have in the cellar, because historically the wine route between Bordeaux and its excellent customer, England, passed through Normandy, and plenty a bottle "fell" off the cart that transported it. Normans are so loyal in their drinking habits, it is said that the wine of Normandy is Bordeaux. In other regions, the wine cellar heavily reflects local production. No cook and/or host is without several bottles of white, rosé, red, and sparkling on hand. All can be served directly from the cellar, though sparkling wine is best served well chilled.

Dominique Léost, a friend and colleague of my friend Marie, has a lively sense of life, which includes his cooking. He is a rarity— the Frenchman who cooks every day—but he enjoys it and uses a lot of imagination when he is in the kitchen. He prefers to cook fresh, but his schedule means that he has things on hand for emergencies. These include different meats in his freezer, along with sea scallops and local trout that he's frozen himself. His refrigerator holds mustard, lardons, ham, dried sausages, pâtés, fruit juice, a few dairy desserts, homemade yogurt, vegetables, butter, and lemons, so that he can whip up one of his favorite cakes, Madame Korn's Lemon Cake (page 44) when he's in the mood. As for Marie, she really has almost nothing in her refrigerator, because either she or Claude cooks fresh every day. I've never opened her refrigerator door (*ça ne se fait pas*—this isn't done!), but if I did I'd counsel her to sell the appliance. There might be a loaf of *pain de mie*, maybe a leftover, or a vegetable. For this couple, one who is retired and the other who is not, each day is a fresh culinary adventure!

Finally, there is Danie's pantry. It's another of my favorites because it isn't just in one spot but in many, and it includes such a marvelous selection of oddities and staples. Danie, you recall, lives on a farm, so from autumn through winter, she has a constantly diminishing stack of squash from the garden outside her back door (one pantry location). In an outbuilding she has tanker-size baskets of onions, walnuts, shallots, and garlic, all her own production. There are cabbages and carrots, too. As for lettuce, Guy staggers planting so she has her supply in the ground, just steps from her back door.

Danie's refrigerator contains the typical grated cheese, bottles of milk, jars of mustard, and cornichons one finds in nearly every

French *frigo*. What makes her *frigo* special, though, is the huge hunk of her rillettes sitting in it, an invaluably delicious luxury. To make them, she slow-cooks goose carcasses with herbs, shreds the meat, and then presses it into big rectangles that look a bit like pâtés. She serves them slightly chilled, to be sliced and spread onto fresh bread. There is almost always leftover foie gras, which anyone would kill for because it's made from her geese, and usually confit, goose cooked long and slowly in goose fat, with herbs for extra flavor (for more on confit technique, see page 184). Alongside that will be air-cured goose ham, and a specialty that makes me weak in the knees: her amazing air-cured goose breast that is stuffed with foie gras then rolled in black pepper. Oh, and there will also be a selection of her jams, which might include blackberry, orange, strawberry, or red currant, and a jar of her vital *hachis*, a blend of parsley, garlic, and goose fat. Even with all of this, Danie's *frigo* looks mostly empty.

I don't snoop when I am invited somewhere for a meal, but I admit to a healthy interest in what my hosts have on hand. With apologies to my dear friends who have revealed to me the intimate facts of what they keep in their *épiceries*, my close observation of their habits, as well as my own proclivity for efficiency, has heavily influenced what is in my own pantry. I include its contents, so that you can always have a flavorful meal within easy reach:

AN IDEAL ÉPICERIE FOR COOKING *COMME LES FRANÇAIS*

In the Cupboard

Flour—cakes, tarts, béchamel, cookies

Sugar—pastries, desserts, caramels

Yeast and other leavening agents—breads, cakes, cookies

Spices—curry, nutmeg, salt and pepper, *quatre épices* (an aromatic blend of allspice, cinnamon, ginger, cloves), juniper berries, turmeric powder, cloves, cumin—all cooking

Vanilla sugar

Almond powder, also called almond flour—what makes so many French cakes light and moist

Semisweet chocolate—sauces, hot chocolate, impromptu *goûter*

Pasta—used in gratins, and always as a meal for children at lunch or dinner, drowned in butter and grated cheese

Couscous—mostly for tabbouleh

Lentils—almost always combined with pork (they cook fast)

Rice—often served as a side dish, considered by the French cook to be a vegetable, also used in salads

Canned tomato sauce—heated and poured directly over pasta or rice, often with some tuna stirred in

Canned tuna—used in tarts, savory breads, salads, sautés

Sardines—eaten on buttered bread, sprinkled with lemon juice

Anchovies—put on homemade pizza, added to tapenade

Olives—green and black, for pizzas, in salad, for tapenade, as appetizers

Eggs—used everywhere, starters to desserts, never refrigerated (even at the grocery store)

Rice cakes

Coffee and tea—coffee for the morning and after dinner; tea for the afternoon

Breakfast cereals—in some homes

Cookies—BN (Biscuiterie Nantaise brand—achingly sweet, industrially produced cookie that most French children die for), petit beurre (the healthier alternative), petit LU (the ones with semisweet chocolate on them are incredible), Hob Nobs (made by the geniuses at McVities—a "rough and tumble" oaty sandwich filled with chocolate, to die for)

Potatoes—if there is a potato, there is dinner

Onions—the basis for most dishes

Shallots

In the Fridge

Lardons (matchsticks or cubes of bacon)—quiche Lorraine, salads, pizzas, sautés, sauces

Grated Gruyère—sauces, pizza, pasta, hot sandwiches (croque monsieur)

Milk—for putting in coffee or pouring over cereal

Yogurt—all flavors, all kinds, all delicious

Butter

Crème fraîche

Heavy cream

Mustard

Mayonnaise

In the Freezer

Some type of seafood—cod fillets, shrimp, trout, salmon

Some type of meat—ground beef, chicken, lamb, fresh sausages—usually from the butcher

Baguette—no meal is complete without bread

Ready-made pastry

A vegetable or two—picked or purchased in season, then home-frozen

Unsalted butter—for that impromptu sauce

Ice cream

Herbs—from Picard

EDITH'S CHESTNUT CAKE
{ GATEAU DE CHÂTAIGNES D'EDITH }

This is the chestnut cake that Edith makes in the winter, when days are short and hearty meals are called for. She can decide she wants to eat this at three P.M., and it will be made and baked by four P.M. It is moist, dense, richly flavored, and completely delicious. Leftovers make a great breakfast!

In order to be so quick about this cake, Edith always has the chestnut cream on hand. And now, thanks to her, so do I. With this in the cupboard, a delicious dessert is not far away!

> Two 17-ounce (510g) cans chestnut cream, to give 2½ cups
>   chestnut cream
> 3 large eggs, separated
> 1 tablespoon mild honey, such as lavender
> 2 tablespoons unsalted butter, melted
> 1 teaspoon pure vanilla extract
> Zest from ½ lemon, preferably organic, minced
> ½ cup (75g) all-purpose flour
> Pinch of fine sea salt
> Confectioners' sugar, for garnish
> Edible flowers, for garnish

1. Preheat the oven to 350°F (180°C) and position a rack in the center. Butter a 9-inch (22.5cm) cake pan. Line it with parchment paper.
2. In a large bowl, whisk together the chestnut cream and the egg yolks until thoroughly combined. Whisk in the honey, butter, vanilla, and lemon zest until combined. Sift the flour and salt over the mixture and whisk just until thoroughly combined.
3. Whisk the egg whites to soft peaks, then fold one-third of the egg whites into the chestnut mixture. Fold in the remaining egg whites and turn the batter into the prepared pan. Set the pan on a rimmed baking sheet, and bake until the cake is puffed and slightly cracked on top, about

40 minutes. To check for doneness, pierce the cake with the blade of a sharp knife—if it emerges sticky, the cake is not quite baked.

4. Remove the cake from the oven and let cool in the pan for about 15 minutes before turning out onto a wire rack. Let cool, then transfer to a serving platter. Just before serving, garnish with confectioners' sugar and some edible flowers (pansies, rose petals . . .).

SERVES 10 TO 12

ROASTED RED BELL PEPPERS WITH GARLIC
{ POIVRONS GRILLÉS À L'AIL }

If I have this sparkling condiment in my frigo, *I have the makings of a great dinner. This goes on a tartine, over pasta, over fresh goat cheese, or as a dip for toast, both great appetizers. You can serve this with roasted chicken, steamed fish, grilled steak . . . I could go on, but you'll find lots more uses for it.*

Make sure that all the ingredients are covered with oil before refrigerating. Remove it from the frigo *about twenty minutes before serving, to allow the oil to return to a liquid state. Use these up within about two weeks.*

> 3 large red bell peppers (for a total weight of 1½ pounds; 750g)
> 3 large cloves garlic, green germ removed, cut lengthwise into thin matchsticks
> 1½ cups (375ml) extra-virgin olive oil, plus more as needed
> ½ teaspoon fleur de sel

1. Roast the bell peppers over an open flame or under the broiler until their skins are entirely blackened, turning them frequently so they roast evenly. Depending on your heat source, this will take about 10 minutes. Place the roasted peppers in a brown paper bag and let them sit for 10 minutes, then peel and seed them. To peel the peppers,

simply rub away the peel with your fingers. Remove any remaining black skin using paper towels or a plastic scraper—do not rinse them. Be sure to remove all the white pith inside the pepper as well. Pat them dry and cut into thin (¼-inch; .75cm) slices, then into ½-inch-long (1.25cm) pieces.

2. Place the pepper strips and the garlic in a medium bowl and add the oil. If it doesn't cover them, add additional oil until they are covered. Add the salt, stir, and your peppers are ready to use. To store, place them in a glass container, cover, and refrigerate for up to 1 month. The oil will solidify. Remove from the refrigerator about 20 minutes before you plan to use them to allow the oil to return to a liquid state.

MAKES ABOUT 2 CUPS (500G) OF PEPPERS IN OIL

CHUNKY OLIVE PASTE
{ TAPENADE }

Nothing says "Provence" more than this savory, highly flavored combination of that region's finest ingredients—olives, garlic, anchovies, and olive oil! Serve this with freshly toasted bread or fresh vegetables, or use it on everything from pizza to roast chicken!

This is a basic tapenade recipe—add the fresh herbs of your choice once you've got it blended together. And if you are using a food processor, process until it's chunky, not to a fine puree (my advice, of course. Do as you like!).

NOTE: *If using anchovy fillets in oil from Collioure, or other excellent-quality anchovies, there is no need to soak the fillets in the white wine, which is done simply to remove some of their salt. If using anchovy fillets packed in salt, the soaking is necessary.*

8 anchovy fillets, preferably packed in oil

¼ cup (60ml) dry white wine, such as Sauvignon Blanc
(needed to soak salted anchovies)

2 cups (300g) best-quality black and/or green olives, preferably
   from Nyons in France, pitted

1 tablespoon capers, preferably packed in salt, rinsed

1 teaspoon Dijon-style mustard, preferably Maille brand

2 cloves garlic, green germ removed

4 to 6 tablespoons (60 to 90ml) extra-virgin olive oil

Freshly ground black pepper

Thyme flower blossoms, for garnish

Fresh bread, toasted, or high-quality crackers, for serving

1. Place the anchovies in a shallow bowl and cover them with the wine (If
   they are salted anchovies. Anchovies in oil don't need to be desalted.).
   Let them sit for 15 minutes, then drain and pat dry.

2. Place all the ingredients except the oil in a mortar and pestle, or in
   the bowl of a food processor, and grind or process until the olives are
   ground to a thick purée. Slowly add the oil until it loosens the purée
   just slightly and is fully incorporated. Season with freshly ground
   black pepper. Transfer to a serving dish, garnish with the flower
   blossoms, and serve with freshly toasted bread or crackers.

MAKES ABOUT 1½ CUPS (375ML) TAPENADE

CHAPTER 13

Meal Plans and More Recipes to Get You Cooking *Comme les Français*

THE FRENCH COOK IS ORGANIZED. MY FRIEND ELOISE sits down with her three children to plan meals three months ahead of time, then puts the plan on a spreadsheet that she prints out as a reminder. Nathalie has certain meals planned for certain nights of the week; Emilie cooks double quantities so she always has home-made meals in the freezer; Virginie is never without the makings for a delicious tartine. Each cook is different, depending on her likes and dislikes, but one thing they all share is that they are never, when it comes to meals, caught unawares. And most every French cook is inherently aware of the season, so part of being prepared is having fresh, seasonal ingredients on hand.

Because of this sense of organization, which is drummed into the French student from first grade onward, a French cook is pre-pared. This takes much of the anxiety out of cooking. To help you develop your inner French cook, I offer you a dozen seasonal meal ideas, with recipes, to get you on the smooth, pleasurable path to cooking *comme les Français.*

1

IT'S A NEW YEAR SUPPER—

JANUARY

Salad with Roquefort and Walnuts (page 255)

Roast Apple and Pear Chicken (page 205)

Green Salad with Classic Vinaigrette (page 96)

Poached Pears (page 256)

SALAD WITH ROQUEFORT
AND WALNUTS

{ SALADE DE ROQUEFORT ET NOIX }

This is Sophie's version of her mamie's endive, Roquefort, and walnut salad. If you don't want to use iceberg, try Belgian endive or another crisp, juicy lettuce. This calls for a Jurançan sec from Charles Hours.

1 tablespoon freshly squeezed lemon juice

Generous 1 teaspoon Dijon-style mustard, preferably Maille brand

Fine sea salt and freshly ground black pepper

2 tablespoons extra-virgin olive oil

3 tablespoons walnut oil

1 big bunch (about ⅓ cup; 3g) fresh chives, minced

1 pound (500g) iceberg lettuce, rinsed, dried, and torn into bite-size pieces

5 ounces (150g) blue cheese, such as Roquefort, chilled

1 cup (100g) walnuts, coarsely chopped

1. In a large bowl, whisk together the lemon juice and mustard with a large pinch of salt and a generous amount of pepper. While whisking continuously, add the oils in a thin stream until the mixture is combined.
2. Whisk the chives into the vinaigrette.
3. Add the lettuce to the bowl and toss until the leaves are thoroughly coated with the vinaigrette.
4. Evenly divide the salad among four salad plates. Crumble one-fourth of the cheese over each salad, and then top with the walnuts.

SERVES 4

POACHED PEARS
{ POIRES POCHÉES }

This recipe was inspired by my friend David Lebovitz, a wonderful au-
thor and pastry chef. Serve these by themselves, or with a gorgeous cookie
alongside, like a nut biscotti. These will keep for about one week in the re-
frigerator, in the poaching liquid.

1⅓ cup (265g) sugar
1 cinnamon stick
3 star anise
5 slices fresh ginger
3-inch strip of lemon zest
1 quart (1L) filtered water
4 firm pears, such as Bosc, cored, peeled, and quartered

1. In a large saucepan, combine the sugar, cinnamon, star anise, ginger, lemon zest, and water and heat over medium-high heat, stirring occasionally, until the sugar has dissolved. Continue to simmer for about 8 minutes, so the spices have a chance to flavor the poaching liquid.

2. Slide in the pears and cover the pan with a round of parchment paper that has a small hole cut in the center.

3. Simmer the pears until tender through but not mushy, 15 to 25 minutes, depending on the firmness of the pears.

4. Remove from the heat and let the pears cool in the poaching liquid before serving.

SERVES 4

2

SHORT MONTH SUPPER—

FEBRUARY

Omelet with Cream and Herbs (page 258)

Sautéed Scallops with Lemon, Garlic,
and Parsley (page 259)

Braised Broccoli (page 76)

Green Salad with Classic Vinaigrette (page 96)

Individual Apple Tarts with Tender Tart
Pastry (page 260)

OMELET WITH CREAM AND HERBS
{ OMELETTE À LA CRÈME AUX AROMATES }

This is about the simplest dinner ever invented—a few eggs, a little cream, some herbs from the garden. You can serve this as-is, or add grated cheese, leftover potatoes that you have browned first, with or without bacon. The sky is the limit for omelet fillings. That said, I think simple is best, which is why I'm offering this recipe. Serve your favorite Chenin Blanc with this.

> 6 large eggs
> ¼ teaspoon fine sea salt
> Generous pinch of piment d'Espelette or hot paprika
> 1 bunch fresh chives or herbs of your choice
> 1 tablespoon extra-virgin olive oil
> 3 tablespoons crème fraîche or non-ultra-pasteurized heavy cream

1. In a medium bowl, whisk together the eggs, salt, and a big pinch of piment d'Espelette.
2. Mince the herbs, and put a bowl over them to contain their flavor.
3. Heat the oil in a 10½-inch (26.5cm) omelet pan or other skillet (nonstick works great!) over medium heat. When the oil is hot but not smoking, pour in the eggs. They will puff up a bit. Cook the eggs, using a spatula to pull the eggs back from the edges of the skillet and tipping the uncooked eggs in the center out toward the edge of the pan. When the omelet is evenly set on the bottom but there is still some uncooked egg on top, drizzle in the cream and sprinkle the herbs over the cream. A French person would consider the omelet done now. If you prefer it to be more cooked, cover the pan, reduce the heat, and cook until it is to your liking. The egg will be completely cooked after 4 minutes.
4. Transfer the omelet to a serving platter by sliding it out onto the platter and folding it after half the omelet is on the platter. Serve immediately.

SERVES 4 TO 6

SAUTÉED SCALLOPS WITH LEMON, GARLIC, AND PARSLEY
{ COQUILLES ST JACQUES AU CITRON, AIL, ET PERSIL }

This is a simple way to prepare scallops, which I like to serve over a freshly dressed and simple green salad (page 96) as a first course. Scallops are in season in the winter months, and this dish on the table in front of a cozy fire makes for a wonderful evening! Serve this with a lightly chilled Entre-Deux-Mers, such as Château Turcaud.

12 ounces (360g) fresh sea or bay scallops, rinsed and refrigerated

¾ cup (7g) fresh flat-leaf parsley or basil leaves, minced

1 clove garlic, green germ removed, minced

1 tablespoon extra-virgin olive oil

3 tablespoons freshly squeezed lemon juice

Green Salad with Classic Vinaigrette (page 96), for serving

Fleur de sel and freshly ground black pepper

1. Remove the scallops from the refrigerator right before you plan to prepare the dish, and pat them dry, if necessary.

2. Combine the parsley and garlic together.

3. Heat the oil in a large, heavy-bottomed skillet over medium-high heat. When the oil is hot but not smoking, add the scallops and the garlic and parsley mixture and cook, stirring and shaking the pan to turn the scallops, until they are turning golden at the edges, 4 to 5 minutes. Remove the skillet from the heat, add the lemon juice, stir and shake the pan, then turn the scallops out onto four plates of green salad, or into a warmed serving dish. Be sure to scrape the garlic and parsley out of the pan onto the scallops. Season with salt and pepper, and serve.

SERVES 4 AS A FIRST COURSE OR 2 AS A MAIN COURSE

INDIVIDUAL APPLE TARTS WITH TENDER TART PASTRY

{ TARTES AUX POMMES INDIVIDUELS À LA PÂTE BRISÉE }

Apple tart is universal in France. This simple tart, which brings this meal to a close, is made special with a drizzle of honey—it adds a floral hint to the apples, an added dimension.

1 recipe On Rue Tatin's Tender Tart Pastry (page 207)

3 medium (5.5-ounce; 165g) apples, such as Cox's Orange Pippins, Reine de Reinettes, Jonagold

2 tablespoons (25g) light brown sugar

3 teaspoons mild honey

1. Line two baking sheets with parchment paper.

2. Roll out the pastry as thin as you possibly can. Cut out six 7-inch (17.5cm) rounds, and transfer them to the baking sheets. Refrigerate for at least 30 minutes and up to several hours. If you plan to refrigerate them for several hours (or overnight), cover the dough with parchment paper, then aluminum foil so the pastry doesn't dry out.

3. Preheat the oven to 450°F (230 °C).

4. Peel, halve, and core the apples. Cut them crosswise into paper-thin slices. Remove the pastry rounds from the refrigerator and arrange the slices from half of an apple on each of the pastry rounds, overlapping the slices slightly and mounding them attractively in the center. Sprinkle each tart evenly with 1 teaspoon of the brown sugar, then bake until the pastry is golden, the apples are golden at the edges, and the sugar has begun to caramelize, 25 to 30 minutes. If you have the baking sheets on two racks, you will need to switch them halfway through cooking so the tarts bake evenly.

5. Remove the tarts from the oven and immediately drizzle each tart with ½ teaspoon of the honey. Transfer to a wire cooling rack and let cool slightly, or to room temperature, before serving.

MAKES 6 TARTS

3

IT'S STILL WINTER BUT SPRING IS COMING—

MARCH

Turnip and Cream Tart (page 209)

Steak with Melted Onions (page 201)

Seared Belgian Endives (page 262)

Green Salad with Classic Vinaigrette (page 96)

Speculoos Ice Cream (page 263)

SEARED BELGIAN ENDIVES

{ ENDIVES GRILLÉES }

This is a quick and delicious way to prepare Belgian endives, which are also called witloof.

With this method, they are searing hot and crisp through, and golden and caramelized on the cut edges. Cut the endives in half right before searing, as they quickly begin to turn a rust color when they are cut. If you don't have almond oil, you can garnish these with a little drizzle of extra-virgin olive oil.

> 1 tablespoon extra-virgin olive oil
> 4 medium Belgian endives
> Fine sea salt and freshly ground black pepper
> Fleur de sel
> Almond oil (optional)

1. Heat the olive oil in a heavy-bottomed skillet over medium heat. Halve the endives lengthwise and place them in the skillet, cut side down and not touching one another. Season with salt and pepper and cook, loosely covered, checking to be sure the endives don't burn, until they are golden on the cut side and completely hot throughout, 5 to 8 minutes. Do not turn the endive. Remove from the heat. Transfer two halves to each of four warmed plates, cut side up. Season with fleur de sel and almond oil, if using, and serve immediately.

SERVES 4

SPECULOOS ICE CREAM
{ GLACE AU SPECULOOS }

NOTE: *When making the custard for ice cream, you must bring it very close to the curdling point in order for it to cook properly. The purpose of the strainer over the bowl is to strain out any beginnings of curdled custard.*

> 6 large egg yolks
> 1 cup (200g) vanilla sugar
> 1 small pinch fine sea salt
> 3 cups (750ml) half-and-half
> ½ cup (145g) speculoos paste (Lotus brand preferred)

1. In a large bowl, whisk the egg yolks, the sugar, and the salt until the mixture is pale yellow and light. Whisk in the half-and-half, and place the mixture in a large, heavy-bottomed saucepan. Place the speculoos paste in a large bowl near the stove, and set the whisk over the bowl.

2. Cook the egg yolk mixture over medium heat, stirring it with a wooden spoon or spatula in a figure-eight pattern, until it thickens and gives some resistance. The mixture will thin out, then will thicken and become smooth so that your utensil glides smoothly across the bottom of the pan. To check whether or not the custard is thick enough, remove your utensil from the pan. If the drops are thick and slow, then the custard is ready. Pour it through the sieve and onto the speculoos paste.

3. Slowly whisk the custard and the speculoos paste together, until they are completely combined. Let the mixture cool to room temperature, then refrigerate until it is chilled through. Transfer to an ice-cream machine, and process into ice cream following the manufacturer's instructions.

MAKES 3 CUPS (750ML) ICE CREAM

4

RAIN, RAIN, RAINY NIGHT SUPPER—

APRIL

Pot-au-Feu (page 19)

Green Salad with Classic Vinaigrette (page 96)

Edith's Profiteroles (page 133)

5

IT REALLY IS SPRING—

MAY

Braised Asparagus with Herbs (page 14)

Fish Fillet in Parchment with Butter Sauce (page 193)

Baptiste's New Potato Fries (page 266)

Green Salad with Classic Vinaigrette (page 96)

Bordeaux Strawberries (page 267)

BAPTISTE'S NEW POTATO FRIES

{ LES FRITES AUX POMMES DE TERRE NOUVELLES DE BAPTISTE }

At the market the other day, Baptiste had fire in his eyes as he described his latest culinary achievement— "They're the best frites you'll ever eat," he said. He described his method and weighed out a kilo of potatoes for me, and I made them that night for dinner. He was right. Easy, beautiful, crispy, delicious.

This serves four as a small side dish, two as a generous side dish. I like to make these and serve them for supper with the Crisp Green Salad with Poached Eggs on page 45.

Coarse sea salt

1½ pounds (750g) new potatoes, scrubbed but not peeled, cut into ¼-inch rounds

3 tablespoons (45ml) extra-virgin olive oil

Fleur de sel

Piment d'Espelette or freshly ground black pepper

1. Preheat the oven to 425°F (220°C) and position a rack in the center.

2. Bring a large pot of salted water to a boil (about 8 quarts water to 1 tablespoon coarse salt). When the water is boiling, add the potatoes and cook just until they begin to turn tender, about 3 minutes. While they're cooking, lay out a double thickness of cotton tea towels on a work surface and brush a rimmed baking sheet with about 1 tablespoon of the oil.

3. Transfer the potatoes from the boiling water to the tea towels, laying them out in a single layer. They'll dry almost instantly. Transfer them to the prepared baking sheet, then brush them evenly with the remaining oil. Sprinkle them with salt and bake until they are golden and crisp, 20 to 25 minutes. Remove from the oven, season evenly with the piment d'Espelette or other pepper, transfer to a serving dish, and enjoy!

SERVES 2 TO 4 AS A SIDE DISH

BORDEAUX STRAWBERRIES

{ STRAWBERRIES À LA BORDELAISE }

This is the typical way to eat strawberries in Bordeaux—slice them into your favorite glass of red! It's simple and makes for an elegant end to the meal. Pour your favorite Bordeaux—I like Château Lapeyronie, a Castillon Côtes de Bordeaux with a lively flavor.

2 pints fresh strawberries, hulled and cut lengthwise into thin slices

1 bottle of your favorite Bordeaux

1. Place the strawberries in a bowl. Pass them after you've served everyone a glass of wine and let each add several berries to their glass of wine.

SERVES 4

6

SUMMER IS ALMOST HERE—

JUNE

Creamy Spring Pea Soup (page 269)

Curried Medley of Spring Vegetables (page 271)

Green Salad with Classic Vinaigrette (page 96)

Sautéed Cherries (page 272)

CREAMY SPRING PEA SOUP
{ SOUPE DE PETITS POIS À LA CRÈME }

*Fresh peas are such a privilege. Here in Normandy they are ready to har-
vest off the vine in early June, and for a week or two, they are magic—
sweet, moist, tender, and luscious. By the end of June their bloom is gone,
they get harder and less sweet, so we enjoy them as much as possible for
that one brief period. We eat them fresh, steamed, and in this beautifully
simple, fresh soup, which is perfect with a lightly chilled Riesling.*

> 1 tablespoon unsalted butter
> ½ small white onion, diced
> Fine sea salt
> 4 pounds (2kg) peas in the pod, shucked (to give about 4¾ cups peas)
> 3 cups (750ml) herb broth (see page 270)
> 6 tablespoons (90ml) crème fraîche
> 1 small bunch fresh basil, for garnish

1. Melt the butter in a medium, heavy-bottomed saucepan over medium
   heat. When the butter has completely melted, add the onions, stir,
   season lightly with salt, cover, and cook until the onions are translucent through and tender, about 11 minutes. Check the onions to be
   sure they aren't browning or sticking to the pan.
2. Add the peas and the broth, stir, and bring to a boil over medium-high
   heat. Reduce the heat so the broth is simmering merrily, cover, and
   cook until the peas are completely tender throughout, about 10 minutes.
   Check the peas—the cooking time will vary depending on their size.
3. Purée the mixture directly in the pan with an immersion blender, or
   transfer it to a food processor, purée, and return to the saucepan. Whisk
   in the crème fraîche and cook just until the soup is hot throughout, but
   do not bring it to a boil. Season with salt.
4. Just before serving, cut the basil into very fine strips. Divide the soup
   among individual bowls and top each with just a few strips of basil.
   Serve immediately.

SERVES 4 TO 6

HERB BROTH
{ BOUILLON D'ARMATES }

Once you've made this the first time, you'll find a million uses for it. Substitute it for stock in a sauce or a soup, add mixed vegetables and it turn it into a soup . . . it makes everything taste better!

20 sprigs fresh thyme

10 leaves fresh sage

4 fresh bay leaves (from the *Laurus nobilis*), or 4 dried imported bay leaves

4 cloves garlic, unpeeled

1 teaspoon sea salt

6 cups (1.5L) water

1. Place all of the ingredients in a stockpot over medium-high heat. When the mixture boils, reduce the heat so it is simmering, and simmer for 15 minutes. Remove from the heat. You may let the broth sit for 15 minutes before straining, for a more intense herb flavor. Otherwise, strain and use immediately.

MAKES 6 CUPS (1.5L) HERB BROTH

CURRIED MEDLEY OF SPRING VEGETABLES
{ COCOTTE DE LÉGUMES DE PRINTEMPS AU CURRY }

You can make this at any time during the year by using whichever vegetables are seasonal.

Serve this delicate dish with an equally delicate Valençay from the Loire, such as Le Claux Delorme by Domaines Minchin.

½ pound (250g) small turnips

4 tablespoons (60g) unsalted butter

2 teaspoons curry powder (see page 172), or as desired

1 small (10-ounce; 300g) celery root, cut into 2-inch (5cm) cubes

8 ounces (250g) young carrots, peeled, if necessary, and cut on an angle into 2-inch (5cm) pieces

1 pound (500g) new potatoes, skins rubbed off

2 cloves garlic, green germ removed, if necessary, minced

Sea salt

1¼ cups (about 300ml) chicken stock

4 very thin slices air-cured ham (such as prosciutto)

½ cup (about 125ml) crème fraîche or non-ultra-pasteurized heavy cream

4 cups arugula leaves, rinsed, dried, and torn into bite-size pieces

1. If the turnips are small, about the size of a large golf ball, leave them whole. Otherwise, quarter them.

2. In a large, heavy-bottomed stockpot, melt the butter. When it is foaming, add the curry and stir. Simmer until the butter and the curry have combined, about 1 minute. Add the vegetables and the garlic and stir until they are coated with the curry butter. Season lightly with salt and pour over the chicken stock. Stir, and let the vegetables cook, partially covered, until they are nearly tender throughout, 20 to 25 minutes, checking and turning them occasionally to be sure they cook evenly.

3. Preheat the oven to 350°F (180°C).

4. While the vegetables are cooking, place the ham slices on a baking sheet. Bake just until the ham begins to curl and the fat becomes translucent, about 10 minutes. Remove from the heat and cut into 2-inch (5cm) strips.

5. About 5 minutes before you want to serve the vegetables, pour the cream over them and stir. Continue cooking, uncovered, until the liquids have reduced slightly, about 5 minutes.

6. Taste the cooking liquids for seasoning. Stir in the arugula, then remove from the heat and divide among four bowls. Top each bowl with several pieces of air-cured ham, and serve.

SERVES 4

SAUTÉED CHERRIES
{ LES CERISES SAUTÉES }

You may use any variety of flavorful cherries you like for this simple preparation.

2 tablespoons unsalted butter
3 tablespoons light brown sugar
2 pounds (1kg) fat, ripe, juicy cherries, pitted
2 tablespoons freshly squeezed lemon juice
Generous ¼ teaspoon freshly ground black pepper, or as desired

1. Melt the butter in a medium skillet over medium heat. Add the sugar, stir, and add the cherries. Cook, stirring occasionally, until they are tender and hot through, about 8 minutes.

2. Using a slotted spoon, transfer the cherries to a bowl and set aside. Add the lemon juice and the pepper to the pan, stir, and cook until the liquids in the pan have thickened and reduced slightly, raising the heat to medium-high, if necessary, to make them bubble; this should take about 5 minutes. Return the cherries to the pan and toss them in the thickened juices, then remove from the heat. Serve immediately.

SERVES 6 TO 8

7

IT'S HOT OUTSIDE—

JULY

Gazpacho (page 274)

Everyday Eggplant (page 275)

Normandy Mussels with Cider (page 277)

Green Salad with Classic Vinaigrette (page 96)

Vine Peaches in Orange Flower Water (page 278)

GAZPACHO

{ SOUPE FRAÎCHE À LA TOMATE }

This basic recipe will wake up your tastebuds! It's very simple, made with basic, seasonal ingredients, and it's an ideal appetizer to cool everyone down!

Make this at the height of summer, when tomatoes are really, really good and everything else is so perfectly fresh. Consider this a basic recipe. Try it, then add what you like the next time, from diced avocado to roasted bell peppers.

On top, I like to float little croutons that I've cut from fresh bread, tossed in extra-virgin olive oil, and baked in the oven until they are crisp and golden. This dish calls for a chilled rosé.

6 ripe medium-size tomatoes, peeled, seeded, and diced

8 ounces cucumber, peeled and diced

1 small clove new garlic

2 small (2½-ounce; 75g) fresh white onions, quartered

¼ cup (60ml) extra-virgin olive oil

1 tablespoon freshly squeezed lemon juice, plus more as needed

1 tablespoon best-quality red wine vinegar, plus more as needed

Pinch of fine sea salt

1 scant cup (8g) loosely packed fresh basil leaves

½ cup (5g) loosely packed fresh flat-leaf parsley leaves

Piment d'Espelette or hot paprika (optional)

Fresh flat-leaf parsley or basil sprigs, for garnish

Fleur de sel, for garnish

1. Place the tomatoes, cucumbers, garlic, and onions in a food processor or blender and process to a coarse purée. The vegetables should be puréed, yet with small bits left for texture. The purée will be quite thick. Transfer it to a bowl and refrigerate for at least 2 hours and up to 4 hours.

2. Remove the chilled purée from the refrigerator. Stir in the oil, lemon juice, vinegar, and salt to taste. Mince the herbs and stir them in as

well. Season again with salt and piment d'Espelette (if using), and additional lemon juice and vinegar, if desired. Ladle into six chilled bowls. Garnish with herb sprigs and a sprinkling of fleur de sel, and serve immediately.

MAKES 6 APPETIZERS

EVERYDAY EGGPLANT
{ AUBERGINE POUR TOUS LES JOURS }

This is a simple, quick, fresh, and light version of a dish we all know and most of us love—eggplant Parmigiana. It came about thanks to Baptiste Bourdon, my favorite market gardener, whose produce makes every dish sing. It came my turn at his stand, and I put in my request for two kilos of his bursting, juicy "coeur de boeuf" tomatoes, and a half-dozen small, taut, shiny egg-plants. He gave me what I wanted, then turned to a crate of tomatoes behind his stand, filled a bag, and said, "Du rabe." This means "extra" and, in this case, very ripe. By the time I got home—a matter of ten minutes' walk—those tomatoes had practically turned to sauce. I removed their skin, trimmed out the heart, and coarsely chopped them. I sautéed onion and garlic, added the tomatoes, and put them on medium heat to cook. Then I took care of the egg-plant. And then I added some cheese and some fresh basil.

You'll find the result here. It was unplanned, dictated by the most fab-ulous vegetables, and so fast that lunch was on the table in under an hour. This dish has become a family favorite—with me because I can whip it up on a school night—with all of us because it tastes so deliciously satisfying! Please, spice and herb this up as you like! I like to serve it with a Plan Pégau from Laurence and Paul Féraud.

¼ cup (60ml) extra-virgin olive oil
1½ pounds (750g) eggplant, rinsed, stem end removed
Fine sea salt and freshly ground black pepper
1 medium (5-ounce; 150g) onion, diced

2 cloves garlic, green germ removed, minced

2 pounds (1kg) very ripe tomatoes, preferably an heirloom variety like coeur de boeuf, peeled, cored, and coarsely chopped

1 fresh bay leaf (from the *Laurus nobilis*) or dried imported bay leaf

½ cup (5g) fresh basil leaves

½ cup (5g) fresh flat-leaf parsley leaves

1 ounce (30g) Parmigiano Reggiano, finely grated (scant ½ cup)

1. Preheat the oven to 450°F (230°C) and position a rack in the center. Brush a heavy baking sheet with about 2 teaspoons of the oil.

2. Cut the eggplant into ½-inch (1.4cm) rounds and set them on the prepared baking sheet. Brush the rounds with more oil and season them with salt and pepper. Bake until the eggplant is softened and golden on the side touching the pan, 12 to 15 minutes. Flip the slices, brush them lightly with oil, season with salt and pepper, and continue baking until they are tender all the way through, 5 to 8 minutes more. Remove from the oven.

3. While the eggplant is baking, heat 1 tablespoon of the remaining oil in a heavy saucepan over medium-high heat. Stir in the onions and when they start sizzling, reduce the heat to medium. Cook, stirring occasionally, until the onions are nearly translucent, about 8 minutes. Stir in the garlic and cook until it starts to turn translucent, 2 to 3 minutes. Add the tomatoes and the bay leaf, stir, season with salt and pepper, and bring to a boil. Cook, stirring regularly so the tomatoes don't stick, until the tomatoes are softened and beginning to form a sauce, about 20 minutes.

4. Coarsely chop the herbs.

5. Place the remaining oil in a heavy, 1½-quart (1.5L) baking dish. Place one layer of eggplant on the bottom. Sprinkle with one-third of the chopped herbs, and pour over one-third of the tomato sauce. Repeat, and then sprinkle half the cheese on the tomato sauce. Top with the remaining slices of eggplant, basil, and tomato sauce, and the remaining cheese. Cover and bake until the dish is hot throughout and the eggplant and tomato sauce have married, about 20 minutes. Remove from the heat and let cool for at least 5 minutes before serving.

SERVES 3 TO 4

NORMANDY MUSSELS WITH CIDER
{ MOULES NORMANDES AU CIDRE }

I love mussels just about any way, and this is my favorite way to prepare them because it's simple and fresh, and it's the way my friends in Normandy do it. You may substitute white wine for the cider. I like to serve this with hard cider, or with a crisp Sauvignon Blanc, like the Aramis Blanc Sec Côtes de Gascogne from Famille Laplace.

NOTE: *Remove the beards right before you plan to cook the mussels, not in advance.*

4 quarts (4L; about 4 lbs) mussels, rinsed, barnacles scraped off the shells, and debearded

1 shallot, minced

2 fresh bay leaves (from the *Laurus nobilis*) or dried imported bay leaves

4 sprigs fresh flat-leaf parsley

10 whole black peppercorns

20 sprigs fresh thyme

¼ cup (60ml) hard apple cider

Freshly ground black pepper

Bread, for serving

1. Place the mussels in a stockpot and sprinkle with the shallots, bay leaves, parsley sprigs, peppercorns, and thyme sprigs. Pour the cider over all, toss, and cover the pot. Bring to a boil over medium-high heat, then reduce the heat to medium and cook the mussels, shaking the pan regularly, until they open. Cook for 1 minute more, about 8 minutes total. If there are mussels that refuse to open after several more minutes of cooking, discard them.

2. Season the mussels with a generous amount of freshly ground black pepper and serve immediately, with lots of bread alongside!

SERVES 6

VINE PEACHES IN ORANGE FLOWER WATER

{ LES PÊCHES DE VIGNE À L'EAU DE FLEUR D'ORANGER }

Pêches de vigne, *or peaches of the vine, are a late-summer delicacy. Their flesh is deep red, their skin fragile and lightly furred, their flavor intensely perfumed and deep, with a slight and pleasantly bitter tannic sensation. They are a connoisseur's peach, an older variety so named because the trees were once planted among the grape vines in the vineyards of the Rhône Valley. They are still cultivated there, harvested at near-total ripeness, packed carefully in wooden crates and shipped in small quantities to distant destinations like Normandy.*

If you cannot get vine peaches, use local, ripe, gorgeous peaches for this dessert.

NOTE: *Lightly chilling the peaches—for 30 to 45 minutes in the refrigerator—makes them easier to slice nicely and gives a refreshing edge to their flavor.*

1½ pounds (750g) lightly chilled peaches, pitted and peeled
2 to 3 teaspoons orange flower water
Fresh peppermint sprigs, for garnish

1. Slice the peaches into ¼-inch-thick (6mm) slices and arrange them nicely in a shallow serving dish. Drizzle them with orange flower water and garnish with the mint sprigs. Serve immediately, so they are still lightly chilled.

SERVES 4

8

VACATION!—

AUGUST

Melon Salad with Shallot Vinaigrette (page 93)

Lamb Chops with Lemon, Rosemary, and Cherry
Tomatoes (page 280)

Roasted Red Peppers with Garlic (page 149)

Green Salad with Classic Vinaigrette (page 96)

Nectarine Sorbet (page 281)

LAMB CHOPS WITH LEMON, ROSEMARY, AND CHERRY TOMATOES

{ CÔTES D'AGNEAU AU CITRON, ROMARIN, ET TOMATOES CERISES }

This is a perfect, and perfectly simple, way to prepare succulent French lamb. The technique is more Italian, the result simply divine! The results here give rosy lamb chops—if you prefer yours cooked more, simply increase the cooking time. It's hot outside, so serve this with a Languedoc from Domaine Mas de la Tour.

> 1 to 2 tablespoons extra-virgin olive oil
> 8 (4-ounce; 120g) lamb chops, at room temperature
> Fine sea salt and freshly ground black pepper
> Heaping 1 tablespoon fresh rosemary leaves, coarsely chopped
> 24 cherry tomatoes, halved
> 1 tablespoon freshly squeezed lemon juice
> Fleur de sel

1. Heat the oil in a large, heavy-bottomed skillet over medium heat. When the oil is hot but not smoking, add the lamb chops and sear for 1 to 2 minutes per side, seasoning as you do with salt and pepper.

2. When the chops are golden, add the rosemary, tomatoes, and lemon juice to the pan, and stir and swirl them around until the tomatoes are softened but still keep their shape, 3 to 5 minutes. Season everything with salt and pepper and remove the pan from the heat.

3. Place two chops on each of four warmed dinner plates, crossing their narrow ends so they look attractive, and top with the cherry tomato mixture. Season with fleur de sel and serve.

SERVES 4

NECTARINE SORBET
{ SORBET AUX NECTARINES }

This is a simple, fresh sorbet that brings summer to the table. Try it with peaches, or a blend of peaches and nectarines. The most important thing is that whatever fruit you use should be very ripe and full of flavor. Note that the nectarines are neither peeled nor sieved, which gives the sorbet a gorgeous, reddish hue.

½ cup (100g) sugar
¼ cup inverted sugar syrup, such as Hey Shuga or Karo brands
1 sprig fresh rosemary (about 5 inches; 12.5cm long)
2 pounds (1kg) ripe nectarines, halved and pitted
1 to 2 tablespoons freshly squeezed lemon juice, or as desired

1. Place the sugar and 3 tablespoons water in a small, heavy-bottomed saucepan. Mix until the water has moistened the sugar and set the pan over low heat. Bring the mixture to a simmer and stir until the sugar has dissolved. Remove from the heat, add the rosemary sprig, and let cool to room temperature.
2. Purée the nectarines in a food processor. Transfer to a bowl, add the cooled sugar syrup with the rosemary, stir to combine, and then re-frigerate until the purée is chilled through.
3. Stir the lemon juice into the chilled nectarine mixture, remove the rosemary sprig, then transfer to an ice-cream maker and process into a sorbet following the manufacturer's instructions. The sorbet is best served the day it is made.

MAKES ABOUT 3½ CUPS (875ML)

9

BACK TO SCHOOL—

SEPTEMBER

Sophie's Lentil Verrine (page 58)

Edith's Rabbit with Dried Plums (page 196)

Here Is a Way to Make Potatoes Special (page 283)

Green Salad with Classic Vinaigrette (page 96)

Sauté of Spiced Autumn Fruit (page 284)

HERE IS A WAY TO MAKE POTATOES SPECIAL

{ VOICI UN FAÇON DE RENDRES LES POMMES DE TERRE EXTRAORDINAIRE }

This very special recipe was inspired by a dish that Edith served one day—potatoes from her own garden, an atypical touch of crème fraîche (she usually seasons with butter or olive oil), and lots of parsley. These are simple, elegant, and an ideal accompaniment to just about anything.

> 1½ pounds (750g) potatoes, preferably Yukon Gold, peeled and quartered
>
> 1 fresh bay leaf (from the *Laurus nobilis*) or dried imported bay leaf
>
> Coarse sea salt
>
> ¾ cup (7g) fresh flat-leaf parsley leaves
>
> Freshly ground black pepper
>
> ⅓ cup (75ml) crème fraîche

1. Place the potatoes, bay leaf, and 2 teaspoons of salt in a medium saucepan and add water to cover. Bring to a boil over medium-high heat, reduce the heat until the water is simmering merrily, and cook until the potatoes are tender throughout. Remove from the heat and keep warm.

2. Just before serving, mince the parsley and stir it into the crème fraîche. If the potatoes aren't blistering hot, heat them quickly over medium heat. Drain and transfer them to a shallow dish. Crush the potatoes with a fork—you just want them broken up. Season them with salt and pepper, pour the crème fraîche over the top, and serve immediately.

SERVES 4

SAUTÉ OF SPICED AUTUMN FRUIT
{ FRUITS D'AUTOMNE SAUTÉ }

Simple and elegant, this is the best of fall fruit, sautéed lightly in butter and heavily doused with spices and a bit of sugar. Serve plain, or with vanilla ice cream or crème fraîche.

½ cup (100g) packed light brown sugar

½ teaspoon ground cinnamon

½ teaspoon freshly grated nutmeg

½ teaspoon powdered ginger

4 tablespoons (60g) unsalted butter

6 medium, tart cooking apples, such as Gravenstein, Winesaps, or Cox's Orange Pippins, cored, peeled, and cut into eighths

3 good-size, not-quite-ripe pears, cored, peeled, and cut into eighths

Freshly ground black pepper or Szechuan pepper

1. Mix the sugar, cinnamon, nutmeg, and ginger in a small bowl. Set aside.

2. Melt the butter in a large, nonstick skillet over medium heat. Add the apples and pears and toss so they are coated with the butter. Sprinkle with the sugar mixture, toss so all the ingredients are combined, cover, and cook, tossing frequently, until the fruit is tender and golden, about 12 minutes.

3. Evenly divide the fruit among six to eight dessert plates, sprinkle with pepper, and serve.

SERVES 6 TO 8

10

FALL IS IN THE AIR BUT WE'VE STILL GOT TOMATOES—

OCTOBER

Tomato Tubes with Mozzarella (page 286)

Cream of Mushroom Soup (page 287)

Green Salad with Classic Vinaigrette (page 96)

Apple and Pear Compote (page 288)

TOMATO TUBES WITH MOZZARELLA
{ CYLINDRES DE TOMATES À LA MOZZARELLA }

This pops off the plate and the palate. It's easy to make, impressive to serve, and delicious! Serve it with a Languedoc white from Domaine du Poujol.

> 5 large, ripe but not soft tomatoes, such as coeur de boeuf, green zebra, or other flavorful variety, cored
>
> 8 ounces (250g) buffalo mozzarella
>
> Generous 1 tablespoon balsamic vinegar
>
> Extra-virgin olive oil
>
> Zest of ½ lemon, minced
>
> 2 teaspoons fresh thyme leaves
>
> Fleur de sel
>
> Freshly ground black pepper

1. Slice off one end of each tomato. Using an apple corer, cut as many tubes from the tomatoes as you can. As you release a tomato tube, place it on one of four small plates in a wide ring. Make sure that some of the tubes are on their sides and some are standing up, if possible.
2. Cut the mozzarella into ¼-inch-thick slices and cut the slices in half.
3. Divide the mozzarella slices among the plates, positioning them in the center so they are surrounded by the tomato tubes.
4. Drizzle the tomato tubes with the vinegar.
5. Drizzle the tomatoes and the mozzarella with oil.
6. Sprinkle the lemon zest over the mozzarella. Strew the thyme leaves over all, and season with salt and pepper. Serve immediately, or let sit for up to 30 minutes before serving.

SERVES 4

CREAM OF MUSHROOM SOUP

{ CRÈME DE CHAMPIGNONS }

This soup is richly, elegantly flavored. I like to serve it with a Pinot Gris from Alsace.

2 leeks, white and tender green parts only, rinsed well and diced

3 tablespoons unsalted butter

Sea salt

1½ pounds (750g) mushrooms, a mix of death trumpets, chanterelles, and button mushrooms, cleaned, trimmed, and coarsely chopped

6 cups (1.5L) chicken broth or homemade stock

1½ cups (375ml) heavy cream

1½ cups (375ml) whole milk

Freshly ground white pepper

1 small bunch fresh chives, minced

1. In a large stockpot, combine the leeks, butter, and a pinch of salt. Cover and cook, stirring occasionally, until the leeks are soft but not golden, about 5 minutes.
2. Add the mushrooms and cook, stirring often, for 5 minutes more. Add the chicken broth, cover, and simmer until the mushrooms are tender and fragrant, about 30 minutes. Taste for seasoning.
3. Purée the soup directly in the pot with an immersion blender until smooth, or transfer it to a food processor, purée until smooth, and return to the pot.
4. Just before serving, add the cream and milk and heat just until the soup is very hot but not boiling, about 5 minutes.
5. Taste the soup and adjust the seasoning. Garnish each bowl with a small amount of chives and serve.

SERVES 6

APPLE AND PEAR COMPOTE
{ COMPOTE DE POMME ET DE POIRE }

This delicious compote is rich with the natural flavors of perfect fruit. Make it and eat it as-is for dessert; spread some over tart pastry before adding other fruit and use it as a filling for crêpes; or serve it hot with roast chicken as a "vegetable" side dish. You can also use it as a filling in the Chaussons aux Pommes (page 150).

4 pounds (2kg) apples, cored, peeled, and cut into chunks
2 pounds (1kg) pears, cored, peeled, and cut into chunks
1 vanilla bean, halved lengthwise
¼ cup (60ml) water

1. Place the apples, pears, vanilla bean, and the water in a large saucepan and set over medium heat. When the water is boiling, reduce the heat to medium-low, cover, and cook until the apples and pears are completely soft, 20 to 35 minutes depending on the varieties of fruit you've used. Check the fruit frequently to be sure that it is not sticking to the bottom of the pan. If necessary, add water, 1 tablespoon at a time, to prevent the fruit from sticking.

2. Remove the pan from the heat. Remove the vanilla bean and use an immersion blender to purée the fruit directly in the pan, or transfer it to a food processor, purée, and return to the pan. If the compote is more liquid than you like, you can continue to cook it over medium heat, stirring almost continuously, until it thickens.

MAKES 6 CUPS (1.5L)

11

IT'S STILL GREEN OUTSIDE—

NOVEMBER

Mushrooms with Chorizo (page 290)

Fish Fillet in Parchment with Butter Sauce (page 193)

Crisp Cabbage Salad (page 291)

Michel's Moelleux au Chocolat (page 131)

MUSHROOMS WITH CHORIZO
{ CHAMPIGNONS AU CHORIZO }

This recipe comes from Luciano Martin, the mushroom grower who has mushroom caves just north of Rouen. He's a vendor at the Louviers market and with his family and friends who include Baptiste, we occasionally have dinner together. No matter where we eat, Luciano keeps us all laughing. Between Luciano and Baptiste, who constantly joke back and forth (they're right across the aisle from each other at the market, too), a good time is had by all! This is a very simple preparation that takes ordinary button mushrooms to new heights. Serve this with a Bergerac red.

NOTE: *If the mushrooms are large, you may need to double the number of rounds of chorizo.*

12 good-size mushrooms, cleaned and stemmed

Fine sea salt and freshly ground black pepper

12 rounds Spanish-style chorizo, or other air-cured salami-style sausage (see Note)

Fresh herbs of your choice, for garnish

1. Preheat the oven to 400°F (200°C).

2. Place the mushrooms in a heatproof baking dish and drizzle about ¼ cup (60ml) water around them. Season with salt and pepper. Bake until they begin to turn tender, about 8 minutes.

3. Remove the mushrooms from the oven and place a round (or two, if the mushrooms are very large) of chorizo atop each one. Return the mushrooms to the oven and bake until the chorizo is hot throughout, about 5 minutes.

4. Remove the mushrooms from the oven and arrange on a serving platter. Garnish with the herbs of your choice. Let cool for about 5 minutes before serving, as the mushrooms will be very hot.

SERVES 4

CRISP CABBAGE SALAD
{ SALADE DE CHOUX CROQUANTE }

If you can get a young, spring cabbage for this salad, you'll be delighted by its sweet freshness. Otherwise, use a regular green cabbage and add ½ teaspoon granulated sugar to the vinaigrette at the same time you add the salt. You'll need about half a head of cabbage for this salad. I love to chill this, and serve it with baked chicken wings (page 78). Note that this is best eaten the day it is made.

1 tablespoon freshly squeezed lemon juice

1 teaspoon Dijon-style mustard, such as Maille brand

Fine sea salt and freshly ground black pepper

½ teaspoon sugar (optional)

5 tablespoons (75ml) extra-virgin olive oil

1 small (3.5-ounce; 105g) yellow or white onion, very thinly sliced

1 small bunch fresh chives, minced

½ good-size head cabbage, cored and cut into ⅛-inch-thick (3mm) slices (6 cups)

1. In a large bowl, whisk together the lemon juice and mustard. Whisk in a generous pinch of salt, some pepper, and the sugar (if using), then whisk in the oil. Add the onion and mix.
2. Add the chives to the vinaigrette. Add the cabbage and toss thoroughly until it is completely moistened with the vinaigrette. Refrigerate until ready to serve.
3. Just before serving, toss the salad, taste, and adjust the seasoning.

SERVES 4 TO 6, GENEROUSLY

12

HOLIDAYS—

DECEMBER

CLAMS IN VINAIGRETTE
{ COQUES À LA VINAIGRETTE }

These are simply delicious and very easy to make. Serve plenty of bread alongside and your favorite Champagne.

½ cup (105g) coarse sea salt or kosher salt
¼ cup (45g) cornmeal
2 pounds (1kg) cockles, Manila clams, or littleneck clams
2 teaspoons white wine vinegar
Sea salt and freshly ground black pepper
3 tablespoons extra-virgin olive oil
3 tablespoons almond oil
1 small bunch fresh chives, minced
1 small clove garlic, green germ removed, minced

1. Purge the clams: In a large bowl, mix the coarse sea salt and cornmeal (which sweeps out the sand inside clams) with 1 gallon water, add the clams, and refrigerate for at least 4 hours. Just before cooking, remove the clams from the water and rinse well.
2. Preheat the oven to 450°F (230°C).
3. Place the clams in a large baking dish and bake until they open, 8 to 10 minutes.
4. While the clams are baking, in a small bowl, whisk together the vinegar and sea salt and pepper to taste. Slowly whisk in the oils until the mixture is emulsified.
5. Whisk the chives and the garlic into the vinaigrette. Taste and adjust the seasoning.
6. Remove the clams from the oven and either transfer them to a shallow serving dish, or serve them in the baking dish directly from the oven. To eat the clams, use a small fork to remove them from their shells and dip them into the vinaigrette.

SERVES 4

THE BUTCHER'S AMAZING LEG OF LAMB
{ LE GIGOT DU BOUCHER }

Mr. Coutard, my next-door neighbor and the best butcher for miles around, lives in a cold, red-and-white universe–his small, impeccably pristine butcher shop—six and a half days a week. He knows his meats, he treats each piece like it's a precious gem, and to watch him trim, slice, tie, and pat everything from a simple steak to a gigot like this, is to see a genius at work. The lamb I get from him is succulent, and this recipe— his—turns it into a gorgeous, tender dish. Try a lush red with this, such as Beaune-Bastion from Domaine Chanson.

I like to serve this with Baptiste's New Potato Fries (page 266, made with older potatoes of the season!).

NOTE: *When you buy the leg of lamb, ask your butcher to separate the bone from the leg but leave it in place, so that you can easily remove it once the leg is cooked.*

---

1 (4-pound; 1.8kg) bone-in leg of lamb, fat trimmed, at room temperature

2 tablespoons extra-virgin olive oil

4 (6-inch; 20cm) sprigs fresh rosemary

5 large cloves garlic, green germ removed, if necessary

Coarse sea salt and freshly ground black pepper

1 tablespoon unsalted butter, cut into 4 pieces and chilled

1. Preheat the oven to 500°F (260°C), or as hot as your oven will go.
2. Truss the leg of lamb with kitchen string so that it makes a nice, solid packet. Pour the oil into a heavy baking pan and spread it over the bottom of the pan. Lay 3 of the rosemary sprigs and the garlic in the pan, then set the lamb atop them. Place the remaining rosemary sprig atop the lamb.
3. When the oven is at the correct temperature (HOT), place the lamb in the center of the oven to roast. Immediately reduce the oven

temperature to 410°F (210°C), and roast for 45 to 50 minutes, depending on how you like your lamb. Forty-five minutes will give you rare-ish lamb; 50 minutes will give you lamb that is pink in the center, more medium. Either way, your lamb will be tender and succulent.

4. Remove the lamb from the oven, season it with salt and pepper, and let it rest in the roasting pan for at least 20 minutes and up to 40 minutes.

5. Transfer the leg of lamb to a cutting board and let it sit for 10 minutes, then remove the twine and the bone (it should easily pull out of the leg). Add 1 cup (250ml) water to the cooking juices, and set the roasting pan over medium heat. Bring the water to a boil and scrape the bottom of the pan to get all the caramelized juices. Strain the juices into a small saucepan and place that over medium heat. Bring to a boil and reduce to the thickness you'd like. Right before you serve the sauce, add the butter, swirling the pan over the heat until the butter has emulsified into the sauce. Taste and adjust the seasoning.

6. Slice the lamb and place it on a warmed serving platter or place individual slices on warmed dinner plates. Drizzle the sauce over the lamb, and serve.

SERVES 8 TO 10

SWISS CHARD WITH GARLIC AND HOT PEPPERS
{ BLETTES À L'AIL ET PIMENTS }

While kale is the "it" vegetable in the United States, Swiss chard is its equivalent in France. It's a different texture and a different flavor, though with hints of that wonderful, green "chlorophyll" flavor that makes you feel so good, healthy, and satisfied when you eat it. I tend to treat Swiss chard like kale, and here is proof—I team it with garlic and hot peppers for a zingy, tender, and flavorful side dish for roast meat, or a base for a poached egg.

1 bunch (about 1 lb; 500g) Swiss chard

2 tablespoons extra-virgin olive oil

2 cloves garlic, green germ removed, sliced into matchstick-thick pieces

¼ teaspoon fine sea salt, plus more as needed

⅛ teaspoon red pepper flakes, or as desired, *or* 1 small hot pepper, minced, or as desired

Fleur de sel

1. Trim the stems from the chard and cut them into small dice. Stack the leaves and cut them crosswise into ½-inch strips.

3. Heat 1 tablespoon of the oil and the garlic in a heavy-bottomed saucepan over medium heat. When the garlic sizzles, stir and cook until it is translucent, 2 to 3 minutes. Add the diced chard stems and 2 table-spoons water, stir, season with the salt, and cook, covered, until the stems are tender, 6 to 8 minutes. Stir them occasionally so they don't stick to the bottom of the pan.

4. Add the red pepper flakes, stir, and cook for about 1 minute, then add the chard leaves, pressing down on them so they fit in the pan. Drizzle in 2 tablespoons water, stir, cover, and cook until the leaves are tender, about 12 minutes. Season with salt, stir again, and increase the heat to high. Stir the chard, shaking the pan, until most of the liquid has evaporated. Remove the pan from the heat.

5. To serve, transfer the chard to a platter. Drizzle it with the remaining 1 tablespoon oil and sprinkle with fleur de sel.

SERVES 4

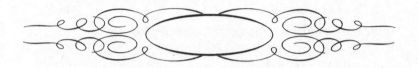

Ingredient Sources

YOU'RE LIKELY TO HAVE GROCERY STORES IN YOUR AREA
that can supply you with all you need to re-create a French *épicerie*,
as well as to cook the recipes in this book. Just in case, though, here
is a list of online sources for the basics.

SPECIALTY INGREDIENTS

The Frenchy Bee
www.thefrenchybee.com

This very French site has everything, including Amora mustard, chestnut paste, wonderful Leblanc nut oils, and green lentils
from le Puy.

Le Panier Francais

www.lepanierfrancais.com

This site offers sel de Guérande sea salt, Pommery grainy mustard, and cornichons, among other typical products.

Simply Gourmand

www.simplygourmand.com

Here you will find marvelous Picholine and Lucques olives.

Whole Foods

www.wholefoodsmarket.com

Here is hoping you have a Whole Foods grocery near you. If not, you can get many ingredients from their website, including:

Orange flower water*
Noirot brand recommended

Capers (packed in salt)
Agostina Recca brand recommended

Chestnut paste
Faugier brand recommended

Phyllo dough
Athens brand recommended

Lavender honey
Le Manoir des Abeilles brand recommended

Lentilles de Puy (green lentils)

---

* This brand is considered to be the best replacement to A. Monteaux, which is nearly impossible to find.

Piment d'Espelette

Speculoos paste
Lotus "Biscoff" brand recommended

Organic corn syrup
Wholesome Sweeteners brand recommended

SPICES

Penzeys Spices
www.penzeys.com

If they don't carry the spice, it probably doesn't exist! Penzeys also has extracts, including vanilla.

FOIE GRAS AND OTHER GORGEOUS POULTRY AND MEAT

D'Artagnan
www.dartagnan.com

Ariane Daguin grew up in the southwest of France, near Auch under the tutelage of her wonderful father, André Daguin, one of France's most talented chefs of his era. Products from this company are absolutely the finest available in the United States.

WINE SHOPS/IMPORTERS

My two favorites:

Kermit Lynch Wine Merchant, Berkeley, California
www.kermitlynch.com
1605 San Pablo Avenue
Berkeley, CA 94702
(510) 524-1524

Specializes in French and Italian wines, a terrific source. If his name is on the bottle, you'll love it.

Table Wine, Asheville, North Carolina
www.tablewineasheville.com
1550 Hendersonville Road
Suite 102
Asheville, NC 28803
(828) 505-8588

This lovely shop specializes in artisanal wines from Europe and the United States. They ship from their shop throughout the United States.

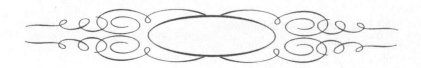

Recipe Index